T. W. Allies

The Formation Of Christendom Vol. 1

The Christian Faith and the Individual

T. W. Allies

The Formation Of Christendom Vol. 1
The Christian Faith and the Individual

ISBN/EAN: 9783742835734

Manufactured in Europe, USA, Canada, Australia, Japa

Cover: Foto ©Lupo / pixelio.de

Manufactured and distributed by brebook publishing software (www.brebook.com)

T. W. Allies

The Formation Of Christendom Vol. 1

THE
FORMATION OF CHRISTENDOM

BY

T. W. ALLIES, K.C.S.G.

VOL. I

THE CHRISTIAN FAITH AND THE INDIVIDUAL

LONDON: BURNS & OATES, Limited
NEW YORK, CINCINNATI, CHICAGO: BENZIGER BROTHERS
1897

LETTER OF APPROBATION

FROM

THE CARDINAL ARCHBISHOP OF WESTMINSTER

Archbishop's House, Westminster, S.W.,
June 4th, 1894.

Very Rev. Dear ———,—Mr. Allies has just republished, in a cheap and popular edition, his volume entitled "The Formation of Christendom." It is one of the noblest historical works I have ever read. Now that its price has placed it within the reach of all, I earnestly pray that it may become widely known and appreciatively studied. We have nothing like it in the English language. It meets a need which becomes greater daily with the increase of mental culture and the spread of education. No English work that I know exhibits the mission of the Church to the world, to the pagan world, to the civilised world, and I might add to the modern world (which is both pagan and civilised in marked degrees), in a more eloquent, a more fascinating, or a more convincing manner. If any man desires to ennoble his own estimate of the Catholic Church, let him read this book. If any man's soul is capable of rising to a lofty ideal of life, as a living member of Catholic Christendom, let him understand the part that Christ has taken (and is still taking) in the formation of Christendom, as is shown from trustworthy sources by the pen of Mr. Allies.

If you desire to enlarge the mind of the youth

committed to your care, to inspire noble thoughts, to kindle generous resolves, to lift up Churchmen to the level of their Church, you cannot do better than commend a serious perusal of this volume. I used to urge, even while none but the expensive first edition was accessible, that it ought to be made a text-book for every ecclesiastical student, whether destined for home or foreign missions, for a Religious house, or for the world. I rejoice, therefore, that at least the difficulty of price has now been removed.

I strongly recommend you to press the perusal of this book upon your ecclesiastical students, and not only upon them, but, as you have opportunity, upon the attention of lay men and women also. In proportion as they take a serious view of life will they become braced and encouraged by this noble portraiture of the Church's life and action in the world, on the Individual, on Society, and on Philosophy.

I am persuaded that nothing wiser could be done than to place this book in the hands of many educated men and women who are inquiring into the claims of the Church, and are searching for an answer to the problems which stand out before their consciences. They need, not controversy, but the light of history, to illumine their soul. They will find it here.—Wishing you every blessing,

Believe me, Very Rev. ——,

Your faithful and devoted servant,

HERBERT CARDINAL VAUGHAN.

CONTENTS

INAUGURAL LECTURE

ON THE PHILOSOPHY OF HISTORY

	PAGE
What is the Philosophy of History?	1
What History itself is	1
Its growth as a picture of human society and civilisation	2–10
Christianity causes it to take a further step	10–16
Philosophic History	16
The Philosophy of History	20
Created by the Christian Faith	24
First instance of it in the treatise *De Civitate Dei*	25
Second instance, Bossuet	26
Guizot	27
Balmez	28
Frederic Schlegel	28
Newman's History of the Turks	29
History in the last three centuries	30
Philosophy of History at present	32

LECTURE I

THE CONSUMMATION OF THE OLD WORLD

SKETCH OF THE ROMAN CIVILISATION	34
I. Its external grandeur	35
The majesty of the Pax Romana	36
Its facilities of commerce	37
Life at Rome: the baths	38
Roman Legislation	40
Internal support of Roman civilisation	41

Contrast with other cities—Athens	41
Antioch	42
Alexandria	43
Roman citizenship, and Rome's mode of imparting it	44
The Colonia	45
Character of Roman sovereignty	47
Majesty of her magistrates	49
Her language an image of this majesty	50
II. Internal conditions of Roman society—Slavery	51
Summary of the slave's social position	52
Effect of slavery on the free population:	
(a) 1. On labour	55
2. On domestic service	55
3. On artisanship	56
(b) On the social and political temper of the free	56
(c) As a fountain of moral corruption	58
Judgment of St. Augustine on the moral and political temper thus generated	63
Condition of men's minds at Rome	64
The schools of philosophy and uncertainty produced by them	66
The idea of God lost	67
Perplexed notion of good and evil	68
Pantheism	70
Idea of human personality lost	72
Idea of Providence lost	73
And of immortality	74
Summary of moral state thus ensuing	75
III. Picture of the above condition of Roman civilisation given by two eye-witnesses external to it	76
1. St. John	76
2. St. Paul	77
Course of human history from the Flood to the Advent of Christ	78
Two incidents at Rome in Nero's time	81
The execution	81
The banquet	82
Morality of the emperors and chief writers of Rome	83
St. Peter, and his coming to Rome	84
On what his presence there was grounded	86

LECTURE II

THE NEW CREATION OF INDIVIDUAL MAN

	PAGE
Empire of Rome the summary of ancient civilisation	88
How St. Peter and St. Paul dealt with it	90
Reconstruction of society with two forces, the knowledge of God and of the human soul	91
Sevenfold idea of God: 1. in His Unity; 2. in His Personality; 3. in His Paternity; 4. as Incarnate; 5. as the Food of man; 6. as redeeming him; 7. as glorifying him, presented as a whole to man	91
The existing civilisation a stranger to this idea	96
Every Christian virtue derived from it	98
How Christianity viewed human morality taken as a mass:	
1. In the motive given to it	98
Contrast between Marcus Aurelius and the Gospel	100
2. In the standard proposed to it	101
3. In the support provided	104
4. In the reward offered	105
How the whole is pervaded by the fact of the Incarnation	107
From the above idea of God springs the distinction between natural and supernatural good	108
And the virtues of Faith, Hope, and Charity	109
Charity, especially, rooted in the Incarnation	110
Newness of this virtue to the heathen	113
Moral purity of the Christian grounded on the Incarnation	114
And the love of husband and wife	115
Christian treatment of man as a member of civil society	115
How it applied the doctrine of the Incarnation to slavery	116
Treatment of man in his relation to equals	119
Obligation of truth grounded on the Incarnation	119
Gentleness, mercy, humility, liberality	119
And in particular, brotherly love	120
Christian treatment of obedience to civil government	121
Rejection of exclusive patriotism	121
Christian idea of the New Creation	122
In the individual and in the mass	123
Christian and Heathen virtue	126
The gift of Grace	128
The seven gifts of the Holy Spirit viewed in Christ as their Well-head	129

CONTENTS

	PAGE
And thence imparted to man	130
The human and the Christian commonwealth a contrast like the natural and the Christian man.	130
Summary of the Christian restoration	131
Contrast between Heathenism and Christianity.	131

LECTURE III

HEATHEN AND CHRISTIAN MAN COMPARED

The above principles illustrated in the lives of individuals	135
Six points common to the Greek and Roman heathen	136
Why Socrates is not taken as a representative man	138
Why not Cato of Utica	139
Why not Epictetus	141
Nor Marcus Aurelius	142
Cicero chosen, and why	144
Sketch of his life and doctrines	145
His treatise on social duties	146
His treatise on the Nature of the Gods	150
Three critical points in his life:	
1. His exile	153
2. His daughter's death	154
3. The break-up of the Republic	155
Transition to St. Augustine	157
Sketch of his life up to his conversion	157
His conversion	159
The death of his mother	162
His subsequent life	165
His genius and character; contrast with Cicero	166
How his mind was penetrated with the thought of Providence	169
His bearing and writings at the downfall of the Roman empire	171
His doctrine as to the City of God	172
Importance of this work, the first Philosophy of History	173
The key to his own life and writings, and to all the change above contemplated, supplied in his treatise *De Vera Religione*	176

LECTURE IV

EFFECT OF THE CHRISTIAN PEOPLE ON THE WORLD

	PAGE
Cicero and Augustine, apart from their genius, fair specimens of Heathenism and of Christianity	178
The revolution wrought by Christianity	179
Description of it by an eye-witness at the beginning of the second century	180
Gradual growth of Christians	184
All the progress took its rise from the Individual	185
Process of change in the thoughts and actions of men produced by Christians	186
1. The Heathen contempt for human life remedied by the martyrs' abnegation of it	186
2. The Heathen impurity corrected by the Virgin martyrs; St. Potamiæna, St. Agnes, St. Afra	189
3. Heathenism with its merely natural end; refutation of it by Christians preferring a future unseen good at the cost of their life	195
4. Inwardness of Christian life and virtue	199
The cardinal virtues completed and transformed by the theological	201
In all this the Christians imitators of one model, Christ	203
Action of the Christian society, as constituted in its Sacerdotium, on the world around	204
Its Unity, Uniformity, and Universality, as derived from Christ, seen in seven attributes	204
1. It rested wholly on the authority of the Sender	207
2. It was a coherent unchangeable system of doctrine	209
3. It was a government of souls	215
4. Which was yet a ministration	217
5. Its success was connected with suffering	218
6. Its sacrifice was bound up with its teaching and all these attributes	219
7. It was supported by the example of its members carrying out its doctrines	220
Summary of what the Christian faith had done in the first four hundred years	222

LECTURE V

NEW CREATION OF THE PRIMARY RELATION BETWEEN MAN AND WOMAN

	PAGE
The Personality of Man the subject with which the Christian Faith dealt	225
But it dealt with him also as a Race and a Society	225
He is himself the most dependent of creatures on others	226
I. The Primary Relation, that between man and woman	226
What it was originally intended to be	226
The first institution of marriage	227
Its seven original attributes	229
God herein the founder of human society	230
II. State of woman in the last years of Augustus	231
Her original condition in Greek society	231
Great declension of morals from the time of the Peloponnesian War	233
Her original condition in Roman society	234
Deterioration of morals from the second Punic War	234
Condition of woman in Persia	235
Among the Israelites	235
Condition of woman in the East and South	237
And among the Germans	237
Divorce followed by remarriage, adultery on the man's side, and polygamy, the three great infringements of marriage	238
Woman considered a minor	239
Her degradation outside of the marriage state	239
Moral state of the world in consequence	240
Efforts of Augustus to improve it	241
Review of his position and means for restoring the family	242
Moral force of the Greek race	243
Of the Roman people	243
Of the Provinces	244
Of the German tribes	245
Of the Jews scattered over the world, and in Judea	246
III. The restoration of woman in herself, springing from the birth of our Lord	246

	PAGE
Restoration of marriage	248
In what the sacrament consists	250
The theory carried out into fact	251
1. Amid the corrupt Heathen civilisation	252
2. Amid the inroads and establishments of the Northern tribes	255
3. Amid the kingdoms of Europe thence formed	256
4. Amid the licence of modern times	257
Complete marriage only in the Church	258
Two results of marriage as a Sacrament	260
First, the restoration of family life	261
Secondly, the education, properly so called, of children	266
Summary of the work accomplished	269

LECTURE VI

THE CREATION OF THE VIRGINAL LIFE

Our Lord's personal character, the mark of Christian imitation	273
Parallel from the present influence of civilisation	274
I. A special feature in our Lord's character	275
Christianity itself, based on our Lord's Virginal conception	275
Mary's own choice of the Virginal Life	276
And our Lord's; on these three facts rested the Christian feeling as to that life	277
This feeling new in the world both as to Jew and Gentile	277
Its source a special imitation of Christ and His Mother	278
Description of the Virginal Life by St. Methodius	280
Summary of it from various writers	281
St. Ignatius and St. Clement of Rome	282
It was not a mere theory, but carried into practice	283
And this in the first three centuries	283
Testimony of St. Cyprian, St. Athanasius, St. Augustine	284
Universality of its production in all times and countries of the Catholic Church	286
The Virginal Life, the condition of all perfect following of our Lord	287

		PAGE
	As a special following of Him it arises at once after Him, and that amongst the most various states and races of men.	289
II.	The special office assigned to Virginity, the propagation of Christianity	291
	The cause of such office being assigned to it	292
	Its development in the secular Clergy	294
	This development arose from within, out of the nature of the clerical office	295
	Its development in the Religious Orders	299
	The Three Vows and their reason	300
	Fecundity and continuity of the Virginal Life	304
	Virginity the Church's marriage	306
	The causes of this	307
	The human and the divine society, and their different motives	308
	The human society as it acts in the propagation of religion	308
	In education	309
	In the works of mercy	310
	The divine society as it acts in propagating religion	311
	As it acts in educating	314
	As it acts in works of mercy	315
	The Virginal Life raises these works from being a profession to an act of devotion	316
III.	Three sentiments as to the Virginal Life in the time of St. Chrysostom reproduced now	317
	Force of an example raised above the natural life on others	319
	The honour and excellence of Virginity, a new element communicated to society	320
	Europe as it was with this element infused into it	321

INDEX 325

INAUGURAL LECTURE

ON THE

PHILOSOPHY OF HISTORY.[1]

WHAT is the "philosophy of history"? There are few persons, if I mistake not, who, were such a question suddenly addressed to them, would not be sensible of some vagueness in their notions, some hesitation in their answer to it. The word "history" bears a certain meaning; the word "philosophy" bears another; but what results from their combination? To which of the two does it belong? Or in what proportions are they blended? Or which predominates? Is the result philosophy; or is it history? Does it narrate, or does it compare and deduce?—It will be my endeavour in the course of this Lecture to give some sort of answer to so radical and primary a question.

I have said that the word "history" carries a plain and definite meaning to the ear. Its subject-matter, indeed, taken in the gross, has not varied from the earliest to the present times. It deals with the whole course of domestic and national life; with races and peoples; their arts and arms; their progress and decline; nay, with the whole temporal destinies of

---

[1] Delivered before the Catholic University of Ireland, Dec. 21, 1854, in presence of Cardinal Newman, its first Rector.

that larger human society, which overleaps all international boundaries, and may be said to constitute one unbroken whole from the earliest recorded time to the present day. History is the picture of civilisation, as that great travail of the sons of men with one another has been called. Not only the man individual, but the man collective, "has gone forth to his work and to his labour until the evening," and history has ever been describing what he has been doing. But as his works have been great or little, simple or complex, broken up, divided, and deflecting from each other, or again converging, and as by some mighty inward instinct and energy co-operating with each other, so has his history been; for it was but the portrait of man, and of the society which he forms with his fellows. Let us take a glance at this course of history, which, we shall find, will lead us to our subject.

In the first beginnings of nations, when the family grows into the tribe, and the tribe into a people, man works as unconscious of any purpose. The sons of Noah went forth to possess the earth, to subdue it, and to cultivate it. The needs of the day prescribe its toil. But that rudimental society as little contemplates itself, or the objects it has in view, as little catalogues or defines them, as does the child. Yet, like the child, it is the creature of habits and tradition; it lives a vigorous, outward, physical life; it has strong generous emotions; it reasons little, but it feels much. Great deeds of personal daring, labours undergone, dangers risked, dwell in its memory. In this, too, it is like a noble youth, whose instincts and impulses are keener and more vivid, perhaps sometimes more attractive, than the balanced thoughts of the grey-haired man. And as this youthful society lives in tradition, and is possessed by it unconsciously, it seeks to give a voice to those memories of which it is full, and so commences history. This is why history in its beginning is ever allied to poetry, and often in its first forms identical with it. Thus we have the hero described as sitting by the seaside, and singing "the glories of men," whose great deeds the divine ballad-singer will presently gather into immortal verse, himself to be the parent of history as well as song, the fountain-head of a matchless language, the ever-living root of the most intellectual of human races. But it was the same beside the birthplace of that ruder race whose destiny it was to govern, rather than to teach, the world. Unhappily no Latian Homer survives to tell us—

> "How well Horatius kept the bridge
> In the brave days of old."

But we know that at the Roman banquets the youth were taught to admire and imitate the deeds of those who had founded, nurtured, or preserved the race of Mars suckled by the wolf; how by such means Lucretia and Brutus became to them names of ever-living power, and from generation to generation the Roman matron drew from the former the dower of chastity, from the latter the Roman citizen the inextinguishable hatred of despotic power. Again, when the northern tribes had descended to break up the Roman Empire, Saxons, and Danes, and Normans, Franks, and Goths, hear recounted at the banquet the deeds of their sea-kings or their chieftains. This is at once their history and poetry.

But society advances a step, and with it history. The Pelasgic tribe settles; the Latian city grows;

the Northman tills the earth. At this period we find chronicles no longer metrical, but recounting briefly those incidents which chiefly strike the imagination; recounting them without coherence or relation of parts; without, as it were, any purpose; with simple juxtaposition. Such, we may suppose, were the *Annales Pontificum*; such, in another clime and time, the Saxon Chronicle. This is but the outward part of history; the recitation of the drama of life, just as it appears to a looker-on, full of its true spirit, but without self-consciousness.

Society takes another step, and it is a great one. Those mysterious powers of race, and language, and primeval institutions, and hereditary laws, and sympathies or antipathies, which date from the very cradle of man, grow up together into that complex, powerful, almost indestructible moral being called a nation. Men are no longer children; they are conscious of themselves, and of a common purpose, an inherited name; a definite and distinctive course of action; of something which belongs to their own race, and land, and tongue, and not to others. Society is become *national*, and forthwith history becomes *political*. Whatever the march of society may be, that of history will be correlative to it.

Let us go back for an illustration to the literature of that land to which we owe so much. Herodotus, so often called the father of history, is an instance of the transition of which I am speaking. He appears to us a man of very active and curious mind, who has the power and the will to seek knowledge everywhere. He verifies to the letter one poet's description of another poet's hero; truly he is the man

"Qui mores hominum multorum vidit et urbes."

He seems to have a greater poet's dictum at his heart, that

> "Home-keeping youths have ever homely wits."

Knowledge was not yet stored up in great reservoirs; he travelled after it from place to place; he saw, and heard, and reflected for himself. It was the fashion once to call him a pleasant story-teller, with fraudulent Greek vision, and credulous ears; but I think this fashion is rightly passed. Rather he listened thoughtfully to all the learning of the Egyptian priests; he gathered up all the traditions that lingered in the oracles, shrines, and cities of Greece; he made all the coasts of the Mediterranean his tributaries, and wove together the parti-coloured treasure into that mixture of chronicle and history, of lively narrative, religious musing, and political lore, which, pass the world through whatever shapes it may, will never cease to charm. Yet there is a clue to all his narrative. He knits together the nations whose history, or rather traditions, he traverses, by their relation to that bitter, everlasting enmity between Europe and Asia, whereof the age immediately preceding him had seen so tremendous an explosion in the expedition of Xerxes.

That very assault on the liberties of Greece had wrought its tribes, in spite of their internal antagonism, into one people, one society; and, but half a generation later than himself, we see what may be termed the *political* history of the ancients reaching a perfection in Thucydides which it never surpassed. This history may be called political, because human society had then fully realised the idea of a people. The highest form of human organisation with which men were familiar was the πολιτεία; nor does it here matter, perhaps, to say that both to Greek and Roman such name was derived from the population of a *city*, and of an adjacent people aggregated round it; rather than from the population of a kingdom, or country, having many cities, towns, and villages living under one law and rule. No doubt the words πολιτεία and *civitas* denote the growth of the commonwealth from the kernel of the city; while "kingdom" derives it from the person of the prince: perhaps the former may be called the Greco-Latin, the latter the Asiatic principle of government. But at least both Greeks and Romans were familiar with great eastern kingdoms, which fully set forth the modern idea of a nation; and Alexander conquered and ruled over such an empire; not to say that from its members several kingdoms, in the modern sense, arose. Society then had become national, and history kept pace with it. Let us see what is the character of this political history.

Its limit is the *nation*, and it deals with all that interests the *nation*. Within the contracted limits of that famous Peloponnesian war passions are stirring, political interests at stake, rivalries are in the field, such as are reproduced now in the larger sphere of Europe. Every form of government may be seen in embryo; every political antagonism runs its petty but well-defined course; and but lately the ablest organ of public opinion in England has twice chosen the funeral oration of Pericles as the liveliest exponent of English feeling over the losses experienced at Sebastopol. Great, indeed, is the charm, where the writer can describe with the pencil of a poet, and analyse with the mental grasp of a philosopher. Such is the double merit of Thucydides. And so it has happened that the deepest students of human nature have searched for two thousand years the records of a war, wherein the territory of the chief belligerents was not larger than a modern English or Irish county. What should we say if a quarrel between Kent and Essex, between Cork and Kerry, had kept the world at gaze ever since? Yet Attica and Laconia were no larger.

Pass over five hundred years, yet history scarcely seems to have enlarged its grasp. It deals, indeed, with an empire materially wider in extent — the wonderful empire of that city which moulded into one dominion all the countries watered by the Mediterranean, the highway of the old world. Thus it might seem to include the *orbis terrarum*. Yet I do not know that in reading the pages of Polybius, of Livy, or even of Tacitus, we are conscious of a wider grasp of thought, a more enlarged experience of political interests, a higher idea of man and of all that concerns his personal or public life, than in those of Thucydides. I am not comparing the qualifications of these several great masters, but trying to trace the idea on which their works are written. And I still find the πολιτεία or *civitas* at the bottom of it. Rome, no doubt, is physically greater than Athens. Her gauntleted hand pitilessly strikes down one after another the fairest of Grecian cities. Syracuse and Corinth, with all their columns and statues, sink before her. Carthage meets her in vain in a hundred battles by sea and land; the result is but that the Roman exile moralises over her ruins. Again, there is a wide difference between a Polycrates or a Peisistratus, and a master of thirty legions, with whom it was ill to argue; but this is a difference of degree;

and not of kind. Still the Cæsar in his almost worldwide dominion reached no higher unity of man than the national unity, and the painter of a servile senate and degenerate people, of a Nero or Domitian, and the empire *super et Garamantas et Indos*, which quivered beneath their rage, had indeed a wider canvas, yet grouped not his figures with a deeper thought than he who described the conflict in the bay of Syracuse, or immortalised the oration over the dead at Athens. In one respect, indeed, this political history of the ancients will never be surpassed, probably never be equalled—I mean as a work of art. I have hitherto been considering history in another point of view; as to its substance, not as to its shape; as to its inward thought, not as to its outward clothing. All of these great masters were genuine artists, and they could work on materials which none can hope for now. They possessed, as instruments of their thought, two languages, very different in their capacity, but both of them superior in originality, beauty, and expressiveness to any which have fallen to the lot of modern nations. It may be that the marbles of Pentelicus and Carrara ensure good sculptors. Certain it is that those masters of ancient thought deemed it not beneath their pains to spend much time on the mode of expression. Those, perhaps, who have but brick to deal with think it useless to mould so ignoble a material, or shrink from an attempt to rival in plaster the forms of marble art. Yet I have often lamented that historians, who would feel insulted at a comparison of their subject-matter with that of Thucydides or Tacitus, should descend to a style which the Greek would have thought unworthy of an Athenian barber, and the Roman of a manumitted slave.

Nor is it only in style, as an expression of thought, that the ancient historians possess so great an excellence. In the narrative—that is, the poetic and pictorial part of history—they have equal merit. Their history is a drama, in which the actors and events speak for themselves. The author is not perpetually intruding himself and his personal feelings, after the egotistic fashion of too many moderns. It is the difference between Shakespeare and a fashionable novel. In the former, characters stand out to the mind, and impress themselves on the feelings by action and suffering; in the latter, we are continually being *told* that the heroes are brave or clever, and the heroines paragons of beauty. As we feel *Othello* or *Hamlet*, so in a battlefield of Livy we comprehend how, while the combatants were fighting,

"An earthquake reeled unheededly away."

The historian is not yet become an untimely moralist or a dull dissertator. He is the great painter of human nature, and in his subject forgets himself.

But on the philosophic part of history—the bearing of events on each other, the relations of cause and effect, the apprehension of great first principles, the generalisation of facts—what shall we say concerning the political history of the ancients? They had faithfully noted whatever belonged to the civil life of man, the political organisation of human society in national centres; but the bearing of nations on each other, the greater whole of humanity itself, they had not reached. Perhaps the course of history within the memory of man had been too short, its experience too simple, its direction too little evident, for such an advance. Something must happen to man, something to society, something to humanity, before such a result could be attained. For history, as we have observed, is the picture of man's civilisation as it *is*; and the reality must take place before its portrait can be drawn. Thus, to find any advance in the idea of history, with an exception which I shall note hereafter, the treatise *De Civitate Dei*, the remarkable work of a great and saintly mind, who has had more influence probably on human thought than any uninspired writer, we must step over a long period of time, during which Europe was reconstituting itself after the convulsions produced by the inroads of the barbarians. At length, after the rise of modern nationalities at the beginning of the sixteenth century, the revival of the ancient literature produced for a time a recurrence, at least in outward form, to the political history of the ancients. Such was the model in the mind of Machiavelli and Guicciardini. But the state of the world had gone beyond this; had advanced to a riper growth. To have been contented with the limited views, the national boundaries of ancient history, because of the exquisite shape and perfect language into which that history was thrown, would have been to sacrifice the spirit to the body, would have been a positive retrogression in the then state of the human mind. Through the long travail of the Middle Ages it had been prepared for something better. Indeed, in those very Middle Ages, and notably in the thirteenth century, there were minds which have left us imperishable memorials of themselves, and which would have taken the largest and most philosophic view of history, had the mere materials existed ready to their hand. Conceive, for instance, a history from the luminous mind of St. Thomas, with the stores of modern knowledge at his command. But the invention of printing, one of the turning-points of the human race, was first to take place; and then on that soil of the Middle Ages, so long prepared and fertilised by so patient a toil, a mighty harvest was to spring up. Among the first fruits of labours, so often depreciated by those who have profited from them, and in the land of children who despise their sires, we find the proper alliance of philosophy with history. Then, at length, the province of the historian is recognised to consist, not merely in the just, accurate, lively narrative of facts, but in the exhibition of cause and effect. "What do we now expect in history?" says M. de Barante; and he replies—" Solid instruction; a complete knowledge of things; moral lessons; political counsels; comparisons with the present; the knowledge of general facts." Even in the age of Tacitus, the most philosophic of ancient historians, no individual ability could secure all such powers. What, then, had happened in the interval? Christianity had happened; Christendom had been formed; mankind had passed through fire and water—a deluge and a passion; the secret of its unity and its destiny had been given to it. The nation was no longer the highest of human facts, patriotism no longer the first of virtues. A reconstructed humanity towered far above the nation, and no one member of the human society could any longer engross the whole interest of man. There was a voice in the world greater, more potent, thrilling, and universal than the last cry of the old society, *Civis sum Romanus;* and this voice was *Sum Christianus.* From the time of the Great Sacrifice it was impossible to sever the history of man's temporal destiny from that of his eternal; and when the virtue of that Sacrifice had thoroughly leavened the nations, history is found to assume a larger basis, to have lost its partial and national cast; to have grown with the growth of man, and to demand for its completeness a perfect alliance with philosophy.

It is true that the breaking-up of the Roman empire—reducing the powers of society into a sort of chaos—long suspended these results. Like the seeds discovered in Egyptian tombs, they lay for hundreds of years, not losing their vital force, but buried, as it were, in the great Christian mind till the hour of awakening should come. The world of thought in which we live is, after all, formed by Christianity. Modern Europe is a relic of Christendom, the virtue of which is not gone out of it. Gregory VII. and Innocent III. have ruled over generations which ignored them; have given breadth to minds which condemned their benefactors as guilty of narrow priestcraft, and derided the work of those benefactors as an exploded theory. Let us take an example in what is, morally, perhaps the worst and most shocking period of the last three centuries—the thirty years preceding the great French Revolution. We shall see that at this time even minds which had rejected, with all the firmness of a reprobate will, the regenerating influence of Christianity, could not emancipate themselves from the virtue of the atmosphere which they had breathed. They are immeasurably greater than they would have been in Pagan times, by the force of that faith which they misrepresented and repudiated. To prove the truth of my words, compare for a moment the great artist who drew Tiberius and Domitian and the Roman empire in the first century, with him who took up its decline and fall in the second and succeeding centuries. How far wider a grasp of thought, how far more manifold an experience, combined with a philosophic purpose, in Gibbon than in Tacitus! He has a standard within him by which he can measure the nations as they come in long procession before him. In that vast and wondrous drama of the Antonines and Constantine, Athanasius and Leo, Justinian and Charlemagne, Mahomet, Zingbis Khan, and Timour, Jerusalem and Mecca, Rome and Constantinople, what stores of thought are laid up—what a train of philosophic induction exhibited! How much larger is this world become than that which trembled at Cæsar! The very apostate profits by the light which has shone on Thabor, and the blood which has flowed on Calvary. He is a greater historian than his heathen predecessor, because he lives in a society to which the God whom he abandoned has disclosed the depth of its being, the laws of its course, the importance of its present, the price of its futurity.

Thus it may be termed a necessity of modern history that it should be philosophic. It must give not only the course of things, but their results; not only the facts, but their reasons. The civilisation which it ought to portray is one immensely advanced beyond that of the ancients; advanced not merely in the material arts which give prosperity to civil life, but most of all in this, that it possesses a tie and bond of the whole race in the Person of its Deliverer, which was so fatally wanting to the old world, and from the absence of which its course was obscure and fluctuating, and its end unapparent. Now, where there is no defined course and no recognised end, the philosophy of cause and effect is scarcely possible. How dreary to chronicle the rise and fall of Assyrian, and Persian, and Macedonian, and Roman dominion, until the key to them was given, until the stone cut out without hands was beginning to fill the earth! Too often has philosophy in the hand of modern writers shown itself ungrateful to the power which made it what it is; nor only ungrateful, but unconscious of its debt. Christendom, that mighty creation of the Church, has left an ineffaceable impression on modern society. It has protected it at once from the excesses and narrowness of such conquerors as the Romans. Never more can one political organisation presume to be the whole of the world, and never again can it restrict man to its own boundaries. Even now, dislocated and convulsed, heaving with half-subdued revolutions, and torn by fatal schisms, Europe feels itself to be one, and the pride of the proudest nation submits to have its history treated but as a part and member of a greater whole. We have kept the term *barbarous* from the old Greek, but we have altered its force. It no longer means that which is strange, foreign to us, but that which breaks away from the universal law of civilised life, shared in common by so many nations; and civilisation itself, the course of man's temporal destinies, can no longer be severed from that ocean of his eternal state into which it is seen to run.

Thus it is that the modern historian looks at society from a higher point of view than the ancient. Its centre and its law do not lie to him in the nation, but in the greater whole of humanity, which the Person of the God-man has revealed to him. He sees before him a collection of nations which has indeed been a republic with a common law, which still has parts and members, common sympathies and antagonisms, wherein no one has a moral or intellectual primacy, but virtues balanced with great defects. It is a mutual give and take; an action and reaction all around him. Here, perhaps, he sees a race at the top wave of its natural strength and energy, full of perseverance, rarely missing success, but proud, hard, and worldly; there another, wherein thought and action interpenetrate each other, more impulsive, frank, and tender, and withal so quick, keen, and homogeneous, that a single feeling will electrify the whole mass, a single man, the secret thought of the nation personified, assume absolute control, and weld them for a time into overwhelming force. A third, with vast and yet unknown powers, of one growth and jet, in force of barbarism, Asiatic, in flexibility of civilisation, European, knit together by an almost unreasoning obedience, and marshalled in a huge military hierarchy aspiring to future triumphs; fourth may come a troop of nations, differing in blood, in language, in social institutions, in their state of progress, but finding a single point of contact, a centre of unity, in the person of a common sovereign, and upholding his throne for centuries with unwavering fidelity. Others, again, seem like the inferior, yet not unimportant, limbs of a great confederacy; they fill up interstices in the huge fabric; while some are great rather in their past renown than in their present power, a *magni nominis umbra*, once rich in arts and arms, and in the thought which rules mankind. In all these a course and progress are ever going on; a common civilisation has its distinctive national colouring; race and religion produce their blended result; and philosophical history has not only to recount facts with rigid accuracy, not only to represent the panorama of war and peace, of outward action and inward development, as it goes on, but to compare and estimate the progress, and weigh the nations in its scales by a standard which they all recognise.

Have we, then, come to the proper subject of which we were in pursuit, and is such a philosophical history identical with the philosophy of history itself? They have, indeed, I believe, much in common; but this latter is, if I mistake not, a yet maturer growth of civilisation. Let me endeavour to specify the distinction between them.

Into whatever alliance history may call philosophy, still, if it be true to its own nature, its basis must be *narration*. It has to set forth events, whether simple or complex, whether striking the imagination by sympathy, or exercising the reason. Take, for instance, the history of a particular nation for a given period of moderate length, say of fifty years. Immediately what a crowd of different subjects force themselves on the mind; war with its thousand incidents, diplomacy, politics, legislation, literature, social economy, religion. This is but a sample. All these require to be described. An accurate and vivid narrative of these must precede the philosophical part of history, the deduction of results, comparison, contrast, generalisation; nor will any amount of philosophic skill in the latter part make up for want of dramatic power in the former. Yet what a medley is here! What a multiplicity of details! Each one of these subjects, the active force of a nation, its politics, its legislation, its literature, its social economy, its state of religion, has its own growth and progress, its philosophical point of view, its manifold facts, and the laws which are their ultimate expression. How is it possible to have unity of conception in such a cluster of different subjects?

It is at this point that the philosophy of history comes upon the stage. Its special force lies in this very unity of conception.

It chooses one of these subjects; it traces such one, as it were, from the cradle, follows it through all the adventures of its course, its trials, conflicts, progressions, defeats, recoveries, completion, and success; draws, as it were, the biography of an idea—gives life and colouring to an abstraction—sums up a chain of facts in their results. "The history of a nation," says M. de Barante—himself so skilful in narration—"does not consist only in the chronicles of its wars and revolutions, in the living portrait of its illustrious men. So far is but the outward drama of history. There may be desired the history of causes that do not appear visibly; certain minds may even prefer it to the history of effects which disclose themselves to the eye. All human things are subject to a progression, the law of which may be sought out in the midst of accidental and variable circumstances. There is an order of facts belonging to each kind of history. Historical interest will turn on the history of a religion, of a legislation, of a science, of an opinion, of an art, as well as on a history, the scenes of which are represented in fields of battle, in the public places of cities, or at the courts of kings. Such histories," he continues, "in which a philosophic genius follows across successive facts the development of an idea or the progress of a cause, have taken their place among the master works of the human mind. Their beauty mainly depends on *unity of conception*, on the author's power to distinguish and arrange facts according to his purpose, according to the object of his researches and his analysis."[1]

In such a work it would appear that history and philosophy have an equal share. It rests on a basis of facts; it results in a science, the scope of which is to set forth the laws by which the political and social world is governed.

How can we attain to the knowledge of these laws? I know, I can even conceive, but one way—by a cautious and conscientious induction of facts, an induction which needs to be as patient, as rigorous, as scrupulous, as extensive, as little warped by preconceived fancies or extraneous theories, as the induction on which the physical sciences are built, and which has been the main instrument of their wonderful advance.

Let me quote here the words of one who has given us in his histories of civilisation in Europe and in France perhaps the most finished specimen of the natural qualities required to produce a Philosophy of History. "What," says M. Guizot, "is the spirit which prevails at present in the intellectual order, in the research of truth, whatever be its object? A spirit of severity, prudence, and reserve, the scientific spirit, the philosophic method. This method carefully observes facts, and only allows itself to generalise slowly, progressively, in proportion as facts are known. This spirit has evidently prevailed for more than half a century" (we may now almost double that time) "in the sciences which are engaged on the material world; it has produced their progress and their glory. Its tendency is at present to penetrate more and more

[1] M. de Barante, *Histoire des Ducs de Bourgoyne*, Preface, pp. 9, 10, 11.

into the sciences of the moral world, into politics, history, and philosophy. On all sides the scientific method extends itself and gains influence; on all sides is felt the necessity of taking facts for one's basis and rule; men are persuaded that they are the material of science; that no general idea can have any real value if it derive not its birth from facts, and be continually nourished by them as it grows to maturity. Facts are now, in the intellectual order, the power in credit." And he adds words which appear to me luminous with truth: "We are cast into a world which we have not created nor invented; we find it there; we look at it; we study it; need is that we must take it as a fact, for it subsists outside of us, independently of us. It is on facts that our spirit exercises itself; it has but facts for materials; and when it discovers their general laws, those laws are themselves facts which it verifies."[1]

I accept these principles fully and unreservedly. I would apply to events of the moral order what a famous philosopher says of physics, that the doctrine of final causes, when actively introduced, spoils them. No doubt, they have a final cause; no doubt, likewise, the whole course of events, as much in contingent as in material things, as much in the actions of free agents as in the unreasoning powers of nature, is foreordered and directed according to that end which is the first in the order of the divine counsels, as it is the last in execution. But it is not given to us, in this stage of our being, to jump at this hidden conclusion. The patient analysis of facts is *our* instrument of knowledge, in politics and history, as in the animal and vegetable world. I can therefore feel no jealousy of

[1] Guizot, *Civilisation en France*, 1re leçon.

facts, no fear of them, in the intellectual order. A half-knowledge, a meagre induction, a hasty generalisation—this indeed is to be feared as the parent of numberless errors; but there is nothing of which I am more intimately convinced than that the order of moral events, when fully disclosed, will be found to be governed by laws far transcending human wisdom to conceive, or the heart of man to admire. In the meantime, if we follow any other guide but facts, we are but dwarfing the Divine Lawgiver to the measure of our fancy.

Indeed, there is a solemnity involved in this view of facts which is seldom recognised. One thing, said the heathen proverb, the Deity cannot do: undo that which is done. And is it not true that all which once has happened, which has become a fact, in so happening passes, as it were, into an irrevocable order of things, and shares the immutability and eternity of the Almighty Maker? Thus it is even with the contingent acts of men, prescinding from the sin which may be involved in them. Once carried into effect, they form part of an universe which is God's creation; the system of which, in its infinitely numerous details, is one vast series of inductions, as to what is His being and His will, for without these they could not have been. The meanest fact around us is one in an infinite series, and bears witness to an infinite power. It is a disclosure of the Eternal; "for the invisible things of Him from the creation of the world are clearly seen, being understood by the things that are made." Those, at least, who so look upon facts are not likely to disregard their importance.

But if the philosophic historian must look to the induction of facts as the scientific method by which alone he can attain to a clearer and fuller view of the laws governing the political and social world, yet there are facts very intimately and universally concerning the actions of men and the course of humanity which come to him guaranteed by authority. Whether the mere observer would deduce them for himself, the experience of the ancient heathen is perhaps sufficient to decide in the negative. But that experience is likewise sufficient to show that, without fully admitting such facts, the course of human affairs was to the most sharp-sighted and reflecting among them dark, cheerless, and even unintelligible. No one can be a great and true historian if his history be not written with a full conviction that three great powers move through the whole course of human events.[1] There is a Divine Providence, which shapes things to its own ends, "rough-hew them how we will," and never leaves the mastery of results to the blind or iron force of chance or fate. There is a free will of man, left sacred in every human breast by that Divine Providence, not the slave of outward circumstances nor of inward pleasure, but the very basis of our moral being, and its inviolable citadel. And there is, by the permission of that same Providence, an ever-active power of evil, universal in his operation, and tempting every human free will to a false pleasure and an unreal good. If the human mind could not discern and recognise these three powers for itself from the mere contemplation of the outward facts of history, yet, at least, when they are disclosed by revelation, it sees infallible proof of their presence in those facts; nor has either of these ever been denied or ignored by the historian without manifest injury to the truth and the com-

[1] Schlegel, *Philosophy of History*, Lect. xv.

pleteness of the view which he takes of human affairs.

Nay, I am prepared to maintain that it was the very discerning and reasoning on these three powers, and their joint operations in human affairs, which gave birth to that philosophy of history of which we are now treating. And how can I better conclude these remarks than by some illustration from facts of the principles which have been here maintained?

When, then, did history first appear divested of what is local, national, and temporary? When did it come forth at length conterminous with the human race, and grasping its whole destiny? Who first allied it with philosophy so as to produce a work which may be referred equally to both? If what I have stated be true, if history be ever the portrait of an existing civilisation, if it cannot forestall the progress of that civilisation, if the mirror cannot reflect till the object be presented to it; if, moreover, darkness and uncertainty brooded over the mind of the ablest and most philosophical of the ancient historians, so that it may be doubted if he recognised either of those three powers which move through all the actions of men, then it is abundantly clear that no philosophy of history could be produced till Christianity had sunk into the minds of men and moulded their thoughts. Now, it is not a little singular that the same great Father, who is usually considered the parent of theology viewed as a science, has likewise given us the first specimen of the philosophy of history. That period of thirty years at the commencement of the fifth century, during which the fertile mind of St. Augustine poured forth so many works to be the seed-plots of thought for future times, was itself one of the most important and decisive in all history. It saw for the first time the capture of imperial Rome, which filled the old world with dismay. That world felt instinctively that it was disappearing. The fountains of the great deep were broken up, and who could tell how much or what would remain standing after the deluge? On all sides the barbarians were bursting in, and the empire which had grown for a thousand years was upheaved from its foundations. He who gave a theory of history at such a time was subjecting it to a rude trial. And again, it is worthy of note that the very capture of the city by Alaric led to the work in question. Rome, said certain Pagan writers, obtained the dominion of the world by the aid of the gods. She is become Christian, and she falls. The objection seemed to St. Augustine to need an answer, and he blends all the treasures of history and philosophy together in giving it in the great treatise *De Civitate Dei*. We are the children of those barbarians, adopted, tamed, regenerated by the Church. We live far on the other side of that gulf into which all that was beautiful, orderly, and peaceful of the old civilisation was about to be cast. We have eighteen centuries behind us, and St. Augustine had four. What judgment should we pass on his work? I will take a summary of it, drawn up by a very able modern historian, that you may see how far it reaches such an ideal of the philosophy of history as I have sketched above. "As to what concerns history," says M. Amédée Thierry, "the following is the idea of St. Augustine. The events of this world are neither fortuitous nor isolated. Divine Providence directs them, forms them into a series, causes them all to concur towards the same end, the triumph of truth and justice, such as they were revealed in the first instance to the Hebrew people, and as Jesus Christ came to confirm and announce them to the nations. Whoever listens to the voice from on high, and follows it, belongs to the people of the elect, the City of God, nigh to which moves the city of the earth, devoted to worldly interests, the city of pride and dominion, the persecutor of the saints, but which not the less labours, by means of which she is ignorant, for the kingdom of God. Thus did Babylon in the east—thus does Rome in the west—both of them queens of nations, both of them announced by prophecies, both of them predestined to spread abroad, the former the revelations of the Old Testament, the latter those of the New. The kingdom of Rome was universal, because such was to be the kingdom of Christ. And as the ancient law was but a preparation for the new, everything in the ancient world converged towards Rome, and the accession of Jesus Christ, just as everything after that accession has concurred to the triumph and the universality of the Christian faith. Never was Rome so powerful as since, by the communication of Christ's religion, she attached to herself the barbarian nations bent formerly on her ruin. The Gauls burnt that Rome which was subject to the false gods; the soldiers of Hannibal would have made her a heap of stones; the Christian Alaric recoils from the destruction of Christian Rome; he makes himself her master, and preserves her."[1]

It is the main idea which is here so valuable. The atmosphere of Tacitus and the lurid glare of his Rome, compared with St. Augustine's world, are like the shades in which Achilles deplored the loss of life

[1] *Histoire de la Gaule*, Introduction, p. 340.

contrasted with a landscape bathed in the morning light of a southern sun. Yet how much more material misery was there in the time of St. Augustine than in the time of Tacitus! In spite of the excesses in which the emperors might indulge within the walls of their palace or of Rome, the fair fabric of civilisation filled the whole Roman world, the great empire was in peace, and its multitude of nations were brethren. Countries which now form great kingdoms of themselves were then tranquil members of one body politic. Men could traverse the coasts of Italy, Gaul, Spain, Africa, Syria, Asia Minor, and Greece, round to Italy again, and find a rich, smiling land covered by prosperous cities, enjoying the same laws and institutions, and possessed in peace by its children. In St. Augustine's time all had changed. On many of these coasts a ruthless, uncivilised, unbelieving, or misbelieving enemy had descended. Through the whole empire there was a feeling of insecurity, a cry of helplessness, and a trembling at what was about to come. Yet in the pages of the two writers the contrast is just in the inverse ratio. In the Pagan, everything seems borne on by an iron fate, which tramples on the free will of man, and overwhelms the virtuous before the wicked. In the Christian, order shines in the midst of destruction, and mercy dispenses the severest humiliations. It was the symbol of the coming age. And so that great picture of the Doctor, Saint, and Philosopher laid hold of the minds of men during these centuries of violence which followed, and in which peace and justice, so far from embracing each other, seemed to have deserted the earth. And in modern times a great genius has seized upon it, and developed it in the Discourse on Universal History.

Bossuet is worthy to receive the torch from St. Augustine; scarcely could a more majestic voice or a more philosophic spirit set forth the double succession of empire and of religion, or exhibit the tissue wrought by Divine Providence, human free will, and the permitted power of evil.

I do not say that the scientific method reached its full perfection in either of these great authors. I do not say that in the latter theory never encroaches on the domain of facts. Nor have I time to touch on the relation which the course of man's temporal destiny holds to that of his eternal, or the bearing of history on theology, and how much the philosopher may assume from the theologian. These great men were, above all, theologians, and if they in any respect stretched their own province too far, the tendency of things has since been so much in the contrary direction that there is little danger of their example in this respect being followed.

Nothing of this sort, certainly, can be charged on a living author—at once statesman, orator, philosopher and historian of the highest rank—who has given to us, on a less extensive subject, a philosophy of history in its most finished and accurate form. The very attempt, on the part of M. Guizot, to draw out a picture of civilisation during fourteen hundred years, and to dissect through that immense and ever-changing period the course of society in so many countries, indicates no ordinary power; and the partial fulfilment of the design may be said to have elevated the philosophy of history into a science. In this work may be found the most important rules of the science accurately stated; but the work itself is the best example of philosophic method and artistic execution united to illustrate a complex subject. A careful study of original authorities, a patient induction of facts, a cautious generalisation, the philosophic eye to detect analogies, the painter's power to group results, and above all, a unity of conception which no multiplicity of details can embarrass—these are some of the main qualifications for a philosophy of history, which I should deduce from these works. Yet while the action of Providence and that of human free will are carefully and beautifully brought out, while both may be said to be points of predilection to the author, he has not alluded, so far as I am aware, to the great evil spirit and his personal operation. Strong as he is, he has been apparently too weak to bear the scoff of modern infidelity, "he believes in the Devil"— unless, indeed, the cause of this lies deeper, and belongs to his philosophy; for if there be one subject out of which eclecticism can pick nothing to its taste, it would be the permitted operation of the great fallen spirit. Nor will the warmest admiration of his genius be mistaken for a concurrence in all his judgments. I presume not to say how far such an author is sometimes, in spite of himself, unjust, from the point of view at which he draws his picture. Whether and how far he be an eclectic philosopher, let others decide: it would be grievous to feel it true of such a mind; for it is the original sin of that philosophy to make the universe rotate round itself. Great is its complacency in its own conclusions, but there runs through them one mistake—to fancy itself in the place of God.

It is, perhaps, these works and their great influence which led to another effort of the philosophic mind in the defence of Catholicism as to its action on society, by the lamented Balmez, too soon removed from Spain and from the Church. With less unity of conception, with less scientific method, above all, far better in its idea than in execution, it yet exemplifies the philosophy of history; more so, I think, than the volume of the celebrated German who has had the honour of giving its name to the science. We miss, indeed, in Frederic Schlegel the accuracy, lucidity, and point, the admirable concentration of the great French mind above mentioned. Yet there is enough in his volume, in its wide stores of thought and immense learning, to justify the title which he has assumed.

St. Augustine, Bossuet, Guizot, Balmez, Schlegel: I have taken these names not to exhaust, but to illustrate the subject. Here we have the ancient and the modern society, Africa and France, Spain and Germany, and the Christian mind in each, thrown upon the facts of history. They point out, I think, sufficiently a common result. But amid the founders of a new science who shall represent our own country? Can I hesitate, or can I venture, in this place and company, to mention the hand which has directed the scattered rays of light from so many sources on the wild children of Central Asia, and produced the Turk before us in his untamable ferocity—the outcast of the human race, before whom the earth herself ceases to be a mother, by whom man's blood has ever been shed like water, woman's honour counted as the vilest of things, nature's most sacred laws publicly and avowedly outraged—has produced him before us for the abhorrence of mankind, the infamy of nations? To sketch the intrinsic character of barbarism and civilisation, and out of common historical details, travel, and observation, to show the ineffaceable stamp of race and temper reproducing itself through the long series of ages, surely expresses the idea which we mean by the "philosophy of history."

We have seen how the strong light of Catholic truth and teaching gave to history its unity and its universality, reducing the nation under the greater whole of the race, subordinating the city of Romulus to the City of God. It was by discerning the growth and progress of that City of God that the Catholic Doctor, St. Augustine, seized upon it as the central point in the destinies of man, which, while dominion passes from country to country and from race to race, remains fixed and immutable. And this idea penetrated and took possession of Christian history for more than a thousand years. At length a violent schism arose, which severed from the City of God a portion of the civilised world. They who were outside felt no longer touched by its glories or soothed by its promises, and the last three centuries have witnessed on their part repeated attempts to construct histories—and philosophical histories too—which either ignore the existence, or disfigure and misrepresent the operation, of the City of God. The grand exploit of these writers is to blot the sun out of the world. Their utmost skill consists in throwing themselves back into the position of the heathen, when there was no *truth*, but every man's *opinion;* their total success would be to banish from their readers' minds, and to exclude from their own, the thought that God had become man, had sphered his truth in a society, and subordinated the whole course of events unto the trial of men, of nations, and of races, in accepting or rejecting that truth, in combating or forming a part of that society. To all such men a philosophy of history becomes by their own fault as impossible, as without their own fault it was to Livy or Tacitus. But there is scarcely a period or a fact of early, or mediæval, or modern history, which this perverted view of things has not misrepresented; and it is necessary to allude to it, since our own country has been the chief seat of the error. None can ask for a nobler intellectual work than to be instrumental in any sort to the restoration of truth to history. May we not hope that this also is a glory reserved for those who have in the midst of them one who sits in Peter's Chair at the centre of the earth, alone immovable where all is fluctuating; who may well possess and communicate to his children the secret of history, for he has seen age after age and people after people pass by him? They are gone, and he remains the same, to be to all future generations what he was to them—truth's pillar, or its witness. *Sedet æternumque sedebit.*

And this would seem to be the special work in history of the present age, and the ages which are to come. If "facts are the power in credit," so never before were they communicated in such abundance to the curiosity of mankind. The predicted times are come upon us; "many run to and fro, and knowledge is increased." The world, indeed, in all its aspects, is ransacked for facts. Not only all that concern the experimental sciences, but all that belong to the moral field of human action, are gathered together before us as in a museum. Life seems too short to exhaust the documents that belong even to a single generation. The ends of the earth are brought to meet, and a tide of travellers is continually going forth to sweep every creek and shore of civilised or uncivilised life, and to lay up the results of their observation for posterity; not to say that every age inherits the riches of its predecessors. In the records of human thought accumulation is ever going on: the individual mind passes away; but the collective mind continues its ceaseless progress. It is said that the greatest philosopher of antiquity availed himself of the power and wealth of his mighty pupil, Alexander, to collect animals for the study of natural history. But the poorest child of modern civilisation is richer than Aristotle with the stores of Alexander at his feet. Rather, the student of history is embarrassed with the boundlessness of the wealth set out before him. It is obvious that the special work of such a period must be to select and combine, to analyse and construct. In this direction a work is possible now which in former days no power of mind could accomplish, because the materials were wanting. A subject of importance may be chosen, pursued through centuries and nations, every fact bearing on it noted, the experience of most dissimilar circumstances calculated; and the result may be to throw a new light on even the leading motives which governed such times and countries. The actors themselves and their contemporaries are usually unconscious of those very motives. "One must be outside the picture," says an able historian,[1] " to know well its striking and characteristic points." It is in such studies, perhaps, that the mind is most sensibly affected by that wonderful mystery of Almighty power, the Providence which rules the free actions of men. Who has not gazed with admiration on a swarm of insects unconfusedly engaged, with ceaseless industry and unity of purpose, in the work of their hive? Who has not felt arrested at the spectacle of the Divine mind which planted this instinct

[1] M. de Barante.

within them, and reveals itself in such effects? But look now on the hive of men, where every one possesses not instinct, but the diviner gifts of memory, understanding, and will—where every one has an origin of action and choice in himself, which is essentially free, which he is ever exercising. And yet no less the whole hive conspire to a work beyond the thought and aim of the individual, beyond that of the mass—every one goes his own way, but all go together a way they wot not of, and man's free will works out God's intention. Gazing on such a scene, we realise the poet's thought, and admire with him

> " La Provvidenza che governa il mondo
> Con quel consiglio nel quale ogni aspetto
> Creato è vinto pria che vade al fondo."[1]

Such is human history in its highest aspect; a most wonderful and entrancing sight. In thus analysing, comparing, sorting, and combining facts, the philosophy of history has a great field open before it. If carried out faithfully and conscientiously, no science can be fraught with more important advantage to mankind. The simple recitation of great deeds will ever possess a charm for the human mind; but the philosophic induction and inference from facts is replete with instruction for the race, and prepares the future against the errors of the past.

But if such be the philosophy of history, my hearers may fairly ask what right or title have I to take any part in so great a work? Now to this I have but one reply. I have not sought a post, but obeyed a call.[2] It is a call the nature of which I had never thought

---

[1] Dante, *Parad.* xi. 28.
[2] The author was appointed, under the rectorship of Dr. Newman, to the post of lecturer on the "Philosophy of History" in the Catholic University of Ireland.

of till it was made; in following it I obeyed another's judgment, not my own. I put my feebleness under the shield of his authority. I recognised him, indeed, as one of the chiefs among the sons of thought, and felt that it was glory enough for me to serve under him. I reflected also that the fortress of error, which we are besieging, is of enormous force; the despotism of self-will, for many a long year ruling undisputed, has filled it full with all the munitions of war; its defenders are proud and stubborn. That the fortress will one day be taken, I know full well; but who will take it, is another story. Many and many a soldier will fall before it; yet, in the day of its capture, their toil, their suffering, their it may be unnoticed fall and unhonoured lot, will not have been in vain. They will have a portion of the success; for they spent in it their force and their life, which is all that the bravest can do. If such be my portion, I accept it beforehand willingly. The soldier who so fights cannot be presumptuous; for his trust is in his commander and his cause, not in himself. It is not his part to judge whether the work is according to his strength; for it comes to him as a duty to be fulfilled, the spring of which is not ambition, but obedience.

It has been my single object in this Address to answer the question, What is the "philosophy of history"? and to lay down some chief rules which should attend the scientific treatment of such a subject. When next I have the honour to meet you, I hope to commence a course in which I shall attempt to apply the principles here touched upon to a great subject of study, the "Formation of Christendom."

THE FORMATION OF CHRISTENDOM.

LECTURE I.

THE CONSUMMATION OF THE OLD WORLD.

THE empire of Augustus inherited the whole civilisation of the ancient world. Whatever political and social knowledge, whatever moral or intellectual truth, whatever useful or elegant arts "the enterprising race of Japhet" had acquired, preserved, and accumulated in the long course of centuries since the beginning of history, had descended without a break to Rome, with the dominion of all the countries washed by the Mediterranean. For her the wisdom of Egypt and of all the East had been stored up; for her Pythagoras and Thales, Socrates, Plato, and Aristotle, and all the schools besides of Grecian philosophy suggested by these names, had thought; for her Zoroaster, as well as Solon and Lycurgus, legislated; for her Alexander conquered, the races which he subdued forming but a portion of her empire. Every city in the ears of whose youth the poems of Homer were familiar as household words owned her sway. Her magistrates, from the Northern Sea to the confines of Arabia, issued their decrees in the language of empire—the Latin tongue; while, as men of letters, they spoke and wrote in Greek. For her Carthage had risen, founded colonies, discovered distant coasts, set up a world-wide trade, and then fallen, leaving her the empire of Africa and the West, with the lessons of a long experience. Not only so, but likewise Spain, Gaul, and all the frontier provinces, from the Alps to the mouth of the Danube, spent in her service their strength and skill; supplied her armies with their bravest youths; gave to her Senate and her knights their choicest minds. The vigour of new and the culture of long-polished races were alike employed in the vast fabric of her power. In fact, every science and art, all human thought, experience, and discovery, had poured their treasure in one stream into the bosom of that society which, after forty-four years of undisputed rule, Augustus had consolidated into a new system of government, and bequeathed to the charge of Tiberius.

It is hard to conceive adequately what a spectator called "the immense majesty of the Roman peace."[1] Where now in Europe, impatient and uneasy, a group of half-friendly nations jealously watches each other's progress in power, and the acquisition of a province threatens a general war, Rome maintained, from generation to generation, in tranquil sway, an empire of which Gaul and Spain, Britain and North Africa, Switzerland and the greater part of Austria, Turkey in Europe, Asia Minor, Syria, and Egypt, formed but single limbs, members of her mighty body. Her roads, which spread like a network over this immense territory from their common centre, the golden milestone of her Forum, under the palace of her emperors, did but express the unity of that spirit with which

[1] Pliny, *Nat. His.* xxvii. 1. "Immensa Romanæ pacis majestate, non homines modo diversis inter se terris gentibusque, verum etiam montes et excedentia in nubes juga partusque eorum et herbas quoque invicem ostentante."

she ruled the earth, her subject, levelling the mountain and filling up the valley, for the march of her armies, the caravans of her merchandise, and the even sweep of her legislation. A moderate fleet of 6000 sailors at Misenum, and another at Ravenna, a flotilla at Forum Julii, and another in the Black Sea, of half that force, preserved the whole Mediterranean from piracy;[1] and every nation bordering on its shores could freely interchange the productions of their industry. Two smaller armaments of 24 vessels each, on the Rhine and the Danube, secured the empire from northern incursion. In the time of Tiberius a force of 25 legions and 14 cohorts, making 171,500 men, with about an equal number of auxiliary troops, that is, in all an army of 340,000 men, sufficed not so much to preserve internal order, which rested on other and surer ground, but to guard the frontiers of a vast population, amounting, as is calculated, to 120,000,000,[2] and inhabiting the very fairest regions of the earth, of which the great Mediterranean Sea was a sort of central and domestic lake. But this army itself, thus moderate in number, was not, as a rule, stationed in cities, but in fixed quarters on the frontiers as a guard against external foes.[3] Thus, for instance, the whole interior of Gaul possessed a garrison of but 1200 men; that Gaul which, in the year 1860, in a time of peace, thought it necessary for internal tranquillity and external rank and security, to have 626,000 men in arms.[4] Again, Asia Minor

---

[1] Champagny, *Les Césars*, iii. 386.
[2] By Gibbon estimated at 120,000,000; by Döllinger (*Heidenthum und Judenthum*, i.) at about 100,000,000.
[3] Champagny, iii. 386.
[4] The *Daily Telegraph*, on August 20, 1864, calculated the number of men in arms in Europe, in a time of peace, at 5,000,000; the calcu-

had no military force: that most beautiful region of the earth teemed with princely cities, enjoying the civilisation of a thousand years, and all the treasures of art and industry, in undisturbed repose. And within its unquestioned boundaries the spirit, moreover, of Roman rule was far other than that of a military discipline, or of a bureaucracy and a police pressing with ever-watchful suspicion on every spring of civil life. The principle of its government was not that no population could be faithful which was not kept in leading-strings, but rather to leave cities and corporations to manage their own affairs themselves. Thus, its march was firm and strong, as one whose empire was assured, but for this very reason devoid alike of fickleness and haste.[1]

Under the peace of so vast an empire, guarded rather by the majesty of the Roman name than by the amount of force employed, the inhabitants of three continents, with ready transit by roads, canals, rivers, and the great central sea at their command, had unexampled facilities of commerce. No theory of free trade could equal the advantages arising from unity of empire; for the public tranquillity being maintained at so slight a cost, this vast dominion was free from a large part of that burden of taxation which presses on modern industry, when the penalty of past wars is felt during even the uncertain periods of intermittent peace. Far indeed was the *pax Romana* removed from that armed jealousy of rival nations, the sole resource of the world after the forfeiture of

lation being taken from the budgets of the several countries. The revenues of these countries were estimated at £314,000,000, of which their armies and navies cost £123,000,000 a year.

[1] Döllinger, *Heid. und Jud.*, i. 34-5. Champagny, iii. 100, gives the disposition of the army.

its spiritual unity, which is termed the balance of power.

Then, on the contrary, from the Rhine and Danube to the deserts of Africa; from utmost Spain to the Euphrates, no war, nor suspicion of war, could arise. Of such a period Tertullian wrote: "The world itself is opened up, and becomes from day to day more civilised, and increases the sum of human enjoyment. Every place is reached, is become known, is full of business. Solitudes, famous of old, have changed their aspects under the richest cultivation. The plough has levelled forests, and the beasts that prey on man have given place to those that serve him. Corn waves on the sea-shore; rocks are opened out into roads; marshes are drained; cities are more numerous now than villages in former time. The island has lost its savageness, and the cliff its desolation. Houses spring up everywhere, and men to dwell in them. On all sides are government and life. What better proof can we have of the multiplication of our race than that man is become a drug, while the very elements scarcely meet our needs; our wants outrun the supplies; and the complaint is general that we have exhausted even nature."[1]

And this Rome herself, the centre, the ruler, the presiding genius of the civilised world—she who, in the words of Strabo, "had taught humanity to man"[2]— what was the life which she bestowed on her inhabitants? Judge of it by the gift of an emperor to his people: of such gifts there were many in Rome. A vast square, of more than a thousand feet, comprehended within its various courts three great divisions.

---

[1] *De Anima*, 30; referred to by Champagny, iii. 196.
[2] See Champagny, iii. 200; Dandolo, *Roma e i Papi*, cap. iii., vol. i. 122.

One contained libraries, picture and sculpture galleries, music-halls, and every need for the cultivation of the mind. A second, courts for gymnastics, riding, wrestling, and every bodily exercise. A third, the baths: but how little the word associated with modern poverty conveys a notion of the thing! There were tepid, vapour, and swimming baths, accompanied with perfumes and frictions, giving the body an elastic suppleness. Then as to their material: alabaster vied with marble; mosaic pavements with ceilings painted in fresco; walls were incrusted in ivory, and a softened daylight reflected from mirrors; while on all sides a host of servants were engaged in the various offices of the bath. The afternoon *siesta* is over; a bell sounds; the Thermæ open. There all Rome assembles to chat, to criticise, to declaim. There is coffee-house, theatre, exchange, palace, school, museum, parliament, and drawing-room in one. There is food for the mind, exercise and refreshment for the body. There, if anywhere, the eye can be satisfied with seeing and the ear with hearing, and every sense and every taste find but a too ready gratification. This feast of intellect, this palace of ancient power and art, is open daily without cost, or for the smallest coin, to every Roman citizen. Private wealth in modern times bestows a few of these gifts on a select number; but poor as well as rich could revel then, without fear of exhaustion, in this treasure-house of material civilisation. For all is the gift of the imperial delegate to the people whom he serves and represents. The establishment is a graceful homage offered by the chosen of the nation to his constituents, who, according to the theory, have invested him with the plenitude of their collective power.

Nor must we here forget the greatest gift which

the Roman empire bestowed upon the human race—
a system of equal law; a system which, in spite of the
force from without, that at last broke up the empire,
still lived on, was first the admiration of the barbarian
conqueror, then instructed him, and finally subdued
him to a willing homage. And that Roman law
should thus have broadened out into an universal
system of equal rights for all, is the more wonderful
because at the beginning it treated the most elementary and necessary rights of man in society as in
the strictest sense national, or rather civic privileges.
If the Roman could legally marry, and possess the
power of a husband and a father; if he could inherit,
acquire, and transmit property, he could do all these
things, not because he was a man, but because he was
a citizen of Rome. The stranger residing within his
borders could do none of them. But when, in the
last century of the republic, Rome became a world-
wide power, and was brought as a ruler into daily
contact with the most different nations, each possessing
its own customs, laws, and rights, this old stern and
most exclusive system of the Twelve Tables became
supplemented, modified, corrected in a thousand details.
Under the ceaseless labour and thought of philosophic
jurisconsults, applying general principles, the science
of *right* was gradually formed, and a barbarous
groundwork of civic privileges, local, arbitrary, relative
in the highest degree, and full of the most galling
inequality, became in process of time, without sudden
change, by the slow and gradual deduction of Roman
genius and Greek subtilty, a complete system of natural
equity, with a sort of philosophic precision and mathe-
matical elegance.[1] This great result had not indeed

[1] See Champagny, iv. 94-102.

been accomplished at the time we are considering, the fifty years which succeeded the Incarnation, but things were in progress towards it. Rome was bringing all civilised nations to have and to acknowledge but one law, and this law not imposed by the power of the victorious nation, but the result of the good sense of all: so that what we now call Roman law was nothing but a great revolt of universal equity against institutions originally peculiar to the Roman people.

For this material fabric of surpassing power and extent rested upon more than material foundations. Rome was not merely the mighty conqueror, but the skilful assimilator of the human race. Her reign would not have acquired and deserved the name of a majestic peace but for this. And to appreciate her power and her merit herein we must look beneath the surface. Perhaps if we compare her for a moment with other great cities which were most distinguished amid the thousands comprised in her dominion, this will be most apparent. We will choose none but the heads of former empires, the chief lights of civilisation.

First of all, Athens. She had been a great naval power, a great emporium of traffic; she was still, as she had been for ages, a great centre of human thought and speculation. Once the tributes of many Greek cities flowed to her, and she became the representative of the Greek name. The most beautiful buildings of the world raised upon her acropolis out of the wealth of her subjects testified to what had been her sway. But she had not the gift of making this sway acceptable to her tributaries. They quickly revolted from her, and her empire passed like a dream. Henceforth her reign was restricted to the arts of peace: painting, music, and sculpture, poetry, eloquence, and philosophy, the natural gifts of the most gifted among ancient races, chose her for their home. The great and wise of the earth loved to visit her, and to spend a time of study within her walls, reverencing the shadow of departed political greatness, but more enjoying the light of present culture and refinement, nay, charmed by the very clearness of the atmosphere, and the hues of a spot renowned for its loveliness,

"Where on the Ægean shore a city stands
Built nobly, pure the air, and light the soil."

Athens was of old and gradual growth; but Antioch was selected by a rich and brilliant sovereign for the head of his empire. She was crowned Queen of the East at her birth; and so long as the kingdom of the Seleucidæ lasted, its princes found in their beautiful Antioch a residence to their mind. They poured out upon her their wealth, and her lovely climate lent itself to every invention of luxury. Seated in a matchless valley between two ranges of lofty mountains, she grew till four cities, each enclosed within its own walls, extended from beyond the deep-flowing Orontes to the heights of Mount Silpius, and her battlements, still towering over craig and ravine, even in their ruins astonish the traveller. All the races of the East found in her their home: there Greek and Oriental civilisation joined hands; and she continued for ages, under Roman dominion, a spot where the wealthy delighted to dwell, her Syrian magnificence embellished by a long series of Roman emperors. Caligula, Trajan, and Hadrian built her baths; Antoninus Pius paved her chief street with Egyptian granite. For more than eight hundred years this glory lasted, until she was taken and destroyed by Chosroes. But what, as a heathen city, are Antioch's contributions to the human race? She was a splendid capital, a choice abode of luxury and power, and nothing more.

Greater yet than Antioch, fairest of all fair cities, yielding to Rome only in size, but her rival, perhaps her superior, in traffic, was Alexandria. Chosen by one of the greatest conquerors and sovereigns to be a military and commercial metropolis, she collected in her bosom the trade of three continents. From the beginning Egyptian, Greek, and Jew had each in her their quarter; but every nation of the empire, and Indians, Scythians, and Ethiopians from beyond it, were represented there. Occupying a broad tongue of land between the sea and the lake Mareotis, from which every fog was scattered by the northern winds that ventilate the Delta in summer,[1] her dry atmosphere preserved for centuries the colour and outline of her buildings unimpaired; not a flute of her pillars or a flower of their capitals was marred by time; and eye-witnesses tell us that no city of the world presented such a scene of beauty and grandeur as that which met the traveller disembarking at the Gate of the Moon, and passing to the Gate of the Sun, from sea to sea, through a street lined with columns.[2] This was crossed by a chief thoroughfare of like beauty and more than four miles long, while her quays lined the two harbours, and exhibited the productions of Europe, Asia, and Africa in abundance, unrivalled by Rome herself. All that the Seleucidæ had done for

---

[1] Strabo, vi. 17.
[2] Achilles Tatius, lib. v. beginning. Diodorus Siculus, xvii. 52. Strabo, vi. 17.

Antioch, and more yet, the Ptolemies had done for Alexandria. They had made her the great school of philosophy and medicine. Her Serapeion and Museum had no equals in the world for grandeur. She joined then in herself the glory of Athens and of Antioch; a seat no less of thought, study, and mental culture than of material wealth. She was the full-grown offspring of Alexander, sharing his double greatness from her birth to her end, and this brilliant life lasted for well-nigh a thousand years, until she yielded to the Arab destroyer. Yet what great contribution did she, too, as a heathen city, leave to the human race?

Greater than Athens, Antioch, and Alexandria, in the material order, Rome excelled them yet more in this, that she had at once the will and the power to communicate to others that which was most precious of all her possessions in her own eyes, in the eyes of her subjects, and in the eyes of posterity: her political and civil rights, her citizenship. Her great instrument in the government of men, her great means of preserving that majestic peace which was the true glory of her empire, was this gift of imparting her own rights in various degrees to the conquered. Her mode of doing this well deserves mention, since it lets us into the secret of her power.

The Latin city which in her cradle had grown upon the ruins of Alba Longa, taking its citizens as the most precious spoil of victory to be her own, had pursued the same policy through seven hundred years of increasing power. Thus all Italy had gradually acquired the right of Roman citizenship. For she, for the first time in history, had created a citizenship independent of material walls and limits. Her rule was not the exclusion of the stranger and the isolation of the city; but to attract, to associate, and to extend. How did she effect this? Let us take an instance. Augustus found the Alpine valleys descending on Italy still in possession of the native tribes. Having conquered the warlike Salesi in the largest and fairest of these, he terminated a series of rebellions by selling for slaves their male population; but in the midst of the valley he planted a colonia. A legion of veteran soldiers, with standards displayed, with their tribunes, centuries, and cohorts, marched to the chosen spot. At their head the augur, the pontiff, the notary, and the land-surveyor took their place. The ground was solemnly marked out according to the sacerdotal laws of Etruria; the omens taken; the lines drawn; officer and private received his portion according to his rank. In the midst of the ground so allotted the sacred plough traced the enclosure without which there could be no legal city, the pomœrium imaging that of Rome. The parallelogram so formed was intersected by two lines, terminating at the four cardinal points, which marked the site of four gates, sacred and inviolable as those of Rome, while at the point of intersection was the forum, the likeness of that whose name had become famous over all the earth. Out of the armed force, which had thus become citizen, the new republic chose duumviri, who were its consuls; and decemvirs, who formed its senate. Three hundred families answered to the three hundred original Roman gentes; thirty decemvirs to the three hundred senators; there was priest for priest, and sacrifice for sacrifice. There was Rome herself in her fourfold aspect of camp, city, temple, and field.[1] It was henceforth Roman soil,

[1] "Campus, urbs, templum ager Romanus."

dwelt in by Roman citizens with all civil and political rights.

Forthwith the new republic became in its district a sentinel, a citadel, a capital of Roman power: the centre of all existing civilisation, and besides, the market-place, tribunal, emporium to all the neighbourhood. Every occupation and business of life drew the natives around to it. There only on marketdays could they exchange their goods and make their purchases; there, if strife arose between neighbours, the law would determine the right. There they saw an image of life, wealth, comfort, and civil peace, far superior to anything which they had imagined. Insensibly it drew them to its bosom, and the aim of their life became to share the privileges which they saw securely possessed by its inhabitants. Rome had planted herself, with all her attributes of power, order, wealth, and peace, before their eyes and within their grasp. How could they fail to stretch forth their arms to the embrace of such a mother?[1]

After nearly two thousand years you may still gaze down from the overlooking mountain on that colonia. Its enclosure remains. Its walls in large part continue as they were then built. Its central square was the ancient forum; its chief streets the intersecting lines drawn by the augur; and before its gate stands the very triumphal arch bearing the name of Augustus, its founder, twenty-seven years before the Christian era.[2] Even in her stones Rome seems everlasting.

[1] Champagny, *Les Césars:* to whom I am indebted for this view of the importance of the colonia in the Roman system of rule. "Coloniæ, nostræ omnes in literis antiquis urbeis quod item conditæ ut Roma." Varro, *De L. Lat.* v. 40. "Coloniæ, quasi effigies parvæ simulacraque populi Romani." Aul. Gell. xvi. 13, quoted by him.
[2] The city of Aosta, seen from the Becca di Nona.

Now what Rome did here in the fairest and most important of Alpine valleys, the great road by which Julius passed to conquer Gaul, and Napoleon from Gaul descended on Italy, that she had been doing for hundreds of years in her own peninsula, wherein during that time she had planted 161 coloniæ and 72 municipia; that she was doing over the broad plains of Gaul, and by the great rivers and thoroughfares of Western Europe, the Rhine, the Rhone, the Tagus, and the Ebro. She propagated herself in France by such cities as Lyons, Narbonne, Toulouse, and Arles; in Spain, by such as Cordova, Tarragona, Merida; in Africa, by Carthage, Utica, Adrametum; on the Rhine, by Cologne and Bâle; on the Moselle, by Treves; in England, by Colchester and London. These are but specimens of her assimilating power, by which she, who had conquered in arms, won and moulded by civilisation, educated by governing, united and exalted by imparting rights. Athens, Antioch, Alexandria did not this, and so lived solitarily, and at length died ignominiously; whereas Rome sowed the whole West with the imperishable seed of her own liberty, law, and self-government, so that her municipal autonomy passed on as a principle of freedom to our living Europe; and throughout her provinces all that were distinguished by wealth, industry, energy, rank of any sort, strove for her citizenship and obtained it, and henceforth had two countries—one that town or district which bore them, the other and the greater, Rome, that queen-mother of ten thousand cities, from whose womb they had been bred, by whose milk they had been nurtured, whose heart's blood—the possession of her original civil and political rights—ran in their veins.

Was the Greek orator[1] wrong when he called the coloniæ and municipia of Rome her true ramparts, ramparts not to the city only, but to the whole empire? "The walls of Babylon were but child's play," he cried, "in comparison with these. Darius once netted a single city on an island within a circle of living men, but Rome has netted the world." And thus she is like the common mother earth, supporting all; or like the ocean, receiving all streams into her bosom without overflowing; where every one has his deserts: and no geographical division prevents merit from being known and honoured. And thus the word "Roman" is become the name not of a city merely, but of a general race, and her guards are her own citizens, the best and most powerful citizens in every city of the world.

Great, then, as in itself was the military power of Rome, it pressed very lightly on so vast an empire, being thrown entirely on the frontiers, while the whole interior was guarded and maintained in tranquillity without soldiers by that sole majesty of her name. Indisputable, all-controlling as was her sovereignty, at the same time it did not efface the variety of subject races, for it left them in general in possession of their own laws, liberty, property, and customs, reserving to itself the right of peace and war, and requiring only that they should have the same enemies and the same friends with herself. It was a patronage,[2] says Cicero, rather than an empire.

---

[1] Aristides, *De Urbe Roma*.
[2] "Regum, populorum, nationum portus erat et refugium senatus. Nostri autem magistratus imperatoresque ex hac una re maximam laudem capere studebant, si provincias, si socios æquitate et fide defendissent. Itaque illud patrocinium orbis terræ verius quam imperium poterat nominari." *De Offic.* ii. 8. This state of things, broken

By so many cities, images of Rome herself, possessing and communicating her privileges, she drew and moulded the various nations after her own pattern; and so, without an ubiquitous police or an army of administrative agents, she gave life, order, and unity to the whole mass, as the centre of all rights, and the disposer of all rewards. "The one thing which I especially admire in you," says the same Greek rhetorician, "is that with so great and strongly constituted a dominion you govern men as freemen, which is entirely peculiar to yourselves. It is no Caria given to Tissaphernes, or Phrygia to Pharnabazus, or Egypt to another, as the private property of one himself a slave; but as the magistrates of a particular city govern its revenues for that city's good, you have made the world one city, and appoint its rulers to preside over and provide for citizens with lawful not despotic power."[1]

We can now better understand the majesty of that omnipresent city as seen in the several magistrates, who by the names of Proconsuls, Proprætors, Procurators, or Præfects, bore her name and power in the several countries. Round their tribunals at Arles, at Cordova, at Carthage, at Thessalonica, at Ephesus, at Antioch, at Alexandria, nations distinct in their origin, laws, and customs, waited with an equally humble obedience, receiving a common law from their mouth. Armed force was not needed, for greater than any force was the name of the goddess Roma, whom they represented. And so the five hundred cities of Asia reverence, without a garrison, a single ruler and his

down in the hundred years preceding the empire, seems certainly to have been, in part at least, restored under the empire.

[1] Aristides, *De Urbe Roma*, pp. 207, 211, 213, 214.

consular fasces. The Greeks with all their wisdom, the Macedonians after all their victories, bow humbly before six rods. The Gauls, who fought for freedom during eighty years, pay tribute and accept prosperity from the Romans, with but 1200 soldiers among them, scarcely more numerous than the number of their cities.[1] Yet these rulers, whose majesty surpasses that of kings, are themselves magistrates owing obedience to another. They serve their appointed time and depart; are responsible for their actions and their judgments to that supreme ruler at Rome who governs the world by his letters.

Is this an unworthy development for those who in their beginning were so unsparing to self, so stern in their notion of duty, so devoted to their country; for which parents were known to sacrifice their children, patriots to devote themselves to death—the city of Marcus Brutus, Camillus, Decius, Fabius, Regulus, Manlius, Curtius, Virginius?

Is not the very language of Cicero and Virgil an expression of this lordly yet peaceful rule; this even, undisturbed majesty, which holds the world together like the regularity of the seasons, like the alternation of light and darkness, like the all-pervading warmth of the sun? If every language reflects the character of the race which speaks it, surely we discern in the very strain of Virgil the closing of the gates of war, the settling of the nations down to the arts of peace, the reign of law and order, the amity and concord of races, the weak protected, the strong ruled; in a word,

"Romanos rerum dominos gentemque togatam."

---

[1] See the speech of Agrippa, dissuading the Jews from war, in Josephus, *De Bello*, ii. 16.

It is with the settled reign and matured policy of Augustus that this peace begins, and it lasts more or less two hundred years in its completeness, and two hundred more in its decline. To it will apply the words of Seneca, that Rome had found most faithful allies in the nations which had been its most obstinate enemies: for in what would its empire consist had it not with wise provision blended the conquered with their conquerors?[1] And a Roman general reminds the Gauls how their country had been a scene of interminable wars and revolutions before the Romans intervened. "And if they were expelled, what else," he added, "would follow, but a struggle between every nation and its neighbour? It cost the good fortune and the discipline of eight hundred years to weld into one mass this empire, which cannot be rent to pieces but with the destruction of those who rend it. Cherish, therefore, and love that peace and that city, which, whether conquered or conquerors, we possess with common rights."[2]

From this glimpse of the external grandeur of the Roman people let us turn to the internal condition of its society.

First and foremost is the great institution of slavery the broad basis on which this mighty pyramid may be said to rest. For not merely was all domestic service performed by slaves, but the cultivation of the land had at this time fallen almost entirely to them, as well as all works of industry involving hand-labour in

[1] Seneca, *De Ira*, ii. 34.
[2] Speech of Cerialis, Tac. *Hist.* iv. 73-4. "Nam pulsis, quod dii prohibeant, Romanis, quid aliud quam bella omnium inter se gentium existent? Octingentorum annorum fortuna disciplinaque compages hæc coa luit quæ convelli sine exitio convellentium non potest. . . . Proinde pacem et urbem quam victi victoresque eodem jure obtinemus amate, colite."

town and country. Even the liberal arts, such as medicine and architecture, were mainly in their hands. Of their number it is difficult to obtain any certain knowledge. It differed probably in the various provinces, being largest of all at Rome, where the servile population was twice, if not thrice, in number the free. Thus, first of all, hand-work was servile; secondly, domestic service; thirdly, industry; fourthly, commerce and the useful arts of life in great part, and even the fine arts in some degree. The conquest of all the countries bordering on the Mediterranean, accomplished in the hundred and fifty years preceding Christ, flooded the Roman world with slaves. Nor were they of an inferior or even markedly different race from their masters. Drawn from Germany, Gaul, Spain, Northern Africa, Syria, Asia Minor, Greece, and Thrace, the vast majority belonged, like their conquerors, to the great Aryan race. There were few of the children of Shem; fewer yet of Ham's unhappy progeny. On the whole, the Roman slave was, in natural gifts of body and mind, fully his master's equal. What then was his social condition?

A slave was a piece of property;[1] an animated instrument, something absolutely belonging to his master, a being absorbed in his master's being, by whom he could be given, lent, pledged, exchanged, or sold. This was the fundamental notion of Roman slavery in particular, that the slave was a thing, not a person; so especially a thing that the Roman word for "chattel" belonged to him peculiarly. He was *mancipium*, a marvellous expression of the hard Roman

[1] The following summary of slavery is condensed from Wallon, and Döllinger, *Heid. und Jud.* p. 704-10. It must be remembered that *Roman* slavery is here treated of, not slavery in general—a question which I reserve for future treatment.

idea, by which the human being became a thing which you could grasp in your hand. Varro, in treating of agriculture, wrote: "There are three sorts of instruments, vocal, semi-vocal, and mute: vocal, which comprises slaves; semi-vocal, oxen; mute, wagons." The principle thus tersely stated by Varro was carried out through Roman law with the most rigorous precision in all its details. As the citizen was the equal of all other citizens in the eye of the State, so he was absolute sovereign within his own house. And the slave was so absolutely his master's property that neither the favour of the people nor the authority of the prince could legally sever the bond. The master could not bind himself to a slave; could not accuse him of theft, because the slave being within his dominion, anything taken by him could not go out of it. The slave had no civil position, no marriage, no paternity. By custom his master allowed him certain perquisites, which he could lay by for himself, and which was called his *peculium;* but this, too, belonged legally to the master. Much more had he no political rights; and an attempt on his part to enter military service or to take any civil office was punished with death. He had no power to receive a legacy; no power of legal action. He could not give evidence, save upon torture; and when he was so called in as a witness, the law carefully provided that any damage done to him by breaking of limbs or loss of life should be repaid according to its money value to his master. His punishment was left entirely in his master's hand. The right of the master had no limitation. There was an old law punishing with death the killing of an ox; but the law made no such provision in the case of the slave; the human being, outside the range of civic rights, had never such value in its eyes. The master, then, might condemn his slave; his sentence itself was subject to no control, and its execution to no impediment. Such executions were carried out publicly under Augustus, and without his interference. The usual mode of inflicting death on the slave was by crucifixion. Not until Hadrian's time was this power taken away by law, on account of the excesses still witnessed. As long as the Romans were their own masters, they never thought of limiting the master's power over the slave.

Cato the Censor, that brilliant example of old Roman virtue, Cicero's model of the old man, was especially remarkable for the exactness with which he carried out the Roman view of the slave being his master's chattel. He saw no difference between animals and slaves, save that the latter were reasonable and docile, and so could be made responsible. When his slaves grew old and helpless, he used to sell or drive them away. And he had them trained like dogs and horses, and at certain times he allowed them to pair. Finding the slave-trade profitable, and loving money more and more, he made his slaves in his latter years buy and train boys, and then sell them again.

Such being the law, in custom and in fact, the ordinary state of the slave was no doubt ruled by the law of interest. It is in the whole mass that the true character of their condition must be seen; and this condition in general represented the influence on which by its nature it depended, that is, the law of property as foundation, and utility as rule. The Roman's custom answered but too well to the law, which gave him the slave for his property, to use him as a thing. This false idea had taken full possession of Roman life.

Such was the condition of that large majority by whose labour society was supported. But must not the superstructure of society correspond to its basis? There could not be a single free Roman household which was not affected by the existence of such slavery as this. Large as was the part of the social domain which it occupied entirely to itself, it fermented through all the rest. The spirit of slavery is never limited to the slave: it saturates the atmosphere which the freeman breathes together with the slave, passes into his nature, and corrupts it. Let us mark this aggressive character of slavery at Rome in three points of view.

(a) 1. First, slave-labour was continually expelling free labour. The land of Italy was originally tilled by a free peasantry. At Rome especially agriculture was held in the highest honour. But the effect of war and conquest had been to exterminate the class of small proprietors both at Rome and in Italy. Their lands went to form the broad estates, *latifundia*, of the nobles; their honourable toils were replaced by the sorry but cheaper tillage of the slave, who was incapable of military service, and without suffrage, the mere instrument of an absent master, and superintended by a steward like himself a slave. Thus agriculture, which had been the nursery of Roman legions for so many centuries, was become servile, and the land of the hardy Sabins had been, in the words of Seneca, delivered over to "fettered feet, bound hands, and branded faces."[1]

2. Again, not only were servants slaves, but slaves were the only servants. There is nothing in domestic

[1] "Impediti, pedes, vinctæ manus, inscripti vultus;" quoted by Champagny, iv. 2.

service of its own nature incompatible with freedom. The happier state of society in which we live allows master and servant to have the same political and civil rights, the same religious duties and hopes. But at Rome the system of slavery had rendered free service impossible, not only by fixing a brand upon it, but because the whole social economy was opposed to it.

3. Once more, slaves were artisans, and held in the city almost as complete a monopoly of the skilled labour by which the various arts of life are carried on, as the ruder field-labour in the country. Industry, retail trade, commerce itself in large part were not free, but conducted by masters through their slaves, who were taught at the smallest cost every manufacture and every art by which the fortune of their lords might be increased.

Labour, therefore, under the three great divisions of tillage, domestic service, and artisanship, had been rendered ignominious because it was the portion of slaves.

(b) But, secondly, what was the social and political temper which slavery generated around and outside of itself? What was the condition and the spirit of the free? This rich man, to whose absolute power the life, the honour, the happiness of so many slaves are committed, without a check upon passion or caprice, what else could he be but a tyrant, regardless of human life and suffering? By the original constitution of the Roman family he was master, with power of life and death, both of wife and children. But when, in addition to this, his household was founded upon slavery, when from his tenderest youth he had been received in the arms of slaves, heard their language, witnessed their habits, and beheld them not merely sacrificed to their master's advantage, but crouching before his feet in helpless impotence, where was he to learn the spirit of a father or of a citizen? And the poor freeman, supplanted by the slave of the rich in the great field of trade and industry, indisposed, moreover, to work of all kinds, as being the portion of the slave, what had he left to him but his quality of a Roman, dependence upon the imperial largess of corn and money, and servile flattery of his patron as client? It is the great work of the emperor to feed the Roman people. It may cost him his throne if the fleet from Africa be delayed too long, bearing corn to three hundred thousand idle and starving citizens. For here, at least, the master of rich and poor, of slave and freeman alike, pays his homage to the universal spirit of servility, and lives in dread of that people as a whole, of whom every single life and fortune are at his mercy. For the lord of a thousand slaves returning some day from his palace-villa on the cool heights of Tusculum, or the lovely shore of Baiæ, may find an order from the emperor granting to him the truly Cæsarean indulgence of choosing his own mode of death. Then will he collect a few chosen friends for the last social feast, discourse on the shortness and uncertainty of life, and order himself to be placed in a warm bath, where the obedient slave-physician, ever at his side, will skilfully open his veins, so that the stream of life may ebb away with the least suffering.[1]

Thus slave and master, patron and client, senator and emperor, form a graduated hierarchy of slavery, the social and political spirit of which becomes the *model*, as well as the *basis*, of society.

[1] Vide the death of Seneca.

(c) Yet all this is as nothing to the fountain of moral corruption opened by slavery in every Roman household. It was not merely that the labour, the time, the health, and strength of the slave belonged to the master; not merely that he might be poorly fed, miserably lodged, beaten without mercy, cast out in his sickness or age, crucified in his youth; it was that the common nature of man in him was not recognised; that the last stronghold in which the moral being resides, the stronghold of purity, sanctity, and conscience, was recklessly invaded and violated. There was, be it remembered, according to the Roman law, and what is more, according to universal Roman custom, no such thing as adultery, no such thing as seduction, no such thing as outrage in the case of male as well as female slaves. In this respect, as in all others, they were the prey of the master. The Roman house was a fortress, within which, as concerns the relation of master and slave, the writ of the law did not run. What passed within it was not merely unpunished; it could not be known. The law of man-property was sacrosanct, and had priority over everything, the law of human nature included. There is an outrage of animals which the English law till lately, as the divine law of old, forbade under pain of death; but that right of outrage itself, if we may so violate all propriety of language to express the utter violation of nature, that right of outrage itself was sacrosanct under the Roman law.

It is needless, then, to dwell on what was the moral character of the male and female slave within the precincts of a Roman palace. "The Roman law by its distinction between a novitius and a veterator informs us of the effect which servitude exercised on the slaves themselves. A slave who had been a year or more in service was a veterator, a used man, and therefore of much less value; for, says the law-book, it is but too hard to improve a used slave, and adapt him to the service of a new master. The dealers, therefore, often passed off a veterator for a novitius. Thus, a year of service was sufficient so to spoil a man that he sunk considerably in value like any other worn-out ware."[1]

But Rome was the centre of the world, and thither from every subject province streamed a host of slaves, the most accomplished and refined, soon to become the most abandoned, of both sexes. In them an inexhaustible supply of fresh victims made up for the rapid waste of life; and a slave-market, fed by a subject-world, was always at the flood. But what was the result to the masters? We find a series of laws passed by Augustus and the succeeding emperors, to encourage, to enjoin marriage, giving rewards and privileges to those who had families, fining and censuring celibacy. But all in vain. Under Augustus the number of unmarried citizens far exceeded that of the married. Poets, historians, philosophers complain that the Roman will not marry; that Roman families decrease in number. But their example is more powerful than their complaint. Horace, and Virgil, and Catullus, and Tibullus, and the very ministers of the monarch who enjoins marriage, remain themselves voluptuous celibates. The utmost tenderness of the most pathetic and inspired of Latin poets is spent on the most profligate of even Roman women, the wife of another, until in the bitterness of his heart he is compelled to denounce her unequalled shame:

---

[1] Döllinger, *Heid. und Jud.*, p. 713.

"Lesbia nostra, Lesbia illa,
Illa Lesbia, quam Catullus unam
Plus quam se atque suos amavit omnes."

But few will marry; fewer still claim the privileges granted to the parent of three children; for the unnameable advantages of the childless far exceed any reward, immunity, or honour which imperial power can devise for the married. And if even in compliance with the imperial law they live in marriage, yet their married life is destitute of its natural fruit; and so Ovid, Lucan, Statius, Silius Italicus, Seneca, the two Plinies, Suetonius, and Tacitus are married but childless.[1] By this, far more than by the suspicious cruelty of Tiberius, or by Nero's thirst for blood, the Roman nobility dies out. The old patrician, the newer noble, the newest senatorian families disappear. In vain are they replenished from the class of knights or even freedmen. The knights themselves, the rich middle class, suffer from the same cause. They are hardly kept up by continual suppletions from below. And lastly, the very Roman plebs has long ceased to be that sturdy race of freemen which seceded to the Mons Sacer. It has been replenished again and again out of the surging tide of slavery. Already Scipio, the conqueror of Carthage, told the populace to their face that he was not to be daunted by the murmurs of those whom he himself had dragged in chains to Rome.[2] They were no longer "the dregs of Romulus," but the dregs of all the provinces who lived on the imperial poor-law, and swarmed by myriads all through the summer day to behold the encounter of gladiators and beasts in the Coliseum, and the race of rival charioteers in the Circus Maximus.

[1] Döllinger, *Heid. und Jud.*, p. 718.
[2] Valerius Maximus, vi. 11; quoted by Döllinger, p. 715.

THE CONSUMMATION OF THE OLD WORLD 61

Thus, while the moral corruption, engendered by the sensual indulgences which slavery threw into the lap of the Romans, was causing the race of freemen in senate, knights, and people to die out, those classes themselves were continually replenished with slave-blood. For instance, the freedmen of the emperors acquired immense fortunes and armies of slaves; and one of them, Pallas, will have a brother, Antonius Felix, marked by one historian as the husband of three queens, and by another as "a monster of blood and lust, who wielded," in Judea, "the power of a king with the mind of a slave."[1] In a short time this slave-blood ran through every vein of Roman society. And thus in the very city of those to whose ears for five centuries the very name of king had been abominable, it was necessary that one man should rule whose word should be law, according to the maxim, "Quod principi placuit, legis habet vigorem;" though, like Caligula, he might sum up his power as being "the right of all things over all men," or like Nero, when seeking poison to destroy his brother Britannicus, he might ask of the poison-vender, "Have I to fear the Julian law?"[2]

But even this was not the worst. There was a portion of the wealthy Roman's house called the Pædagogium, that in which the young male slaves were brought up, with a certain varnish of education and accomplishments. Seneca gives the portrait of one. "Dressed out like a woman, he struggles with his years: he must not go beyond the age of youth; he is kept back; and though his figure be massive like

---

[1] Tacitus, *Hist.* v. 9.
[2] "Monenti Antoniæ aviæ, tanquam parum esset non obedire, Memento, ait, omnia mihi et in omnes licere." Suet. *Cal.* 29. "Sane legem Juliam timeo." Suet. *Ner.* 33.

that of a fighter, he has a smooth chin, where the hair is rubbed away, or plucked out by the root."[1] I forbear to quote what follows. In a word, as Nero must surpass all other men, while every wealthy Roman may possess his harem of male slaves, the emperor has a harem of freemen.[2]

Thus slavery, after stamping all honest labour with ignominy, and vitiating in its source the social and political spirit of the free, had this further result, that it destroyed the general morality, and in doing so caused the population to decay with a force which no remedial laws could prevent; no filling up from its own ranks counterbalance.

And through every part of the slave-law runs an utter disregard of human life. Man as man has lost his value. He is become the cheapest of all things. In the amphitheatres lives are mown down by thousands yearly, and all Rome gloats over the spectacle of blood. Within the prison-house, which slavery has made of each private family, the vices, luxury, and caprice of masters waste away generation after generation in their first bloom and vigour.

Here, then, in the midst of this Roman empire, so grand in its outward tranquillity, under whose guardianship the civilised nations of the earth aspire not in vain after the blessings of universal peace, we find a despotism without limit in the internal relations of society, in the master over the slave, in the father over the wife and children, in the patron over the client, that is, the rich over the poor, and in the prince over the subject; and with the despotism a moral corruption and a disregard of human life, which

[1] Seneca, *Ep.* 47; quoted by Döllinger, p. 719.
[2] "Ingenuorum." Suet.

THE CONSUMMATION OF THE OLD WORLD 63

are eating away the population, and undermining the foundations of the State.

It was the world of Nero prolonged in the minds of those outside the Church to his own time which St. Augustine saw and described to the life, when a chorus of voices arose from the worshippers of the old gods in favour of a state which gave them an abundance of material goods. What wonder that they, to whom Jupiter with his cupbearer Ganymede was the model of one sex, and Venus with her lover Mars of the other, should be touched by no moral turpitude in such a government? "Only let it remain," they said, "only let it be still abundant in wealth, and glorious with victories, or better still, secure in peace. Why obtrude upon us this notion of sin? What we care about is that wealth should increase, to provide these daily supplies. Poverty is weak, and wealth is strong, and it is natural that strength should command weakness. The poor may well obey the rich, if they be fed by them, and enjoy a quiet idleness under their patronage. Let a universal suffrage approve not those who provide for its good, but who supply its pleasures. Impose no hard command, but do not prohibit enjoyment. Kings should regard not their subjects' morality, but their obedience; and provinces obey their rulers not as models of virtue, but as yielding material sway, and providing for material needs. Their tribute should be not sincere loyalty, but servile fear. The province of the law is to protect property, not to interfere with private vice. Bring to trial whoever has injured the estate, or house, or life of another, or been troublesome to him; but may he not do what he likes with his own? or with those who join him voluntarily? Give us in abundance the instruments of public licentiousness for all who choose to enjoy them, or for those specially who cannot have them to themselves. There cannot be too much of large houses, rich feasts, and revelry by day and night. We will have no restrictions on our theatres, no squeamishness as to the pleasures which they offer. Count that man a public enemy who likes not such prosperity. But should he attempt to meddle with it, let a free people close their ears to him, pluck him from his place, and sweep him from the earth. Count those for true gods who have provided and preserved such gifts for the people. Let them have what worship they desire, ask for such games as they like, wherein their worshippers shall be companions or instruments. All we ask of them is to suffer no enemy, no plague, no calamity to interfere with such prosperity."[1]

But what is the mental condition of which these things are the token? On what root do they grow? The actions of men are the results of what they believe, hope, fear, and desire. We have seen how Roman heathenism was acting. What then was its belief?

First of all, the whole of this heathenism[2] which Rome inherited, represented, and sustained, was destitute of what we mean by religious doctrine, and of teachers whose office it was to promulgate and propagate such doctrine. It had nowhere a moral authority: what it possessed was only transmitted ceremonies and fables. To take, for instance, the most universal of religious rites, the rite of sacrifice. The reason and meaning of the institution were everywhere lost. So priests and priesthoods existed everywhere, interwoven

[1] St. Aug. *De Civ. Dei*, ii. 20.
[2] Döllinger, *Heid. und Jud.*, p. 652.

with the civil government, as in all the Hellenic cities, and in Rome herself especially; but nowhere was it imagined that "the priest's lips should guard knowledge, and that they should seek the law from his mouth, because he is the messenger of the Lord of hosts."[1] Religious rites were separated from what we understand by religion, that is, the obedience and homage of heart and will to God, and from morality, not to say that they were too often connected with the most flagrant breach of moral purity. Nowhere accordingly were the priests moral or religious teachers; and what the priests were not, the philosophers sought to be. And as this great gap in the moral life of a people yawned everywhere frightfully open and void, the few in every age who thought for themselves and busied themselves with the problem of human life, sought to fill it up. "They who seek wisdom," says Cicero,[2] "are called philosophers; nor is philosophy anything else, if you take the meaning of the word, than the study of wisdom. Now wisdom, as defined by the ancient philosophers, is the knowledge of divine and human things, and of the causes which contain these things; nor do I understand what he who censures this study would praise. For whether you seek the mind's entertainment, and its relief from anxieties, where is there any to be compared with that derived from studies which embrace the whole field of a virtuous and happy life? or whether you seek the grounds on which constancy and virtue rest, either this is the art whereby to obtain them, or there is none at all." Philosophers, then, aspired to be theologians and moralists of nations, whose priests performed, indeed, what should have been religious rites,

[1] Malachi ii. 11.   [2] *De Officiis*, ii. 2.

but had ceased to teach the doctrine which gave meaning to those rites. But as these philosophers recognised no standard, no common authority, each, according to the variety of human thought, pursued his own theories, selecting from his predecessors' opinions, changing or reversing them at his pleasure. Thus if we take only the three prevailing philosophic systems at Rome in Cicero's time, the Stoic, the Epicurean, and the Academic, the whole field of morality, in the words of Horace, "Quid pulchrum, quid turpe, quid utile, quid non," was completely broken up. It was a mass of endless variety and contradictions: so that as to the cardinal point of the end for which all other things are to be sought, St. Augustine remarks [1] that Varro could point out no less than two hundred and eighty-eight different opinions into which the three classes ramified, who placed this end in the mind, or in the body, or in both. As there was scarcely any opinion which could not claim some man of ability, not without a certain following, for its author, and as all opinions stood on the same foundation of mere reasoning from that common human nature which each interpreted differently, the result could only be, as it was, the destruction of all moral certainty in thinking minds, and the acquiescence of the vulgar in a practical system of religious rites, which carried with them no moral force or value, and in which man had no intelligent belief.

But, secondly, the study of religion and morality being the proper study of philosophers, they had one and all lost that notion which is the keystone of the arch that supports both religion and morality, the notion of an immaterial and personal God. If, amid perpetual

[1] *De Civitate Dei*, xix. 1.

inconsistencies and contradictions, some at some time appear to set forth their belief in one God, the orderer and ruler of all things, yet their conception of such God would seem to be material, or at least pantheistic. Thus Cicero makes Velleius, in the person of an Epicurean, expose, not without reason, the conflicting theories of no less than twenty-seven of the most famous philosophers, comprising, in fact, every name of note from Thales to his own time, which he entitles not so much sober judgments as delirious dreams; which, however, seem all to agree in this, that they do not recognise a God at once immaterial and personal.[1] And being without the notion of a personal, immaterial God, it is not wonderful that they should likewise have no grasp of the soul's enduring personality. The greater part believed it to perish at death; but those who deemed of it most highly, deemed it something of fiery, aerial, or ethereal nature; or like the harmony of a musical instrument, or a portion of the universal world-soul, which after death was dissolved again into that from which it had sprung, as a flask filled with water in the sea when broken returns the severed portion to the surrounding element.[2] The notion of immateriality of spirit was one which they did not conceive, either as concerns God or the human soul.[3] But from this it followed likewise that they had lost the notion of sin, which is "anything done, or said,

[1] *De Natura Deorum*, i. 11-15. The philosophers whose delirious dreams on the subject of the Godhead are so noted, are, Thales, Anaximander, Anaximenes, Anaxagoras, Alcmæo, Pythagoras, Xenophanes, Parmenides, Empedocles, Protagoras, Democritus, Diogenes Apolloniates, Plato, Xenophon, Antisthenes, Speusippus, Aristoteles, Xenocrates, Heracleitus, Theophrastus, Strato, Zeno, Aristo, Cleanthes, Persæus, Chrysippus, Diogenes Babylonius.
[2] Döllinger, ut sup., p. 593.
[3] Champagny, iii. 335; Döllinger, p. 340.

or desired against the eternal law."¹ This eternal law is the divine reason. The goodness of the human act depends principally on its conformity to the eternal law, and by consequence its malice consists in being discordant from that law, that is, from the divine reason or will, which alone is the rule of its own act, as not being directed to any superior end.² But since in this great sea of ignorance the notion of a personal God had been lost, the notion of His reason or will, as the rule of government in the whole universe, which He had created, was gone with it.³

Again; as to the nature of good and evil, there prevailed the utmost uncertainty and contradiction. For the supreme good had become unknown to them; their horizon was limited to the visible world, and in the visible world evil was so mixed up with good, and to the mass of men indeed appeared to exercise so equal a contest with it, even if it did not gain the mastery, that they were inclined to attribute to it a coeternity with good, and to connect its origin with matter, not with a fault of the will. This error, which prevailed almost universally, indicated a confusion between the notion of moral and of physical evil. Or again, they identified evil with the imperfection or weakness of the faculty of knowledge, as Socrates maintained that all sin was ignorance. Of the will's freedom, or of its perversion, they had no clear view; none, therefore, of the doctrine of human merit or demerit as proceeding from the right or wrong use of the will. The perception of the divine personality being lost, the perception of the human personality was greatly weakened, and no

---

[1] S. Augustine, tom. viii. 378.
[2] S. Thomas, Sum. 1, 2, 19, 4, and 21, 1, and 1, 63, 1.
[3] Id. 1, 2, 91, 1.

philosopher could detach himself from a certain pantheistic leaning. In this state of things the notion of morality, of duty, which still remained confused and as it were without an object, was but the stamp of the divine reason ineffaceably impressed on the human reason, the work of His hands. Thus the names of virtue and vice, of good and evil, still remained, while the existence of that Being to whom alone they had reference had ceased to be an object of faith.

Cicero, with all the books of Grecian wisdom before him, constructs an ethical system, in which he makes as good as no use of his knowledge of the Godhead. Now Cicero, without being himself a philosopher, was yet perhaps "Rome's least mortal mind," and it was his purpose, after studying the whole field of Grecian thought, to present to his countrymen what he found most worthy of value. He was an eclectic, who, with a vast treasure-house at command, selects a picture here, a statue there, a rich mosaic, a costly table, an inlaid couch, the work of men long passed away, for his own intellectual museum; and as he died in the last half-century before the Christian period, his writings serve to show us what Grecian and Roman antiquity was as to morals and religion. "In his work upon duties,[1] he passes with short mention over the duties of man towards the Godhead, though he does indeed assign them the first rank before all others: in what they consist we do not learn. Nowhere is theology brought into an inward connection with morality, nor are moral commands and duties rested on the authority, the will, the model of the Godhead. His motives are always drawn merely from the beauty and excellence of the *honestum*, from the evil and shamefulness of

[1] Döllinger, *Heid. und Jud.*, p. 571.

outward body which is mortal; for that outward shape does not exhibit your real being; but the mind is the man, not that figure which the finger can point out. Know therefore that you are god, if indeed he is god who has vigour, sense, memory, providence, who as much rules, directs, and moves that body over which he is set, as the supreme God this universe; and as God, Himself eternal, moves a partially mortal universe, so the everlasting mind moves a frail body." And a little further on: "Since, then, what is moved by itself is clearly eternal, who can deny that such a nature has been given to souls? For everything is soulless which is moved by external impulse; but that which has soul is moved by internal motion, its own motion, for this is the proper nature and force of soul. And if soul be the one only thing which moves itself, then was it never born, and is eternal."[1]

And so the ignorance which divested God of His creative power, by the same stroke divested man of his personality. In Greek and Roman philosophy man had not only ceased to be a creature, being conceived either as emanation of the world-soul eternally transfused through material forms from generation to generation, or as a product of the earth's slime warmed into life by the sun's heat; but likewise, emanation or production as he was accounted, like all other living things, he could hardly in his short transit through the world be held to have a personal subsistence: or if this be allowed him, it must be allowed to all other living things, and at the same time was deprived of all moral value, being utterly extinguished at death by resumption into the world-soul.

It is but a part of the same error as to the divine

[1] *Somn. Scip.* 8, 9.

nature, that the notion of a divine providence observing and directing the course of the world, rewarding or punishing the actions of men, had likewise been lost. The wisest and the best of the heathen used with regard to such a providence the language of doubt. Perplexed with the frequent triumph of the evil, and suffering of the good, and without faith in a future state of retribution, doubt on this point was their best, and despair their ordinary state of mind. Thus Tacitus, describing the persecution and death of the virtuous Soranus, contrasts the conduct of a friend and client, a Stoic philosopher, at Rome, who was bribed to betray his patron, and amply rewarded for his hypocrisy and treachery, with that of a friend in the provinces, who remained faithful to him, and defended him, and for this was stripped of all his goods and banished; and he ends with the bitter sarcasm, "Such is the equity of the gods towards good and evil actions."[1] And what Tacitus here says, the historians and philosophers of Greece and Rome all thought.

It is in vain to seek for any certain hope of immortal life beyond the grave in Greek or Roman literature. Cicero, pleading, mocks such a belief as absurd; but the pleader addresses himself to the general standard of human feeling and opinion. Cicero philosophising, wherein he addresses an eclectic audience of higher minds, would fain believe it, but dies at sixty-three, before he has made up his mind. Virgil, as a poet, sets forth the old tradition, in which a certain sort of future life with an accompanying retribution appears; but he significantly dismisses his guests through that ivory gate which he says transmits falsehood. And, indeed, in what was such a life

[1] Tacitus, *Annal.* xvi. 33.

to consist? Was Achilles for ever to drive his chariot, and Homer to recite his verses, in the pale moonlight beneath the earth? What object in the future world did polytheism offer to satisfy the aspiring soul of man? Its gods were deified men, who carried out the enjoyment of every human lust with superhuman power. Could the human heart love and adore that Jupiter whose private life was the consecration of all wickedness? whose government did not distinguish between good and evil? Rather Nero as emperor was a fitting representative of Jupiter as god. And as to the material deity of the philosophic mind—that is, under the name of spirit, a fluid finer than ether, and devoid of will—was it more possible for Plato or Cicero to love and adore such a god than for men now to love and adore the law of gravitation?

In fact, despair and depression had seized on the higher class of minds, while the lower wallowed in gross sensuality. And the whole may be summed up in one word, "there was wanting the consciousness of sanctity in God, and the need of sanctification in man."[1] In other words, their state was the contradiction of the precept, "Be ye holy, for I am holy."

Man, then, had lost his Maker, and in losing his Maker had lost himself. In proportion as the knowledge of God had been darkened to him, the knowledge of his own soul had been darkened also. If he admitted that he had a soul, it was such a soul as he gave likewise to the animals: a soul whose union with the body was broken at death, never to be restored; a soul which, if it survived that shock, survived not with a separate conscious existence, capable of its own joy or sorrow, reward or punishment, but as reunited to that

---

[1] *Heidenthum und Judenthum*, p. 633.

world-soul, of which it had been a portion temporarily detached and enclosed in a fleshly prison. This was the root of that profound contempt for human life which ruled the heathen society. Hence the slave perished undeplored, unvalued, on the rack, in the underground workhouse, of disease, of over-labour, the sport of his master's or his mistress's passion or caprice. Hence the rich man, after indulging every fancy, and revelling to satiety in every pleasure, would "die of weariness."[1] Hence suicide was deliberately proposed by the most moral of heathen philosophic systems as an escape from pain, disease, bereavement, or disappointment. Hence the noblest, bravest, and wisest of the Romans surrendered first the political liberties of their country under Julius and Augustus, and then every security of individual life under Tiberius, Caius, Claudius, and Nero. And thus man, "noble in reason, infinite in faculties, in form and moving express and admirable, in action like an angel, in apprehension like a god, the beauty of the world, the paragon of animals," was become in his own eyes without value: his labour, the profit of a master; his death-agony, the pastime of a mob; all his destiny on earth, the sport of chance, the victim of despotism, the instrument of blind fatality; and at last his body the prey of destruction, his soul absorbed as a drop lost in the ocean of being.

It has been my purpose hitherto to set before you two pictures of the Roman empire: one of its greatness, the other of its littleness; one of its material unity, extent, and magnificence; the other of its moral poverty and desolation; both touched in as few strokes as possible from the writings of its own

[1] "Fastidiose mori."

historians, poets, moralists, and philosophers. But there exist two descriptions of the same great power, drawn by two contemporaries who were eye-witnesses of what they described, yet at the same time outside of it, antagonists, not portions of its society. And it is further remarkable, that their descriptions, though both taken from the moral point of view, dwell, the one specially on the exhibition of material power, the other specially on the exhibition of moral dissolution. Nor will the intrinsic force of these descriptions be lessened to any thinking mind by the fact that they express not merely the opinions of eye-witnesses, but the judgment of inspired writers. One of these witnesses, summoned to Rome on a capital charge in the reign of Domitian, thus afterwards described what he had seen: "The waters which thou sawest, where the harlot sits, are peoples, and multitudes, and nations, and tongues;—and the woman which thou sawest is that great city which holds dominion over the kings of the earth:—Babylon the great,—who says in her heart, I sit a queen, and am no widow, and may not see grief;—for her merchants were the princes of the earth, for by her sorceries all the nations have been led astray;—and the kings of the earth, who committed fornication and wantoned with her, shall weep for her and mourn over her,—saying, Alas, alas Babylon, that great city, that strong city;—and the merchants of the earth weep and mourn over her, because no one any longer buys their freight; freight of gold and silver, and precious stone, and pearl, and fine linen, and purple, and silk, and scarlet, and all sweet wood, and every ivory vessel, and vessel of most precious wood, brass, iron, and marble, and cinnamon, and odours, and ointment, and frankincense, and wine,

THE CONSUMMATION OF THE OLD WORLD 77

and oil, and fine flour, and wheat, and cattle, and sheep, and horses, and chariots, and slaves, and souls of men."[1] Do we not see here the long line of a triumph defile before us, and Caractacus walking in chains, and the forum full of the slaves of all nations, and the world's shipping which crowds the Tiber from Ostia to Mount Aventine, and Nero's golden house, and his banquets in the gardens of Agrippa, and countless thousands calling for their human prey from the piled-up seats of the Coliseum?

The other description was addressed to the Christians at Rome by one who afterwards lived two years at least there, and having been acquitted once by the Emperor Nero, returned thither to suffer a glorious martyrdom. "The wrath of God is revealed from heaven against all impiety and injustice of men, who keep down the truth concerning God by their injustice. Because what is known of God is manifest in them; for God has manifested it to them. For the invisible things of Him from the creation of the world understood by what He has made are plainly seen, likewise His eternal power and Godhead; so that they are without excuse. Because when they knew God, they did not glorify Him as God, nor give thanks, but grew vain in their thoughts, and their foolish heart was darkened: for, calling themselves wise, they became fools; and they changed the glory of the incorruptible God into the likeness of the image of corruptible man, and of birds, and quadrupeds, and reptiles. For this cause God delivered them over to the desires of their heart, to uncleanness, so that they dishonoured their own bodies in themselves: who changed God's truth into falsehood, and worshipped

[1] Apocalypse, xvii. 15, 18; xviii. 2, 7, 23, 9-13.

and served the creature more than the Creator, who is blessed for ever; Amen. Wherefore God delivered them over to ignominious passions: for their women changed the natural use to that which is against nature: and likewise their males, leaving the natural use of the female, burnt in their desires towards each other, men with men working out that which is unseemly, and receiving in themselves the fitting recompense of their error. And as they thought not good to retain God in their knowledge, God delivered them up to a reprobate mind, to do what was not fitting: full of all injustice, malice, fornication, avarice, wickedness, full of envy, murder, strife, deceit, malignity, whisperers, backbiters, hated of God, insolent, proud, puffed up, inventors of evil things, disobedient to parents, unwise, covenant-breakers, without natural affection, implacable, unmerciful, who knowing the justice of God, understood not that they who do such things are worthy of death, and not only they who do them, but they who consent with those who do them."[1]

What makes especially for our purpose here is that the apostle has grouped into one mass the whole heathen world, which he tacitly signifies to be under the headship of Rome, to be represented and summed up in Rome, in that he writes thus to the Christians at Rome. Viewing with one rapid all-embracing glance the whole progress of man since the nations were divided after the Flood, he considered their actual moral state at the time he wrote as a penal state, the punishment of idolatry. And he traced the cause of this idolatry as not being ignorance, but a corruption of the heart which turned away from the knowledge of God, in order that it

[1] Romans i. 18-32.

might indulge in desires forbidden by that knowledge. And as men would not read the book of the world, spread ever open before them, and pointing to one Creator, Ruler, and Judge, because they desired gods of their own making to sanction deeds after which they lusted, God more and more withdrew Himself, whom they would not have, punished more and more this affected ignorance with the moral corruption which had been its first cause, until the world had universally become that which St. Paul beheld and described it under Nero. We must here further remark the exact identity of the description with that which we had before drawn from the heathen writers themselves. As to the facts of the case, Cicero, Seneca, and Tacitus alone, not to speak of the long array of Greek and Roman authors, would supply us with inexhaustible details of the picture thus summarily drawn by St. Paul and St. John.

We have, then, before us two great facts as the result of human history for more than two thousand years after the Flood: the parallel growth of a brilliant civilisation, and of an intense moral corruption. For these things advance and flourish together, not civilisation in one tribe and place, and moral corruption in another; but as the civil life becomes refined, and the political life develops and assumes shape, and man builds cities and calls the places after his name, the moral life becomes weaker, ancestral virtues decay, the sanctions of religion are less regarded, belief in the unity of God gives way to idolatry, and idolatry dissolves every moral bond. In all the heathen nations this experience repeats itself:[1]

[1] See Rosmini, *Filosofia della Politica*, pp. 286-8, for a passage on the decline of the human race.

in all, the tradition of a golden age, when justice dwelt on the earth, succeeded by ages of silver, brass, and iron, bears witness to it. Rome, gathering together into her mighty empire so many scattered limbs of the one human family, summed up and represented this result in its most striking form. She had, on the one hand, all the arts and conveniences of life; a network of roads made her forum the world's centre, and her sea was a highway for all nations to exchange their commerce. Her name was peace as well as strength from the Rhine and Danube to the African desert, from the Atlantic Ocean to the Euphrates. Within these immense boundaries, "peoples, multitudes, nations, and tongues" held her for supreme arbitress, and the daily journals of her capital made known the acts of her rulers. Nay, far more, she was preparing one civil law for all these regions and races; and the poet has expressed her truest praise when he cried in rapture:—

> "Fecisti patriam diversis gentibus unam;
> Profuit injustis, te dominante, capi;
> Dumque offers victis proprii consortia juris,
> Urbem fecisti, quod prius orbis erat."[1]

On the other hand, all this splendour, all this greatness, was for the few. This world-wide society was built upon slavery, and felt its foundations tremble beneath it day by day. Every house contained within it victims and enemies. No law nor any custom protected the labour, the honour, the life of the slave from his master; no law nor any custom protected the property, the liberty, the life of the master from the suspicion or enmity of the prince. But penetrating beneath these outward coverings into the human

[1] Rutilius.

heart itself, what do we find there? An impurity and a cruelty, the details of which are sickening; a doubt or an infidelity which makes religion a hypocritical routine. Man has ceased to believe in the unseen, to hope in the future, to desire what is beyond the needs of his body and the gratification of his tastes. In a word, while the State rules over the fairest regions of the earth, and possesses boundless wealth with unrivalled power, the life of man is become valueless because his soul is ignored, and his existence upon earth seems, in his own eyes, without meaning or object.

In Nero's time a stranger from a distant province is passing one day through the streets of Rome. He finds them in unwonted commotion, for one of the principal thoroughfares is lined with soldiers who keep back an agitated crowd.[1] In their countenances anger and terror, sympathy and fear, rule by turns; even Nero's guards almost waver and yield to the emotions of the multitude, as between their lines marches a long procession of four hundred men, women, and children, preceded and followed by fresh troops. They are slaves, and they are marching together to a common execution. What was their crime? They are the family of Pedanius Secundus, prefect of the city, who has been murdered in his house by one of his own slaves. The deed had been done either because the master, having promised the slave his freedom, and received the price, had refused to execute the agreement; or because the slave, as another report said, enamoured of a fellow male slave, the victim of his master's abandoned passion, could not endure a rival in this unnatural tie. Where a

[1] Tacitus, *Annal.* xiv. 42-5.

master had been killed in his own house by one of his slaves, whatever might have been the cause, the law of Rome ran that every slave in the house, male or female, old or young, should be put to death. On this case the senate has debated. A famous patriot has insisted that the law should take its course, chiefly on ground of the public security. "Our ancestors," said he, "suspected the disposition of slaves even when they had been born and bred on our country estates or in our own household, and had imbibed at once affection for their masters; but from the time that we have been embracing whole nations in our families, who have different religious rites, and foreign religions, or none at all, there is no means of keeping down that seething mass of corruption, save by terror." This pleading prevailed: the law was left to take its course; and lest the public pity should be more yielding than the prudent ferocity of the senate, the emperor has lent the assistance of an armed force to carry out the decision.

In the evening the stranger is proceeding by the Campus Martius. He finds, as he goes along, the squares and public places resplendent with torches. The emperor's freedman, Tigellinus, gives a banquet to-night on the lake of Agrippa, in the gardens close by the Pantheon.[1] There, says Tacitus, a platform has been erected, moved by ships superbly decorated with gold and silver, whose crews are formed of the most abandoned slaves, each having his station according to his age and skill in the practice of debauchery. The country has been ransacked for birds and game, and fish has been brought even from the ocean. On the borders of the lake are buildings filled with ladies of

[1] Tacitus, *Annal.* xv. 37.

rank, who invite every comer; on the opposite side a band of harlots make no secret of their persons. Wanton dances succeed; and as night comes on, a blaze of light, with a concert of music, breaks over the lake. There in person the Emperor Nero revels in every turpitude; but not yet satisfied until a few days afterwards he had solemnly espoused one of that abominable crew named Pythagoras. The emperor puts on the bridal veil; the augurs assist; the dowry is paid; the genial bed is displayed, and the nuptial torches lighted: "all," says the historian, "is public, even those endearments which natural marriage veils in secrecy."

And, in order to give the measure of the world's morality at that time, it must be added that the abominable crime thus committed by her emperor in the face of Rome lies equally upon the memory of fifteen out of sixteen who first wore the purple.[1] Julius with his matchless genius, Augustus with his wise good fortune, Trajan the great ruler in peace and war, and Hadrian with his varied talents, and Titus the delight of the human race, and Antoninus Pius in spite of his surname—were no less stained with this blot than those emperors who seemed to exhaust the capacity of human nature for crime, Tiberius, Caligula, Nero, or Domitian. Out of the sixteen there is but the husband of Messalina and Agrippina who escapes at least this pollution. And to the fifteen emperors

---

[1] See Gibbon, ch. iii. p. 100, note p. For Antoninus Pius, see Döllinger, *Heid. und Jud.*, 718. Marcus Aurelius, in his *Meditations*, lib. i. 16, praises his father for having overcome this vice: Παρὰ τοῦ πατρὸς—καὶ τὸ παῦσαι τὰ περὶ τοὺς ἔρωτας τῶν μειρακίων.—It was reserved for the first Christian who became emperor, Philip, *exoletos vetare*. See note of Champagny, *Les Antonins*, vol. iii. p. 346, quoting Lamp. in Alexand.

we must add the greatest names of Latin literature, Horace, and Virgil, and Catullus, and Cicero.[1]

And the stranger who beholds this double triumph of cruelty and lust, this utmost disregard of human life joined with the utmost debasement of man's dignity as a moral being, why has he come to Rome, and what is he doing there? Poor, unknown, a foreigner in dress, language, and demeanour, he is come from a distant province, small in extent, but the most despised and the most disliked of Rome's hundred provinces, to found in Rome itself, a society, and one, too, far more extensive than this great Roman empire, since it is to embrace all nations; far more lasting, since it is to endure for ever. He is come to found a society by means of which all that he sees around him, from the emperor to the slave, shall be changed. He will first teach that slave, now the secret enemy in every household, to be "subject to his master with all fear, not only to the good and gentle, but also to the froward;" and reciprocally he will teach the master "to give to his slave that which is just and equal, because he has himself a Master in heaven."[2] But more, under the effect of his teaching, that great work of injustice and oppression, which had grown up, flourished and increased in all nations, will be dissolved as it were of itself, and the master accept the slave to equality of civil rights; while at the same time towards the sovereign power, which had made its will the rule of law, he will learn to exercise an obedience compatible with a freeman's liberty, and a new virtue will find for itself the new name of loyalty.

---

[1] It does not seem possible to extricate Cicero from this crime after the testimony of Pliny in his letter to Pontius, lib. vii. 4.
[2] 1 Pet.

But what remedy will our foreign teacher apply to the disease prevailing all around him, the contempt of man as man, and of human life? What power of persuasion does he bear within him which was wanting to those philosophers, men of ability, learning, and eloquence, who from age to age, and out of every clime, had sought in Rome, as the world's centre, to establish a doctrine and gather a following? They have come with many varied gifts of human genius, and after shining for a while and attracting attention, have dropped away, and their followers after them. But the stranger of whom we are speaking has none of these gifts. He has neither the wisdom nor the eloquence of the Greeks; he is even without the learning of a cultivated mind: a fisherman by trade, poor, old, obscure, a foreigner of the most despised race, how can he succeed as a teacher among these lords of the world? He has two things within him for want of which society was perishing and man unhappy: a certain knowledge of God as the Creator, Ruler, Judge, and Reward of men, and of man's soul made after the image and likeness of this God. This God he has seen, touched, and handled upon earth; has been an eye-witness of His majesty, has received His message, and bears His commission. In this name he will speak to Nero and his court; to the patrician, the freeman, and the slave; to the female sex, the victim and instrument of the corruption around. He will speak; the few will listen and believe; the many will reject. Presently persecution will arise; he will be tried, condemned, and crucified on a hill overlooking the city. But in that death he will take possession of the city lying beneath him, which from him will receive the germ of a new life. In that city, the centre of idolatry, heathenism, and tyranny, and of all the corruption that is in the world through lust, he will have been the first of a line of rulers which is never to cease, and which, while the crown of temporal empire falls away from the Capitol, will substitute for it the spiritual rule of purity, gentleness, and charity over the whole earth.

But whence had this despised foreigner received the double knowledge of God and of the soul so miserably lost—as we have seen—to this brilliant Roman civilisation?

In the latter years of Augustus, when the foundations of the imperial rule had been laid, and the structure mainly raised by his practical wisdom, there had dwelt a poor family in a small town of evil repute, not far from the lake of the remote province where this fisherman plied his trade. It consisted of an elderly man, a youthful wife, and one young child. The man gained his livelihood as a carpenter, and the child worked with him. Complete obscurity rested upon this household until the child grew to the age of thirty years. Then he is suddenly found in the cities, villages, and fields of his native country, preaching a new kingdom, based upon a new doctrine. This doctrine proclaimed that hitherto the whole world had gone astray, calling evil good, and good evil, fixing its desires on wealth, honour, and prosperity, seeking for rest and enjoyment in visible things, and in this idolatry forgetting God, its Creator, and its End. But the new Teacher declared that every man possessing within himself an undying soul was made for something infinitely greater than the visible world contains. And He further affirmed, in proof of His doctrine, that He himself would suffer the most despised and abject of deaths in the sight of all men, abandoned and rejected: that, lifted up in scorn upon the cross as a malefactor, He would draw all men unto Him, and make all things new upon the earth.

For He would create a new society of men, founded upon the imitation and communion of His passion, the passion of a God-man. And He should Himself be the rule and model not only of the society in general, but of every member, according to His words: "If any man be willing to come after Me, let him deny himself, and take up his cross and follow Me. For whosoever wills to save his life shall lose it, and whosoever loses his life for My sake shall find it. For what is a man profited if he gain the whole world, and lose his own soul? or what shall a man give in exchange for his soul?"

What He had foretold took place. He suffered the death reserved to the vilest slave, whose life we have seen held of no account, and in so dying appeared the weakest, the most despised, and rejected of all men. This death the stranger we have mentioned above had witnessed, and likewise that resurrection which followed it: had witnessed both the man in suffering and the God in power. From His lips, when risen again, he had received authority to form this new society, resting on the Teacher's person and example: and in the strength of this word alone, the self-sacrifice of God for man, revealing visibly the Saviour in the Creator, he had come to Rome to inaugurate, in the seat of the world's corrupt empire, the everlasting kingdom of charity.

LECTURE II

NEW CREATION OF INDIVIDUAL MAN BY THE CHURCH

THUS the empire of Rome was the summary and definitive conclusion of the ancient world. In it the old heathen civilisation culminated. It was the product of all man's labour, invention, suffering, and experience downwards from the division of the nations after the Flood, until the time when Rome gathered up and reunited so many limbs of the great human family. And it rested upon the slavery of the majority. Outside of the narrow range of citizenship man was a thing in the eyes of his fellow-man; an instrument, not a person. And even within the circle of citizenship the State treated the Individual as devoid of personal inalienable rights. For the false principle of disregarding man as man lay at the foundation of the human commonwealth itself. Slavery was its most offensive and most ruinous result; but it ruled even the highest political relations of man with his fellow-man. The dignity and value of man as a reasonable soul, the image of God, were not known; but in their stead were substituted the dignity and value which he might possess as a member of the political body. But thus viewed, the part is inferior to the whole. And so it came to pass that the State violated not only the interests of the stranger and the sojourner, but made even the citizen in himself and in his family, as well as in his property, a sacrifice to its unlimited sovereignty. And with the change from republic to empire, after the savage acts of successive proscriptions, this principle obtained still greater mastery; for whereas the old republic only debarred from fire and water, that is, drove into banishment, the most criminal, except in a very few cases, the emperor ceased to regard not only the goods but the lives of men. And as was the whole, so were the parts; for in the family the father was the master of wife and child, whose rights were not co-ordinate with his, but gave way to them and merged in them. The husband had an unlimited privilege of divorce. Cicero repudiated the mother of his children for a young and rich bride, and then, after a year's marriage, expelled her in turn; and the virtuous Cato divorced his wife in order to bestow her on his friend. For indeed all these miseries had a deep abiding cause. The fountain of all truth and right was concealed to men. The Judge of the earth was not seen to sit upon His throne. Men had in their thought broken up the Ruler and Rewarder of the world into numberless idols, whose range was limited and their rule conflicting; and the human conscience amid this moral twilight groped after the scattered fragments of truth and justice. Here and there indeed Polytheism itself bore witness to its own fatal error; as where, in the city which was the eye of Greece and the university of heathenism, it inscribed an altar to the Unknown God. And Tertullian[1] could appeal against the

[1] *De Testimonio Animæ*, i. " Novum testimonium advoco, immo omni literatura notius, omni doctrina agitatius, omni editione vulgatius, toto homine majus, id est, totum quod est hominis. Consiste in medio anima—Sed non eam te advoco, quæ scholis formata, bibliothecis exercitata, academiis et porticibus Atticis pasta, sapientiam ructas. Te simplicem, et rudem, et impolitam, et idioticam compello, qualem te habent qui te solam habent, illam ipsam de compito, de trivio, de

schools and the philosophers to the simple unlettered soul, to the language of the street and the manufactory, to men's household words in joy or sorrow, for testimony; as when they said, "If God will," "God grant it," "Good God," "God bless you." Yet practically the eclipse of the truth on which man's spirit should live was all but total, and the reign of sensual indulgence unbounded. The whole of man was given to the goods that met the eye. He tried them in all their richness and variety, plunged into them, was speedily satiated, and was then ready to "die of weariness." This was the world in which St. Peter and St. Paul raised the standard of the Cross. How did they deal with it?

First of all, they did not set themselves to re-establish directly the political, the social, the domestic, or the individual rights of man. Indeed, they did not speak of rights at all, but of duties. Society was in rapid progress to dissolution because it knew not its Superior: they essayed to stop the decay by revealing that Superior. When the golden chain between heaven and earth should be once more suspended, the earth could rest upon it and be secure. They disclosed God in His most wonderful and most touching attribute of compassion and love, dying upon the cross, the universal victim, and embracing with His outstretched arms the race whose nature He had assumed, whose death He had endured, and whose liberation He had accomplished. This and no other was the rock on which they prepared to build that new society. This divine Person they set forth to be at once the model

textrino totam.—Nam te quoque palam et tota libertate, quia non licet nobis, domi ac foris audimus ita pronuntiare, Quod Deus dederit, et Si Deus voluerit;—Deus bonus, Deus benefacit, tua vox est."

of every private man, and the bond of the whole mass. Setting aside all question of *rights* in a world where the most precious rights of the individual, the family, and the society were utterly disregarded, they enjoined every duty with a reference to this great Exemplar. The regeneration of man himself was their remedy for a world in ruins.

To this end they reconstructed society with two forces. They disclosed God on the one hand, and His creature, the human soul, on the other; but God clothed in human flesh and the human soul raised to a participation of this incarnate God. These were their two factors, and in their teaching every human duty became the result of the joint application. The soul of man viewed in its immense capacity for joy or suffering, in its eternal duration, by nature of which the whole visible universe faded into insignificance before it, and in its triple unity of a being which has reason and will, wherein consists its likeness to the Triune Maker, this soul of man was the unit which the Creator and Redeemer of men, having first assumed it into His own Person, took to remould the moral fabric by the hands of His Apostles and their spiritual successors.

The gods many and lords many who divided the allegiance of the heathen nations, while they encouraged a boundless and often most degrading and most immoral superstition in the vulgar, had become contemptible to thinking minds. Instead of these an adequate object for every intellect and every heart was to be provided. Such an object was presented in the great doctrine of one God set forth to all mankind in the beginning, but now republished. The gods of Greece and Egypt, old Saturn who devoured his children, Isis and Anubis with all their barking crew, disappeared like a wrack of stormy clouds before the brilliant rise of that sun. That great doctrine of the divine unity, which came to Noah's children as their birthright, stamped with the judgment of the Flood, and which, when already obscured by the retrograde nations, was heard in fear and awe by Israel amid the thunders of Sinai—that bond and stay of man, "the Lord thy God is one God"—came forth in softer, soul-penetrating tones from the gentle height of Thabor; for there, not merely joined, as of old, with this declaration of unity, but now visibly represented and embodied in the Son of God, appeared the equally needful and most precious doctrine of the divine Personality. Equally needful; for then, as now, outside of the Christian pale, the whole moral atmosphere was charged with pantheism, and that which modern infidelity recurs to, as the result of a long induction from the laws of matter, had for ages been the fostered dream of many an eastern sage; while the acuter minds of Hellas, in spite of the popular Hellenic longing for personal and visible gods, had rested in this as the solution of their poets' imaginative mythology. And most precious doctrine assuredly; for pantheism, in destroying the divine personality, sweeps away by the same stroke in man that which gives him his only value—the undying personal existence, the produce of an inward self-acting root and cause, the subject of an eternal retribution. But intertwined inseparably with the doctrine of the divine Unity and Personality, came forth at the same time, for the consolation and joy of man, the inexpressibly attaching doctrine of the divine Paternity, which said, "This is My beloved Son, in whom is all My pleasure." For hence all fathership is named in heaven and earth, and because of this eternal Fathership and Sonship the only-begotten Son came before the nations as the First-born of many brethren, whose delight was to be with the children of men, and who was not ashamed to call them, the children of Adam, brethren: "Se nascens dedit socium." Who can imagine, far less describe the thrill with which the heart of man first met that most unimaginable mercy of the Incarnation? When the words of the Archangel fell on our Lady's ear, "The Holy Ghost shall come upon thee, and the power of the Most High shall overshadow thee, and therefore that Holy which shall be born of thee shall be called the Son of God," does it not give the greatest idea which we can have of the strength which grace had infused into the creature, that the message did not take away her life with joy, and that she was able to answer, "Behold the handmaid of the Lord; be it done unto me according to Thy word." Who then can picture the emotion which the echo of that word produced on the heart of man?—how Greek or Roman, Scythian or Barbarian, bond or free, learned or unlearned, rich or poor, prosperous or miserable, heard it with amazement, and forthwith these petty differences of a fallen state and a temporary exile disappeared as their eyes opened on that unanticipated universe of the divine grandeur and beneficence? And yet it stopped not there. The truth that God had become incarnate did not flash upon the soul of man save in conjunction with another truth as little to be imagined, a refinement of divine love, which the angels might well desire to look into, since never from the beginning of creation had such a thought occurred to a created mind. This

God, who out of love had made Himself man, would give Himself in that assumed nature to be the food of His creature. That creature, whose soul is full of infirmity, whose flesh is frailty and weakness itself, requires for his soul as well as his body a daily replenishing, a daily instrengthening, a daily union with that essence, presence, and power by which alone it lives. And out of the Incarnation itself flows forth this perennial yet daily fountain; and the nations knew not that God was among them, until they knew that the same God was likewise their food: not only "Se nascens dedit socium," but "convescens in edulium." Is the divine mercy satisfied? Not so; but in these depths there is a farther depth. The God who is incarnate, the God who is the food of man, is seen hanging between heaven and earth in the uttermost torture which the human frame can bear, a victim; a victim for the innumerable sins of men from the first sin of Adam and Eve to the last sin which the last child of Adam shall commit a moment before the final judgment. The life who is the Light of men is their Sacrifice too: the grain of divine wheat which is to be their food must first be ground in the mortar and baked in the fire of suffering; and out of the whole race of man one specimen of created nature shall voluntarily choose that death which is the supreme mark of divine displeasure, the utmost punishment for sin, the state of an executed criminal, and make it the sin-offering to efface the spot of guilt which was ineffaceable, and to deify the nature which was condemned. We must add to the hymn of the divine benefits, "Se moriens in pretium." Yet we do not end here: and this surpassing sphere of wonders has yet a fitting crown. He who conveys to man the divine Unity, Personality, and Paternity; who is become the Brother, the Food, and the Sacrifice of man, is likewise, and finally, and for ever, not only his Rewarder, but his Reward. Nothing else but Himself, nothing short of God, does He offer to the intellect and the heart of man, misled by a thousand false lights, wasted upon a thousand false goods. Here only He ends where all is endless: " Se regnans dat in præmium."

Such was the sevenfold vision of the divine majesty and mercy which burst upon the astonished nations when St. Peter and St. Paul raised the standard of the Cross in Rome, their Queen. For this divine doctrine came all together, not detached and piecemeal, but forming one great whole, accordant and indissoluble, since the harmony ran through all. At one and the same moment the nations had God preached to them as One God, personal, nay the source and root, and marvellous exemplar of all personality, as in the absolute unity of His own divine essence personal distinctions were revealed: the Father, for He had made them after the image and likeness of that Son who now, in the fulness of time, was formed in flesh as that divine man, of whom Adam had been the first sketch; the Saviour, for none other but He who made had now redeemed, by His thirty-three years' labour and suffering on the earth, with the cross embraced in thought each moment, and at last embraced in fact; the Vivifier, Supporter, and Strengthener, for He gave His own Flesh and Blood for their food, and yet the same one God, the ultimate crown of blessedness to this redeemed race; in whose ocean of being they should one day be plunged, yet not absorbed, for every life should be distinct in that all-penetrating life; every human eye behold for itself the King in His glory; every human heart embrace Him for itself; every human voice swell the accordant notes of that triumphant hymn; every human person share in due degree the glory which the eye and heart of man should be strengthened to contemplate.

The existing civilisation was an utter stranger to this help which came to it from above. There was nothing in the dominant empire, or in the region of barbarous tribes or apostate nations lying beyond it, which gave any such promise. Heathenism had worked itself out, and was not dumb but powerless to satisfy, much less to restore and exalt man. For not only had all sense of human responsibility been weakened by the multiplicity of deities into which men had broken up the one incommunicable Name, but they had not merely divided, they had also degraded to their own level the object of their worship. Man is responsible only to the Infinite One, but Infinity cannot be divided; and the gods of Greece, and Syria, and Egypt, and Rome, and of all the heathen nations, at least at that time of deep moral decline which marks our Lord's advent, were not man's makers, but themselves made by him, who had lost the sense of his own creatureship. They were but reflections of his own mind as it was kindled by sensuous beauty, thrilled by the sight of Nature's calmness, order, and majesty, engrossed in war and agriculture, or before primeval tradition faded away, was yet touched by mystic dreams of another world. All had become emanations of the earth, foul clouds of human passion steaming up from her fertile bosom. This illumination, on the contrary, which burst forth afresh with intense splendour from the Cross, this

NEW CREATION OF INDIVIDUAL MAN 97

sevenfold radiance of the Most High, was of another birth, plainly descending from above. In part, no doubt, it had been disclosed to the ancient world, and the nations at their very beginning, when they shot forth from the trunk of Noah's race, had received a great and precious deposit of truth, wherein the Unity, Personality, and Paternity of God were conspicuous parts, and wherein another great doctrine was foreshadowed in the rite of sacrifice. And it is the great and exceeding guilt of heathenism, that having this truth, it corrupted, distorted, and finally lost it. Heathenism has been well called nothing else but "the continuation and carrying out of the Fall;"[1] and assuredly it affords the most convincing and ever-abiding evidence of that mystery, so hateful to the philosophic mind, that is, the natural pride of man. But this one complex and interwoven idea of the Incarnation, the Blessed Eucharist, the Atonement, and the Beatific Vision and enjoyment of God, associated with the former truths in the preaching of the Cross, is assuredly a gift from heaven to earth which affords as strong evidence of its own divine origin, as heathenism affords of the Fall. If, as is beyond doubt, the rational creature, ever more and more falling away from its Creator, speaks of an earthly influence which, left to itself, draws irresistibly downwards; so likewise, the rational creature, brought back and restored to its Creator, speaks of a power

---

[1] "Obgleich das Heidenthum eigentlich nichts anderes ist als die Fortsetzung des Urfalls, oder die durch den Einfluss des Satans instigirte weitere Entwickelung des in die Natur-egoität getretenen Menschen, welche die Menschheit von Gott abzuführen und in das Verderben zu stürtzen bemüht war, so ist dasselbe doch gleichwohl keinesweges als ein völliger Abfall und eine eigentliche Negirung der Religion zu betrachten." Molitor, *Philosophie der Geschichte*, 4 Th. § 160.

from above tending upwards. And so, as every heathen vice was the direct product of idolatry, every Christian virtue is the direct result of the Christian revelation as we have above considered it. Morality to the Christian bears a constant reference to the dogma of the Incarnation, lives by it, and perishes when severed from it. ·The vision of God which the Christian Faith communicated to the human soul possessed and transformed it. A Divine Person laid hold of the nature of man, and became, as it were, a soul within the soul: henceforth in Him, His example, His life, and His death, what had been the imperfect virtues of the natural state obtained a new root. Man's life had no fewer sorrows than before, but all were viewed in the light of God's passion; man had equal need of help from his brother man, but the Master of charity had first given His life for His enemies; and those of His followers would be likest Him who should approach nearest to the sacrifice of self.

Let us see how these principles were practically applied to the circle of human life.

First let us consider the tissue of human acts, affections, and energies in the mass, before we proceed to dwell on its several parts.

And, again, this morality in the mass may be looked at from four points of view: its motive, its standard, its support, and its reward. We will take each in its order.

1. As to the motive of morality, this sevenfold vision of God told on it with great power by restoring at once the idea of creatureship on man's part, and of beneficent providence on God's. In that wide sea of ignorance wherein the heathen nations lay tossed, man

knew not whence he was, how he came upon the earth, to what he tended. The common idolatry mixed up the earth and its productions, the stars, and the gods in an existing whole, or system, if that which had no unity could be so called, without knowing its origin or determining its relations. Such was the state of the mass, while among cultivated minds one widely-spread philosophy declared specifically that the gods meddled not with human affairs for government, reward, or punishment. Another substituted the notion of Nature for that of God, stripping Him thereby of personality. To idolater and philosopher alike man was not a creature, but a substance among other substances above or below him, a portion of the whole, a physical portion of a physical whole, the former without responsibility, as the latter was without providence. But in this vision which the Christian faith disclosed man saw himself clearly, distinctly, and in the most vivid light a creature, at a certain time called forth out of nothing, formed with sovereign wisdom and power, sent into the world, guided, guarded, watched over in it; and then, moreover, a creature to God so precious, that after creating him He would be made Himself man and die for him. Redemption, if it did not explain Creation, cast round it a light which drew man towards God with an invincible attraction. And with the idea of creatureship man recovered the complete idea of duty; not an idea of that merely which was fitting for the good of human society—for so much as this, so long as he was a social animal, he could not wholly lose— but an idea of that great primary relation in which he stood to God as the work of His hands. Thus only the value of his acts as a free agent stood revealed to him: thus only their consequences. God, creatureship, duty, and judgment for the acts of free will came upon him together, and formed a new motive of his life. How distinct the two voices sound! Marcus Aurelius gives us that of the old heathen world. "There is one light of the sun, though it is distributed over walls, mountains, and other things infinite. There is one common substance, though it is distributed among countless bodies which have their several qualities. There is one soul, though it is distributed among infinite natures and individual circumscriptions. There is one intelligent soul, though it seems to be divided."—" How small a part of the boundless and unfathomable time is assigned to every man! for it is very soon swallowed up in the eternal. And how small a part of the whole substance! And how small a part of the universal soul! And on what a small clod of the whole earth thou creepest! Reflecting on all this, consider nothing to be great, except to act as thy nature leads thee, and to endure that which the common nature brings."—" Man, thou hast been a citizen in this great state; what difference does it make to thee whether for five years or three? For that which is comformable to the laws is just for all. Where is the hardship, then, if no tyrant, nor yet an unjust judge, sends thee away from the state, but Nature who brought thee into it? The same as if a prætor, who has employed an actor, dismisses him from the stage. 'But I have not finished the five acts, but only three of them.' Thou sayest well; but in life the three acts are the whole drama; for what shall be a complete drama is determined by him who was once the cause of its composition, and now of its dissolution; but thou art the cause of neither. Depart, then, satisfied, for he also who releases thee is satisfied."[1] Human life becomes desolate, morality evaporates, under such teaching. Would you hear what bound it up, what gave it an abiding motive, a distinct course and end? It is that other voice of the great Teacher, surrounding man's life with the tender care of the Father. "Are not two sparrows sold for a farthing? and not one of them shall fall on the ground without your Father. But the very hairs of your head are all numbered. Fear not, therefore; better are you than many sparrows." A Father and His children succeed to that notion of a physical whole without sympathy or succour for its parts. But it is in redeeming that the Father is disclosed. And the Son whom He has sent is likewise the Judge. It is not a simple notion of duty which has been elicited, but a desire of pleasing God manifested as the redeeming God. The abiding presence of One who is at once Creator, Father, Redeemer, and Judge surrounds men, no longer units and atoms before an unbending necessity, but persons before a personal God. This thought at once rules the present and embraces the future, as St. Paul says: "We know that if our earthly house of this tabernacle be dissolved, we have a building from God, a house not made with hands, eternal in the heavens. Therefore we labour—whether present or absent—to be well pleasing to Him: for we must all of us be made manifest before the judgment-seat of Christ, that every one may receive the things done in the body, according as he has done, whether good or evil."[2]

2. Again, what standard of morality was there placed before man in that old heathen world? It is

[1] Marcus Aurelius, *Thoughts*, xii. 30, 32, 36; Long's translation.
[2] Cor. v. 1, 9, 10.

here that the false gods told with most demoralising effect. It is here that Marcus Aurelius with his spectral form of fatalism called Nature, and Epicurus with his gods who knew not human affections, nor cared for human life, nor considered human actions, were more moral at least than Jupiter, Juno, Venus, Apollo, Mercury, Isis, Baal, Mylitta, and a thousand others. For their power and immortality lent consecration to every foul deed wrought by the imitation of their worshippers. It must not be forgotten that the multitude looked upon these as examples. But let us turn to the highest reason of the contemplative mind, and see what guide it proposed. "Of human life," says Marcus Aurelius again, "the time is a point, and the substance is in a flux, and the perception dull, and the composition of the whole body subject to putrefaction, and the soul a wheel, and fortune hard to divine, and fame a thing devoid of judgment. And to say all in a word, everything which belongs to the body is a stream, and what belongs to the soul is a dream and vapour, and life is a warfare and a stranger's sojourn, and after fame is oblivion. What, then, is that which is able to conduct a man? One thing and only one—philosophy. But this consists in keeping the genius within a man free from violence, and unharmed, superior to pains and pleasures, doing nothing without a purpose, nor yet falsely and with hypocrisy, not feeling the need of another man's doing or not doing anything, and besides accepting all that happens, and all that is allotted, as coming from thence, wherever it is, from whence he himself came, and finally waiting for death with a cheerful mind, as being nothing else but a dissolution of the elements of which every living being is compounded. But if there is no harm to the elements themselves in each continually changing into another, why should a man have any apprehension about the change and dissolution of all the elements? For it is according to nature, and nothing is evil which is according to nature."[1]

This is all which that great, most accomplished, thoughtful, and, save only to Christians, benevolent prince could devise for the guidance of man through life. But now, instead of these false gods, who we know were demons; instead of these gods serenely careless of mankind, the produce of faithless impiety; instead, too, of the genius within man, a something at least no stronger or wiser than man himself; who was the Christian's guide, standard, example? Before him rose, in beauty unimagined until then by man, the man-loving God—the God who dies upon the Cross—the God whose teaching is His own suffering—the Legislator who writes His law upon men's hearts by obeying it Himself. There were heathens who talked of the imitation of God, and they meant the following that divine principle of reason in man, by which, as they thought, he shared a common nature with God. It was a vague phrase, which, seemingly raising man above himself, left him really to his own innate power alone. But in the sight of God's Throne and Tribunal, which was likewise His chair of teaching—in the sight of the Cross—to imitate God became the most definite of all instructions. For there was spread before men the whole life of the thirty-three years; the boyhood passed in obscurity, and the manhood in labour; the teaching, requited with opposition, terminated with the Cross; the complete exemplar of humility, obedience, self-sacrifice, the spotless mirror

[1] Marcus Aurelius, ii. 17.

of purity. This was man, the guide and teacher of men, and this likewise was God. And if Marcus Aurelius had stooped to examine what was passing in Lyons, one of the cities of his own empire, and by his own order, about the time the words above quoted were written by him, he would have found men and women who could not only direct their life according to the pattern of that God-man, but could die not only serene in the midst of terrible torments, but full of the liveliest hope and the firmest certainty, because His image was impressed upon the heart, and the desire of seeing Him conquered at once all love of the world and all fear of death.

3. But the one abiding difficulty of the heathen was the weakness of his moral nature. In the perpetual strife between body and soul the body continually won the battle. And it was not only an incessant fall, but one in which there was nothing to arrest the descent. In vain the philosopher cried to him: "Live with the gods. And he does live with the gods who constantly shows to them that his own soul is satisfied with that which is assigned to him, and that it does all that the genius wishes, which Zeus hath given to every man for his guardian and guide, a portion of himself. And this is every man's understanding and reason."[1] But the reason was itself the traitor. It was always failing at the critical moment. When the body pressed it hardest, reason gave way. When the mind desponded, reason fluttered for a while and then sunk with it. Reason, said philosophy, was the man himself; but it was no more than man, and a greater than man was wanted. It was here that the Creating and Redeeming God came

[1] Marcus Aurelius, v. 27.

in with constant power and efficacy. The Apostle, describing this very conflict under which the heathen continually sunk, exclaimed, "Who shall deliver me from the body of this death?" and he answered his own question: "The grace of God through Jesus Christ our Lord." And again: "I have strength for all things through the instrengthening Christ."[1] This indwelling of the Redeeming God, by which a continuous never-failing support for every day's trials and work was bestowed on the creature, was the very substance of Christian life. It was at once visibly represented and imparted in all the seven sacraments of the Church; was the very mystery of the most divine and excellent of them all, intended for his daily sustenance. For in Baptism redeemed man was buried and raised again with the Incarnate God; in Confirmation strengthened by Him; in Penance absolved by Him; in Marriage blessed by Him; in Order consecrated as His officer by Him; in the Holy Eucharist fed by Him; in Unction anointed for the last conflict by Him. And the vital breath on man's part of this union so visibly expressed on God's part was prayer, which is the constant disclaiming of power and sufficiency in his own nature; the constant request of power and sufficiency from a higher nature, and that the God who had not only created but redeemed him, and who, still more, in the work of redemption had become man. So that into every part and fibre of Christian morality, into the work of every day, the thought of every hour, into the whole domain of man, his affections, words, and actions, the grace of God incarnate descended as a life-stream.

4. The fourth general view of Christian morality

[1] Rom. vii. 24; Phil. iv. 14.

which we were to take was the reward proposed to it. And here an intrinsic value, and that immeasurable, was given to every human act by the end assigned to it. For in Greek and Latin heathenism all human life was struck with worthlessness by its severance from any life to come, of which the course and nature should depend on its actions here. Nor can any more universal reason be assigned for the cruelty, the impurity, the extremes of luxury and poverty, of sensual enjoyment and of suffering, which abounded everywhere, than the loss of faith in a future life of retribution, wherein the person of the man who did well or ill should be restored. Most plaintive and touching in their doubt near akin to hopelessness are the very aspirations of the wiser and better among them; as when, after delineating the noble character of Agricola, Tacitus cries, "If there be any place for the shades of the pious—if, as the wise will have it, great souls are not extinguished together with the body—mayest thou rest in peace!"[1] But the imperial stoic philosopher boldly said, "Thou existest as a part; thou shalt disappear in that which produced thee, but rather thou shalt be received back into its seminal principle by transmutation:" and again, "To conclude, always observe how ephemeral and worthless human things are, and what was yesterday a little mucus, to-morrow will be a mummy or ashes. Pass, then, through this little space of time comformably to nature, and end thy journey in content; just as an olive falls off when it is ripe, blessing nature who produced it, and thanking the tree on which it grew."[2] Would you gather, in a word, the wondrous change which Christian faith brought on human

[1] Agricola, 46. [2] Marcus Aurelius, iv. 14, 48.

NEW CREATION OF INDIVIDUAL MAN 107

life, pass on to the anticipated tribunal of Him who is at once Creator, Redeemer, and Judge, yet Brother and Kinsman of man. "When the Son of Man shall come in His majesty, and all the holy angels with Him, then shall He sit upon the throne of His majesty: and all nations shall be gathered together before Him, and He shall separate them one from another, as the shepherd separates the sheep from the goats: and He shall set the sheep on His right hand: but the goats on His left. Then shall the King say to them that shall be on His right hand, Come ye blessed of my Father, possess you the kingdom prepared for you from the foundation of the world. For I was hungry, and you gave Me to eat; I was thirsty, and you gave Me to drink; I was a stranger, and you took Me in; I was naked, and you covered Me; I was sick, and you visited Me; I was in prison, and you came to Me. Then shall the just answer Him, saying, Lord, when did we see Thee hungry, and fed Thee; or thirsty, and gave thee drink? And when did we see Thee a stranger, and took Thee in? or naked, and covered Thee? or when did we see Thee sick or in prison and came to Thee? And the King shall answer and say to them, Amen, I say to you, inasmuch as you did it to one of these My least brethren, you did it to Me. Then shall He say to them also that shall be on His left hand, Depart from Me, you cursed, into everlasting fire, which was prepared for the devil and his angels. For I was hungry, and you gave Me not to eat; I was thirsty, and you gave Me not to drink; I was a stranger, and you took me not in; naked, and you covered Me not; sick and in prison, and you did not visit Me. Then they also shall answer

Him, saying, Lord, when did we see Thee hungry, or thirsty, or a stranger, or naked, or sick, or in prison, and did not minister to Thee? Then shall He answer them, saying, Amen, I say to you, inasmuch as you did it not to one of these least, neither did you do it to Me. And these shall go into everlasting punishment; but the just into everlasting life."[1]

Here observe how the acts of daily human life are invested with an importance far transcending their natural measure, since on them depends a futurity without limit. Nor only so, but they are connected with the human nature assumed by God, since the acts done to His brethren are counted by Him as done to Himself. That work of the Incarnation is not an act done once for all, and then receding back into distance of time; but a state touching, and by its touch transforming, every human life and every relationship of human life, man and man's society in every time and place. That human life at Bethlehem, Nazareth, and Golgotha surrounds us all, connects us altogether now with its sympathies, affections, and kinsmanship. The kingdom promised as the sequel of this earthly life, made up of trials, is an inheritance prepared of old for brethren, as well as a reward given to combatants; and the King who gives it connects it inseparably with His own sonship, His human nature, and His sufferings, as in that high and transcendent promise wherein His own description of eternal life culminates: "To him that overcometh will I give to sit with Me on My throne, as I also have overcome, and am set down with My Father on His throne."[2]

We have seen the light cast from this sevenfold

---

[1] Matt. xxv. 31-46.   [2] Apoc. iii. 21.

vision of God on man as a moral agent in general. Let us now consider this light as it falls upon man in his different relations. And first as it falls on the individual.

The intellect of man tends naturally to truth, which is its object, desires to possess it, and aims at it. The will of man tends naturally to good, and desires equally its possession. But this truth and this good are both of the natural order; and the natural power of man's intellect and will is limited to this order. Now the light we have above mentioned disclosed to man God as the Author of a supernatural order, and a multitude of truths concerning that order comprehended in God and deduced from Him; disclosed to him likewise God as the Author of supernatural good, and the possession of this good as the further and higher end of his own being, superadded to the natural end. Thus this light in its operation upon the soul of man distributed itself into three virtues: that of Faith, lifting man's intellect to the knowledge of God, not only as his Creator, but as his Redeemer and his Reward; that of Hope, lifting his will to the desire of such a good; that of Charity, uniting actually his will with the good itself. These three virtues, Faith, Hope, and Charity, cognate as having the same object, purify, enlarge, and exalt the natural powers of the soul, raising them immediately to God, as the first Truth, the Giver of beatitude, the infinite Good Himself. In the order of generation Faith is first, for the intellect must apprehend before the will can desire; Hope succeeds, for the will must desire before the desire can be terminated in the possession of the good itself, which is the final union of charity. But in the order of perfection Charity is supreme, since it alone touches that Truth and that Good which the others aspire after.

But the God who is the object of these three virtues is He who not only creates but redeems; who is become visible in His Son; who by that Son imparts sonship to those whom He redeems. As to Faith, among those things hoped for of which it is the substance, and those things unseen of which it is the evidence, the economy of redemption takes so large a place that the word often stands by itself for the profession of Christianity. As to Hope, the possession of eternal beatitude, after which it aspires, is so entirely the gift of God in Christ, that we are said to be saved by it.[1] But let us take especially Charity, since, inasmuch as it unites with God, it becomes, as it were, the informing power or soul of all other virtues, without which none of them can merit eternal life, and so is the proper mark and character of the Christian. Now everywhere this habit of charity in the Apostolic writings is referred back to the example of Christ in becoming man for us—in teaching, labouring, suffering, and finally dying for us. It is our Lord Himself who first sets forth the Incarnation as the proof of unsurpassable love on the part of the Creator. "God so loved the world that He gave His only-begotten Son." It is our Lord Himself who first made the appeal from the divine love to the human, on the eve of His passion. "A new commandment I give to you, that you love one another; as I have loved you, that you also love one another. By this shall all men know that you are My disciples, if you have love one for another."[2] But the commandment was an old one, and together

[1] Rom. viii. 24. [2] John iii. 16; xiii. 34.

with the love of God, out of which it flowed, was, as He had before declared, even the great commandment of the law, on which the whole law and the prophets depended. How then was it new? It was new in its motive and new in its standard; for it ran no longer, "Thou shalt love thy neighbour as thyself," but "as I have loved you." The imitation of Himself, therefore, was the motive; the standard was God becoming man for man's sake, and as man dying for Him. He makes the application so that none can mistake it. "This is My commandment, that you love one another as I have loved you. Greater love than this no man hath, that a man lay down his life for his friends. You are My friends, if you do the things that I command you."[1] Thus out of loving our neighbour as ourself in the old law is developed by means of our Lord's passion the martyrdom of charity in the new law. St. John draws the same conclusions thus: "By this hath the charity of God appeared towards us, because God hath sent His only-begotten Son into the world that we may live by Him." Here is the first point of the divine love, God becoming man. But there is a second; for he urges more strongly, "In this is charity, not as though we had loved God, but because He has first loved us, and sent His Son to be a propitiation for our sins." Here is the second point, the passion of God become man. From both he concludes: "If God hath so loved us, we ought also to love one another." And again: "In this we have known charity, because He hath laid down His life for us; and we ought to lay down our lives for the brethren."[2] Nor is St. Paul behind St. John in putting forth this

---

[1] John xv. 13.   [2] 1 John iv. 9-11; iii. 16.

motive when he says: "God commends His charity towards us, because when as yet we were sinners Christ died for us." And on this he rests the spring of the interior life: "The charity of Christ constrains us, judging this, that if one died for all, then all were dead. And Christ died for all, that they also who live may not live to themselves, but unto Him who died for them and rose again."[1]

And as the Incarnation of the Son of God and His death are put forward as the standard of the divine love to man, and as the motive of an answering love on the part of man to God, so the love thus called forth is a quality produced in man's will by that Third Person who is the Love of the Father and the Son; for "the charity of God is poured forth in our hearts by the Holy Spirit, who is given to us."[2] Thus it is not only a special virtue, but, as extending itself to all the acts and habits of the soul, is the root at once and the perfection of all virtues. It produces so exactly the fruits of divine grace that theologians have a hard matter to distinguish the habit of charity from grace itself. And it has a single object before it, God; its relation to creatures being determined by its relation to God. Thus, being the first operation of grace, it as completely penetrates and underlies the whole Christian character as the soul is in every part of the body, the life of the whole. And so charity alone is called at once "the new creation," "the fulfilment of the law," "the bond of perfection."[3]

---

[1] Rom. v. 8; 2 Cor. v. 13.   [2] Rom. v. 5.
[3] Compare together Gal. vi. 15, v. 6, 1 Cor. vii. 19, with Rom. xiii. 8–10, and Col. iii. 14. By the former three texts it appears that St. Paul names "the new creation," "faith which works by love," and "the keeping the commandments of God," as equivalents. In the fourth he calls charity "the fulfilment of the law;" and in the fifth, "the bond of perfection."

To complete our view of this virtue, we must remark how entirely new it was to all the heathen nations. There is not in Greek and Roman life, nor in any system of philosophy, the remotest approach to any virtue like Christian charity. And the reason of this is plain. For there being two rules of human actions, the reason of man, and the absolute reason of God, or the eternal Law, they had lost the conception of any rule but the former. They had ceased to conceive of God as the supreme rule which should regulate human reason; ceased to aspire to Him as the absolute good. Nor, indeed, so far as they held His unity, did they hold Him to be a personal God at all. Thus that movement of the soul towards Him and towards the rational creature for His sake, which is the proper act of charity, was not only far beyond their power as a supernatural act, but found no disposition of their will or their understanding to it.

And here we might terminate this portion of our argument; for if Charity be in such sense the seal and character of the Christian, that without it all other virtues are of no avail in the sight of God, and if it have so intimate a connection with the Incarnation and Death of Christ as to be a gift of God resulting from these, it might seem that nothing further could be said. Yet it will be well to continue our review so far as to see how other virtues are exhibited in relation to the same great objects of faith.

And I will take next the virtue of moral purity, because it was one almost as little known to the whole heathen world as charity. It was here that the degradation of man was most complete. In the mass of men the body had made the mind its subject, and men had become the slaves of sensual enjoyment. On the other hand, and as a reaction from this, the highest philosophy denied that the body was a part of the man, or that together with the mind it made up the man, and asserted that the real man was the reasonable soul, which used the body as an instrument. But here, from the opposite side, it dishonoured the body, for an instrument is but a means to an end, and has no intrinsic value. Now, the Son of God, by assuming a human body, consecrated the body for ever: by taking it, as well as the soul, into indivisible union with His Godhead, He showed it to be a part of human nature which has its own intrinsic value and dignity. And His disciples inculcated the virtue of moral purity as based upon the Incarnation and its result, union with God. It was the whole man who was taken into this union, not the rational soul only, but the body likewise. And more even than this. It was from the Body of the Lord, in virtue of its personal union with His Godhead, that the union of His members with Him proceeded: for "we are members of His Body, of His flesh, and of His bones;"[1] from His Body that their perpetual food was drawn in the greatest of Christian mysteries. And so, as a part of this teaching, Christians were told, "The body is for the Lord, and the Lord for the body; and God, who raised up the Lord, shall likewise raise us up through His power. Know you not that your bodies are members of Christ?—Now he who adheres to the Lord is one Spirit with Him.—Know you not that your body is the temple of the Holy Spirit, who is in you, whom you have from God, and are not your own: you have been bought with a price. Therefore glorify God in your body and in your spirit, which are God's."[2] This is the ever-abiding source of Christian

---

[1] Ephes. v. 30. [2] 1 Cor. vi. 13, 15, 19, 20.

purity; and the fixing of this doctrine with all its consequences in the minds and hearts of men was of itself a moral revolution. It is a direct result of the Incarnation, and not only grew out of it at first, but rests for ever upon it.

Pass next to the first and tenderest relations of the family. The love of husband and wife is placed on the basis of Christ's love to the Church, and the obedience of the wife to the husband on that of the Church's obedience to Christ. Thus these duties, forming the groundwork of natural society, have a supernatural motive given to them. "Wives, be subject to your own husbands as to the Lord; because the man is head of the woman, as Christ also is head of the Church, and He is Saviour of the body: but like as the Church is subject to Christ, so also let wives be to their own husbands in everything. Husbands, love your own wives, as Christ also loved the Church, and gave Himself for her."[1] And he proceeds to exalt marriage by representing it as a type of the most sacred and intimate of all conceivable unions, the union of the Incarnate God with His Church. What a doctrine to be promulgated out of the midst of that Rome whose emperor at the time had murdered an innocent and virtuous wife, and had taken the profligate wife of another, to become presently her murderer likewise: of that Rome, where, the satirist says, that wives counted their divorces by the years of their marriage!

We have touched on the Christian treatment of man as an individual, and in the society of home. Let us now continue the delineation of that treatment as it affected man in civil society. We will begin with the deepest humiliation of man as viewed in his

[1] Ephes. v. 22–26.

natural rights. What did the Apostles say to this outcast of Roman society, this refuse of the heathen world, the slave?

Slaves formed, it must be remembered, a probably large majority of the human race; and, moreover, the institution made an essential part of Greek and Roman civilisation, which simply could not exist without it. For society is built upon manual labour, and such labour was deemed unworthy of freemen. And the character of the institution itself was, that men were regarded not as persons but as things. Did the Christian teachers set themselves to reverse directly this enormous wrong? Did they urge upon the slave to claim and to recover his indefeasible rights as man? The way in which they dealt with this remarkable difficulty, which met Christianity at the threshold and encountered it everywhere, offers a striking illustration of the entirely inward genius of the Christian faith, and how completely it sought to restore society by remoulding individual man. "Slaves," was the command, "be obedient to your masters after the flesh with fear and trembling, in simplicity of your heart, as unto Christ; not with eye-service, as men-pleasers, but as slaves of Christ, doing the will of God from the heart with good-will, as being slaves to the Lord and not to men; knowing that whatever good thing any one may do, this he shall receive from the Lord whether he be a slave or a freeman."[1] Thus it feared not to consecrate the most unhallowed relation of man to man by representing that the slave's obedience to the master, if performed with pure intention, was an obedience to Christ Himself. The Prince of the Apostles extends this duty especially to

[1] Ephes. vi. 5-8.

unkind masters, supplying the supernatural motive. "Servants, be subject in all fear to your masters, not merely to the good and kind, but to the perverse. For this is praiseworthy if for conscience-sake towards God any one endure pains, suffering wrongfully. Since what glory is it if, when committing faults and being buffeted for them, you endure it: but if you suffer for doing good, and endure it, this is pleasing before God. For unto this you were called, inasmuch as Christ also suffered for us, leaving to us an example that you should follow upon His footsteps."[1] But the most instinctively and sublimely Christian recommendation concerning slavery is perhaps that given by St. Paul, when he says: "Let every one remain in the calling in which he was called. Wast thou called being a slave? care not for it: but even if thou mayest become free, use rather thy slavery; for the slave that is called in the Lord is the Lord's freeman; and so he who is called, being a freeman, is the slave of Christ. *You have been bought with a price: become not the slaves of men.*"[2] Now, bearing in mind what slavery was; to what perils and sufferings it exposed both man and woman, and how at any moment it might require the sacrifice of life itself for the preservation of moral purity; could any religion use this language unless it came directly from God, and felt itself able to renew human nature from its very heart's core by the supply of a boundless grace from its Author? These words bear witness to the implanting of an inward and spiritual freedom in the slave's inmost heart. Whatever he might suffer, he could put himself in the place of the Lord of heaven and earth suffering unjustly before Pilate and Herod;

[1] 1 Pet. ii. 18-21.   [2] 1 Cor. vii. 20.

and he had the conviction that every one who suffered with Him and for Him should likewise reign with Him.

The exhortation given to masters is the counterpart of that given to slaves. "Masters, afford to your slaves that which is just and fair, giving up threats, knowing that you also have a Master in heaven, and with Him there is no respect of persons."[1]

Thus Christianity did not command the slaveholder to enfranchise his slave, but it commanded him, instead, to treat that slave as a brother: that is, leaving the legal bond as it was, it imposed a moral check, making the slave a person, not a thing, in the eye of his master; and a person equally dear as himself to the common Master; a person for whom account was to be rendered by him to the common Master; and a person, likewise, to whom a kindness done would be interpreted by Christ as done to Himself.

Such was the doctrine which the Cross, the punishment of slaves, brought into the Ergastulum and the Pædagogium of the Romans. How long would the underground prison-house, and the still fouler den of infamy in the palace, last before it? As we hear these words of St. Peter and St. Paul, we feel that the bright light of heaven had shot into the darkest nook of earth, and kindled a never-dying flame of faith and hope in breasts long condemned to a misery without relief. An imperious Fabiola would henceforth be no match for a loving Syra. The mistress of Christian slaves might indeed make her apartment a place of martyrdom; but it could not henceforth be a mere torture-chamber or slaughter-house.

Having thus, by a wholly internal restoration, repaired the basis of man's society with man, in his

[1] Col. iv. 1, and Ephes. vi. 9.

treatment of inferiors, Christian teaching went on to deal with him in his relation to equals. Thus it placed the obligation to truth not on a conventional point of honour, but upon the Incarnation itself. "Putting off falsehood, speak truth each with his neighbour; for we are members one of another."[1] And the same idea is elsewhere expressed as to the peculiarly Christian grace of truth. "Do not use falsehood towards one another; because you have put off the old man with his deeds, and have put on the new, who is renewed unto knowledge according to the image of his Creator;"[2] where falsehood seems made of itself the criterion of fallen man.

In the same way the virtues of gentleness, mercy, long-suffering, meekness, and humility are urged by the example of Christ. "Put on, as the elect of God, holy and beloved, tender compassion, goodness, humility, meekness, long-suffering, supporting one another and forgiving one another, if any have a complaint against another; as Christ also forgave you, so do you also."[3]

So likewise the standard of liberality in assisting the poor, which is set before men, is no less than the act of Christ Himself in becoming man for us. "You know the grace of our Lord Jesus Christ, who for our sakes became poor, being rich, that by His poverty you may become rich."[4]

In short, every act of daily life, however seemingly insignificant or indispensable, was to be penetrated with this thought. "Whether you eat or drink, or do anything, do all to the glory of God." "Whatever you do in word or in deed, do all in the name of the Lord Jesus, giving thanks to our God and Father

---

[1] Ephes. iv. 25.
[2] Col. iii. 10.
[3] Col. iii. 12-13.
[4] 2 Cor. viii. 9.

through Him." And every condition in which man might be was to be seasoned with the reflection, that what was present was merely temporary. "This I say, the time is short. It remains that those who have wives be as though they had not; and those who weep, as though they wept not; and those who rejoice, as though they rejoiced not; and those who buy, as though they possessed not; and those who use this world, as though they used it not; for the fashion of this world passes away."[1]

But the temper and habit of mind towards others which Christianity specially created out of the example of our Lord Himself, and which may be said to sum up the whole of man's conduct to his fellow-man,[2] is brotherly love, kindness, or charity. Thus it is directly out of their filial relation to God, obtained for them by the unspeakable sacrifice of His Son, and in virtue of the power given by Him through that Son, which he terms "regeneration from an incorruptible seed,"[3] that St. Peter calls on the disciples to "purify their souls in the obedience of the truth, through the Spirit, unto unfeigned brotherly love, and so out of a pure heart to love one another earnestly." No such conception as this of the relation between man and man is to be found in the whole heathen world. They had neither the thing nor the name for it. It is a derivation to man from the Sonship bestowed on him by God in Christ, which encircles the whole brotherhood with a new tie, and draws them together in a bond unknown to those for whom Aristotle thought, or Cicero compiled the thoughts of others.

[1] 1 Cor. x. 31; Col. iii. 17; 1 Cor. vii. 29-31.
[2] This is expressly said by St. Paul, Rom. xiii. 8-10. See also 1 Pet. i. 17-23, and 2 Pet. i. 5-7, and 1 Thess. iv. 9. The first and last make φιλαδελφία and ἀγάπη identical. [3] 1 Pet. i. 22.

While thus creating a new virtue for the practice of those who were to be associated in a new brotherhood, the attitude of the Christian society to the existing civil society is specially remarkable. It was a new doctrine to all the heathen subjects of Nero, when St. Paul declared that "every soul should be subject to higher powers; for there is no power but from God," and "the powers that are are ordained by God, so that he who resists this power resists the ordinance of God."[1] Thus the duty of obedience to civil government was established on its only true basis by declaring that civil authority is not the result of agreement between men, but of divine appointment, and therefore claims submission to itself, not on account of the temporal consequences only which would attend denial, but for conscience-sake. This principle alone could stay the interminable fight of adverse factions which rent asunder cities and republics in old times, and supply the only stable foundation of a really Christian order. Here again the supernatural motive reinforced the natural conditions of society. And the example of our Lord Himself was before men, who recognised the divine authority of government when unjustly accused, by observing to His judge, who represented the Roman emperor, "Thou wouldst not have any power against Me unless it were given thee from above."[2]

Yet the same Christian teaching which thus consecrated civil authority and fulfilled the whole circle of duties between man and man by the divine virtue of fraternal love, removed by a consequence of that very virtue that exclusive regard to the greatness and welfare of one's own country which formed the heathen's patriotism. No other consideration will bring out more

---

[1] Rom. xiii. 1.   [2] John xix. 11.

fully the kind of that supernatural order which our Lord established by the teaching of His Church, or exhibit more distinctly how the spiritual and most inward renewal of the individual man is connected with the advance of the whole society. For instance, if there be any relation which is dear to men in the natural order, it is that of country; which, indeed, to those who have consciously or unconsciously rejected the supernatural order becomes the leading passion, devotion to which is their standard of what is great and good. Patriotism to the Romans was the first of virtues; and there is a nation of modern times which often recalls to mind the heathen greatness of old Rome, in the minds of whose people patriotism likewise seems to be the symbol of all greatness and the test of character in man. Now, it can scarcely be doubted that Christianity did not allow this exclusive feeling of patriotism at all. It would not allow the denizen of an eternal kingdom to give to an object of the natural order the devotion which is due only to the mystical body of Christ. "Our commonwealth, or citizenship, or political life," for the word means all this, says St. Paul, "is in heaven;" and again: "You are fellow-citizens of the saints and of the household of God." "You have approached Mount Sion and the city of the living God, the heavenly Jerusalem;" whereas here you have "no abiding city, but seek that which is to come."[1] The people of Romulus believed in the immovable rock of the Capitol; the people of God believe in the immovable rock of Christ. The Christian's country, so far as he could

---

[1] Phil. iii. 20, ἡμῶν τὸ πολίτευμα; Ephes. ii. 20, συμπολῖται τῶν ἁγίων; Heb. xii. 22, προσεληλύθατε πόλει Θεοῦ ζῶντος xiii. 14, οὐ γὰρ ἔχομεν ὧδε μένουσαν πόλιν.

have one in what was represented to him as a journey, was the Church of God, in its vast extent of all the souls who had been, are, or are to be of that divine commonwealth. For these he laboured and prayed, suffered and died; with these was all his sympathy; and to add to their number his highest joy. In that magnificent vision of the City of Peace he swept away as unworthy of a thought the divisions which had arisen from human sin. To him there was neither Greek nor Jew, circumcision nor uncircumcision, barbarian, Scythian, slave nor free; but Christ was all things and in all.

For the very idea under which Christianity presented itself in the teaching of the Apostles was the new creation of all things springing out of the love of God, exhibited in the Incarnation of His Son, and implanted in the hearts of men by His Spirit as a consequence of the Birth, the Life, the Death, and the Resurrection of Christ. The whole order of morality was based upon the personal union of the Godhead and Manhood in the God-man. The natural Sonship of Christ as man led to the adopted Sonship of men His brethren. The work which the Holy Spirit wrought in the highest degree in our Lord's Incarnation, effecting the union of the divine and human natures in the Person of the Eternal Son, He worked in a lower degree, but in the same order, in the redemption of each individual. For it is the participation of the divine nature communicated to the soul by the gift of habitual grace which constitutes that adopted Sonship, on which rests the whole operation of the Christian, the whole merit of eternal life.

This divine generation was declared by our Lord in His words to Nicodemus to be necessary for every one who would even enter into His Kingdom. Of this entrance He spoke as a new birth, as true and real as the natural birth, for "that which is born of the Spirit is spirit," just as "that which is born of the flesh is flesh." The state of man in it is called by St. Paul "a new creation." For creation is the passage from not being into being. And being is twofold—the being of nature, and that of grace. Now, the first creation was that in which creatures were made by God from nothing in a natural being. The new creation is that by which they are produced in the being of grace, because those who are without grace are nothing before Him. Thus the infusion of grace is a creation. The sons of this new creation are viewed and described collectively by St. James, in words which rather shadow out than delineate distinctly some untold and inconceivable magnificence of design, while he connects them with the Incarnation of the Son and the gift of the Spirit. For, after declaring that every good giving and every perfect gift is from above, descending from the Father of Lights, he adds: "Of His own will has He begotten us, in order that we might be a sort of beginning of His creatures."[1] By entrance into this state of adoption, all relative superiority or inferiority arising from nation, sex, or civil condition is done away;[2] for what are these to a creature renewed after the likeness of his Creator?

Again, let us compare what this adoption is in the individual with what it is in the mass. In the individual, as we have seen, it is "a new creation;" in the mass it is entitled "the Body of Christ."[3] For as the origin and seed are supernatural, so are the growth

---

[1] John iii. 6; Gal. vi. 15; James i. 16, 17.
[2] See Gal. iii. 26, and Col. iii. 9.   [3] 1 Cor. xii. 27.

and termination. The soul, new created in grace, has new desires, affections, hopes, and fears, directed towards the objects now disclosed to it, and the mass of souls thus new created grows up into a Body, which takes the name of its Head, because it is first formed and then ruled by the Spirit of its Head.

Further, let us contrast both the individual in this state of adoption with the individual as he was before in the broken and impaired state of the Gentile world, and the Christian commonwealth with the Gentile commonwealth.

As to the individual, there is man in his state of fallen nature wasting himself away in desires which deceived him with a false appearance of good; the pendant to which is man in his new state of adoption created according to God in justice and true sanctity.[1] As to the mass, the Apostle collects in one view the whole heathen world, summing them up in clear, decisive words as "the nations walking in the vanity of their minds, having their understanding darkened, being alienated from the life of God through the ignorance that is in them, because of the blindness of their hearts, who in their callousness have given themselves up to lasciviousness to work every uncleanness with greediness." As a contrast he sets before men the Church, as springing directly from the gifts of Christ at His ascension; for as part of these gifts, administered through all time by the Holy Spirit, came the whole arrangement of the ecclesiastical ministry, the appointed guard against error, "until we all arrive into the unity of the faith and of the knowledge of the Son of God unto a perfect man, unto the measure of the age of the fulness of Christ."[2]

[1] Ephes. iv. 22-24.   [2] Ephes. iv. 17-19 and 13.

Thus it is that the Christian commonwealth—in order to show how entirely supernatural a creation it is, how absolutely the work of God redeeming, how exactly and definitely an organic whole—is termed "the Body of Christ." And of such a title there is full justification in the fact that in every individual composing it the root is the grace of adoption, not an imitation merely, but an actual participation of that immeasurable grace which is bestowed on Christ incarnate, which in the mass grows up to what the Apostle calls by the name of the material created thing most wonderful in the universe of God, the Body of His Son. In what other words was it possible to show so clearly how the Christian people was the reduplication of the incarnate God?

Let us trace some of the social consequences hence arising. How could those whose whole spiritual existence lay in the possession of this adopted Sonship —of this brotherhood embracing the redeemed out of all races and countries—suffer their hopes, desires, and sympathies to be confined within the limits of a particular nation? Man, no doubt, will ever love his country with a natural love; but it is a natural love alone. It cannot rise above its source. The nation is a result of the dispersion of the human family at Babel, and therefore a result of human division and sin. Its attraction, its manifold ties and organisation, begin and end with this world. The hopes and fears participated in it have their beginning and their end here. With this life it ceases itself, and is never reproduced. How could those who were exalted by their very state as Christians to be "fellow-citizens of the saints and of the household of God" make the nation their home, and sink to be mere citizens of Romulus?

And descending from the commonwealth to the individual, let us trace the conception of virtue itself as it would be formed by man in his fallen state, and as it is formed by the Christian.

Plato and Aristotle, Cicero and Epictetus, whom we name as representing the whole heathen world, had no other rule for their actions than the natural reason of man. By nature, as we have already said, their intellect tended to truth, and their will to good; but the truth and the good were confined to the natural order which they saw around them. Thus they had well divided the whole sphere of human action among the four cardinal virtues: prudence, which is the reason directing itself rightly in the choice of means; justice, directing man to what is due and right in all his conduct towards others; temperance, which restrains all the passions of the part in him which desires, and fortitude, which arms him with firmness against all passions of the part which fears. And the good which they had in view was the good of the individual and of society as limited to this present life. And as, when so limited, the good of the multitude is superior to that of the individual, the highest form of good which they could set before them was the well-ordered human commonwealth, and to this therefore, if need were, the good of the individual must in all cases be sacrificed. Thus the wealth, power, and extension of the State, and its just government, were the highest result of the virtue which they contemplated, and man had in himself no intrinsic value which could outweigh or vie with this result. Their whole virtue consisted, therefore, in obedience to the dictates of reason within this sphere.

But now Christian Grace came upon this same natural reason, elevating all its powers to a higher end and a superior good, and bestowing on it, in accordance with such end and good, a rule above itself, the divine reason, which is the absolute good. In and by the gift of adoption it disclosed God to the soul as loving each soul with an infinite love; and as the love of God is not barren, as bestowing on its object a quality answering to that love. This was the virtue of Charity, the affection on man's part answering to its cause, the previous love of God, the creature's movement to meet the Creator's embrace. The Holy Spirit Himself, the perfect Gift, began all by implanting grace in the soul, and in this grace charity rooted itself, and became the mother of all other virtues, because it directed them all to the end of pleasing God. The parallel between Nature and Grace is complete.[1] Just as the natural light of reason is something before and beside the virtues acquired by the right use of it, and directed to the end which it sets before them, so this infused light of grace, this participation of the divine nature, is something before the virtues which spring from it, before even Charity, which, however, taking possession of the will, becomes the exact representative of Grace. And as the political good was the highest object at which natural reason aimed, so reason, informed by Grace, aimed at an object connatural to grace, the possession of God Himself, the full inheritance belonging to the adoption. Yet it did not exclude those virtues of human society, prudence, justice, temperance, and fortitude; but whereas in their natural state they are tendencies rather than virtues, and do not always cohere together in the bond of prudence, but rather men are brave, or

---

[1] St. Thomas, *Summa*, 1, 2, q. 110, a. 3.

temperate, or just, or prudent, by a sort of natural disposition, here, on the other hand, Charity, the mover of the will by Grace, produced these virtues on a new stock, with a perfect ripeness, cohesion, and completeness; produced them with the spontaneity of an affection, and the unfailing force of a divine origin. It produced them on a new stock, for in the eyes of Charity the political good, to which in their natural condition they were related, was in itself transitory, and subordinate to a higher good; and so Charity bestowed on their acts the value of this higher good. And it produced their several acts with perfect ripeness, cohesion, and completeness, because it took possession of the whole will, and was the motive power of all actions.

And here again the highest form of Christian excellence was seen in prophecy as attached to the Person of Christ, its well-head and fountain, and streaming forth from Him upon His brethren, when it was said [1] that on the Flower arising from the root of Jesse should rest the sevenfold spirit of wisdom, understanding, counsel, fortitude, knowledge, piety, and fear. For inasmuch as the reason of man has two perfections, one natural, according to the light of reason, and one supernatural, according to the light of grace, though this second perfection is greater than the first, the first is more perfectly possessed by man.[2] For whereas he has full and complete possession of reason, he knows and loves God but imperfectly by the light of Grace in the reason. So that a special divine instinct is necessary to quicken the action of reason, and therefore the Holy Spirit breathes these gifts as a Spirit, transforming the intellectual and moral virtues, which the heathens themselves named and in some sort possessed,

---

[1] Isa. xi. 1, 2.   [2] St. Thomas, *Summa*, 1, 2, q. 68, a. 2.

into movements of His own in the will. Thus the motives respectively guiding the heathen and the Christian were, for the first reason in its rectitude, for the second the Holy Spirit moving the reason in perfect accordance with its freedom. The virtue of Charity held all these gifts together, by which all the powers of the human soul were guided into willing obedience to the divine prompting. And the bestowal of them on each Christian in various degrees was an emanation from the fulness with which they rested on His divine Head.

And to complete what we have to say we must add that so far as the virtue of Christian Grace exceeded the virtue of natural reason in the individual, so much did its consummation in the mass exceed anything which the human commonwealth could reach. These virtues are of a different origin, a different order, and point to a different end, both in the individual and in the mass; but further, in the natural polity the good of the individual and the good of the whole do not concur. The State is perpetually sacrificing for objects of its own those whom it treats not as members, but as instruments, and this without respect to their moral goodness, as, for instance, the victims of war, and those who perish in the conflict with their wiser or stronger fellows in the struggle for advancement in life. But in the divine polity of sons adopted through the grace of the only-begotten Son, the good of the individual and of the whole perfectly concur. There none are treated as instruments to be used, broken, and thrown aside, on whose ruins others may rise, but the incorruptible Seed grows up into an impregnable Kingdom.[1]

Thus when Christianity came into the ruined fabric

---

[1] 1 Pet. i. 23, σπορὰ ἄφθαρτος; Heb. xii. 28, βασιλεία ἀσάλευτος.

of human nature and society, it appealed to no violated rights; it set up no political means of redressing wrong; but having presented the one God in an effulgence of moral glory, it attached itself to the individual human soul as a counterpart to this vision of God: and the doctrine of a dependent immortality, a continual but never-ceasing gift of a self-eternal Giver, drew man, as a magnet, upwards: this faith knit again the creature to the Creator by the bond of the Redeemer; and wove all round about dislocated, enfeebled, perishing human nature and collapsing society these "cords of a man," who was likewise God: until, as those minute creatures in the eastern seas by infinitesimal accretions form beds of coral which rise to be isles and continents, so this mass of human souls, each one of whom was leavened with a divine life, formed a society of which likewise that divine life became the standard and all-pervading force.

In the time of heathenism the world of sense which surrounded man flattered and caressed all his natural powers, and solicited an answer from them; and in return he flung himself greedily upon that world, and tried to exhaust its treasures. Glory, wealth, and pleasure intoxicated his heart with their dreams: he crowned himself with the earth's flowers, and drank in the air's perfume: and in one object or another, in one after another, he sought enjoyment and satisfaction. The world had nothing more to give him; nor will the latest growth of civilisation surpass the profusion with which the earth poured forth its gifts to those who consented to seek on the earth alone their home and their reward: though indeed they were the few, to whom the many were sacrificed. The Roman noble, with the pleasures of a vanquished world at his feet, with men and women from the fairest climes of the earth to do his bidding—men who, though slaves, had learnt all the arts and letters of Greece, and were ready to use them for the benefit of their lords, and women the most beautiful and accomplished of their sex, who were yet the property of those same lords—the Roman noble, as to material and even intellectual enjoyment, stood on a vantage-ground which never again man can hope to occupy, however

> "Through the ages an increasing purpose runs,
> And the thoughts of men are widened with the process of the suns."

Cæsar and Pompey, Lucullus and Hortensius, and the fellows of their order, were orators, statesmen, jurists and legislators, generals, men of literature, and luxurious nobles at the same time; and they were this because they could use the minds as well as the bodies of others at their pleasure. Not in this direction was an advance possible. But man's exaltation came upon another level, and was of a different order. He had long known the excess of sensuous, artistic, and mental enjoyment, and wasted away under it: he was now to learn the greatness of suffering for a moral end, and to rise by it. The sum of the teaching I have so slightly sketched above was this: that in all this world, so brilliant and enticing when untried, yet so fleeting and fallacious upon trial, there was but one thing of real and abiding value, the personality of man; and this personality resided in something the operations of which indeed met the eye, while the substance was invisible. The soul of man, his person, the chief work of his Maker, stood out over against the now disclosed being of that Maker Himself, the source of all personality. This soul the new doctrine took as its basis, and leaving for the time the mass, addressed itself to the unit of which the mass was composed. It laid hold of that in man which was at once most his own yet most divine, his own character, and the copy of God's image, his spirit. National divisions, divisions of caste and class, divisions of freemen and slaves, vanished before an identity which underlay them all, which not only made all equal who possessed it, but raised them all to a divine brotherhood. For the force with which this idea struck the world lay in the fact that this soul, the body's eternal indweller, was once more revealed to man at the moment that the Word of God, executing the counsel which had been intended before the world's foundation, joined it to His Divine Person by a most unspeakable and transcendent union. The equality and brotherhood contained in man's descent from a common father became of quite another value when that common father himself was seen to be but the type and first sketch, as it were, of the Restorer, the Man from heaven, the true Father and Head of the race. But what shall we say when to this likewise was to be added that He was its Redeemer? When Adam sunk into mystical sleep, and Eve in that slumber came forth from his side by the word of the Most High, it cost the Creator nothing; but when the true Eve came forth from the true Adam asleep upon the Cross, it cost the Almighty suffering unspeakable, itself the last fruit and crown of long labours and sorrows. Thus the knowledge of the soul was linked in this teaching with the knowledge of the human birth, the toilsome life, and the painful death of the soul's Maker and Redeemer; and it was only from the mouth of God, first incarnate and then dying on the Cross, that this knowledge had power and fruitfulness to restore and new-create man.

And the one adequate object which, instead of "this palpable array of sense on every side encountered," was now presented to man was an eternal union with this God who had so wonderfully created and redeemed him. This teaching preached to him labours, troubles, and sufferings on earth, instead of the paradise which the heathen sought there: but it made earth the way and not the end; the exile, not the home; the place of merit, not of reward: and it fixed the drooping eye and discouraged heart upon that Person who had Himself borne the burden and heat of the day, and now waited to crown, after a short period of conflict, those who followed Him. And as the whole restoration sprung from the act of God redeeming, so in every man it consisted in the work of God sanctifying. There was exact correspondence between the source and the quality of the salvation thus brought. As the source of it was the eternal Son of God entering into the world as man, and becoming the new Head of the human race, so the quality of it was the eternal Spirit of God planting in each man the gift of Sonship, that divine quality of grace, which should be the root of all the affections and actions of man, the guarantee and the earnest of his union with God.

The decay had reached man's heart, and the remedy reached it too: the decay had touched the powers of life, and the remedy poured life in full stream on the seat of the disorder. Man himself had fallen to pieces, and man himself was restored by the hand of God, not as of old creating, but now suffering; not calling out of nothing, but from a ruin drawing a masterpiece. This force there was in almighty power assuming weakness, and divine majesty clothed in humility.

LECTURE III

HEATHEN AND CHRISTIAN MAN COMPARED

HAVING dwelt upon the principles which distinguished the great heathen world of nations before our Lord's coming from the principle which was the mother idea and the generating force of the society which He came to found, let us now pass from precept to example and from doctrine to life. Let us slightly review the former principles as they showed themselves in the conduct of men, and contrast them with the latter in the characters formed by it.

When we look over the five hundred years which elapsed from Solon to Christ, we are at first sight confused by the multiplicity and contradiction of religious and moral opinions and doctrines which arose in them. Of seeds so diverse it would seem that the harvest must be equally various. When, again, we look at the conduct and actions of men, how great in one respect is the divergence! Gather up, as far as human scrutiny can, and ponder on an individual human life as it lies before you in history, and then what a distance, for instance, between a Socrates and an Alcibiades, a Julius Cæsar and a Cato of Utica! Some would seem to follow with more or less fidelity a moral rule before them and a moral law within them, resisting their passions with more or less success. Others with equal knowledge seem to discard obedience to any moral rule or law, and to give themselves up to the pursuit of whatever appears to them valuable or desirable without stint or limit. There is obviously room here for an unerring judgment to pronounce sentence of very different degrees.

But if we look beneath the surface of these rival philosophies and various systems of thought, and if we further endeavour to range these various lives under certain points common to them all, we shall find, I think, that of the whole mass of the Greek and Latin races during the five hundred years mentioned above, certain things are true in common, which are of no slight importance or inconsiderable bearing on the lives and actions of men. I will put them under six heads.

First, neither men in their conduct nor authors in their writings recognise one God, the Creator and Rewarder of men. And by this I do not mean that many philosophers did not seek to reduce the vulgar idolatry of the day to the notion of one God; but that, even if they did so, their god was a physical, not a personal God; not the Creator of men, but at the utmost the former of them out of pre-existent matter, coequal and coeval with the divine being or essence infused through it; and further, not their Rewarder, but rather something which precluded the very notion of retribution, because it did away with a distinct existence, namely, the World-soul, into which after death their separate lives were sooner or later absorbed.

Secondly, none of them direct their actions in view to a future life. By which, again, I do not mean that the vision of a future life did not hover before the minds of many, and the possibility even of reward and punishment after death, but that these truths were no longer grasped with a hearty faith, nor asserted with unhesitating confidence. They were theories, which Plato might propound or Zeno deny, and Cato study the night before his suicide; but from a living belief they had become visions out of the ivory gate, which man, walking in the broad and palpable light of day, disregarded. Practically, the thoughts and desires of men were limited to this present life and its objects.

Thirdly, the best and most virtuous, those who were looked upon as models in their day, proposed to themselves no higher standard than the virtues of prudence, justice, fortitude, and temperance, within the sphere of the actual society in which they lived, that is, as limited to the course of this world.

Fourthly, they looked to no higher good than the good of the political life, as the end of these virtues. The human commonwealth's security and well-being, progress in physical strength and wealth, in order, peace, and the enjoyments of life, was the object to be obtained. Those were the least selfish and the most virtuous who kept this end in view, rather than any private advancement of their own.

Fifthly, in practising these virtues, and in attaining this end, as their starting-point was human reason, the intellectual principle in man, so they looked to no other force to sustain them. They had lost the notion of any divine assistance given and infused into man in addition to his natural powers. And in saying this I am mindful of the Stoical notion of the demon or genius of each man. But this was a part of himself, the diviner part, by which he shared, as it were, a spark of that great fire which animated the universe.

Sixthly, the notion of sin, that is of disobedience to

a law and a lawgiver superior to man and to the whole constitution of human society, but impressed upon man's inmost nature, eternal and unchangeable, was grievously impaired and almost extinct within them. There was substituted generally for it the notion of crime, that is, infringement of positive law enacted by man.

These, then, are six heads of that general resemblance which, in spite of their individual differences, the great men of Greek and Roman antiquity bore to each other. These constitute a certain level, out of which they do not rise, and they make the choice of a representative man, in whom to consider that great world of human thought and action, of less importance than at first sight it might seem.

The character which perhaps first of all others presents itself for selection is that of Socrates. His name as a moral teacher, and the lustre of a death unequalled for sublimity in the whole range of heathen history, point him out at once. Yet are there great difficulties in his case. Not only is his period too remote for a review which closes four hundred years after his death, but the real Socrates is still a problem of history. We have him as depicted by two of his chief disciples, and it is hard to say in their portrait how much is artistic effect and how much the real man. I will not dwell upon the fact that popular reports of immorality rested on his fair fame from his own time downwards. Put it, if you like, that these were slanders so often tracking the footsteps of the great and good. But the plain old soldier, who is the less imaginative, and perhaps therefore more trustworthy, delineator of his character, does tell us things of him which make it hard to believe that he had any sense of moral purity at all. Those who study the position assigned to him by Xenophon in the visit which he volunteered to the hetæra Theodota, and that which he occupies in the same writer's Banquet, can only, I think, come to this conclusion. There are expressions abundantly scattered through the Dialogues of Plato which tend to the same point. It is for all these reasons therefore, of time, of uncertainty as to the real man and what he taught, and of the dubious moral light in which he stands in the works of his own disciples, that I pass him over.

Now, passing to the generation immediately preceding our Lord, we find a school at Rome which laid especial claim to the possession of a virtue equal to all the emergencies of life. And in that very school we find a noble Roman, inheritor of a great name, who may be considered the most faithful representative of old Roman political traditions, as well as of the higher morality which the corruption of universal empire had so grievously impaired: a senator who in evil times was a worthy specimen of what the Senate had been when that body was the greatest tribunal of justice in the world, the most devoted to the good of the State which it governed. Cato of Utica's life, as it lies for us sketched in Plutarch, may be considered the model of a life grounded on the dictates of natural reason. Of dauntless courage, and of no mean capacity in the field, in his civil life he is inflexibly incorrupt. A devoted brother, kind and considerate towards all with whom he is brought into relation, that is, being citizens and equals; for of his conduct to slaves, the blow given to one on the night of his death, so severe that it caused an inflammation of his hand, impairing the force with which he dealt his own death-stroke, does not give a pleasant impression. In the whole course of his life he has before him the good of his country as a constraining motive. Once he seems to rise above even this, where he censures Cæsar's attack upon the Germans on grounds of universal justice, telling the Senate that they ought to deliver Cæsar into the hands of those who had been unjustly assaulted, that they might expiate the offence, and not bring a curse upon the city.[1] There are but two blots in all this life recorded. The one, that this generally high-minded senator, while he prosecuted Muræna for obtaining the consulship by corrupt means, let off the other candidate Silanus, who was equally guilty, but was his brother-in-law; the other, that he made use of the unlimited right of divorce possessed by the Romans of his time to repudiate his wife Marcia, in order to gratify his friend Hortensius, who had fallen in love with her, though after his death, when she was a rich widow, he took her back again. With these exceptions, perhaps, it may be said that whatever Roman virtue could do, Cato of Utica, up to the time of his death, had done. Why, then, not take him for a representation of heathen man? In this I am influenced by two reasons: first, that his writings having perished, we have no means of fully judging his principles from his own mouth; secondly, that the mode of his death undoes much of his life's grandeur, and sets him lower than many others apparently greatly inferior to him in their personal character and in the conduct of their domestic and civil life. For consider what his suicide meant. Agonised at the issue of the civil war, he had exclaimed, "How dark and uncertain is the will of heaven! Pompey, when

[1] Plutarch's *Life of Cato of Utica*. See also Merivale, i. 453.

he did nothing wisely or honestly, was always successful, and now that he would preserve his country and defend her liberty, he is altogether unfortunate."[1] But the mode of death which he selected was an act in accordance, indeed, with the Stoical doctrine carried out by Zeno and Cleanthes, approved afterwards by Epictetus and Marcus Aurelius, of "the open door," but in itself the definitive rejection of a belief in a providence over the affairs of men. It was a practical admission that man had no inward freedom of the will which tyranny could not reach; a practical assertion, moreover, that so far from being a creature placed by God in a certain post which he was not to desert—an image repeatedly used by the better heathen—he was his own master, an independent being, who had nothing to live for if he were deprived of political liberty. Cicero, so often timid in action, so often a moral coward, redeemed in his death much that was wanting in his life, and when he stretched his neck out of his litter to meet without swerving the blow of Antony's assassin, is far more human, more religious, and more noble than Cato, who ponders during the night over the immortality of the soul, and kills himself in the morning because he cannot stoop to meet the wrath or the clemency of Cæsar, his equal once, now the lord of his once-free country, and the disposer of his own lot.

This same Stoical school presents us at a later period two persons, one remarkable as a master of thought, one as uniting thought with action in a sphere the most exalted and most difficult, the government of the Roman empire at the period of its greatest extension—Epictetus and Marcus Aurelius, the former a philo-

[1] Plutarch's *Cato of Utica.*

sopher of no mean name, whose conduct seems to have been consistent with his theory; the latter a ruler who, with his adopted father and predecessor, stands at the very head of all heathen sovereigns. Why not take one of these as a specimen of what heathenism could do? I reply, as to Epictetus, that he left nothing in writing; and we only know him by the remains gathered up by disciples, which are, however, sufficient to convey accurately his philosophical system, while at the same time his life is very obscure, the particulars of it little known, and the chief events uncertain. But many might think Marcus Aurelius, as combining both thought and action, as ruling for nearly twenty years with absolute power, yet with general justice, clemency, fortitude, and vigour, the greatest of empires, to be the very person in whom heathen virtue culminated. Nevertheless, I think an examination of those private thoughts called his *Meditations*—perhaps the most interesting book which heathen literature has left to us, because it discloses the secret recesses of a heathen soul—would show that such a choice would not be the best that could be made. In truth, there are the same objections at the bottom to Marcus Aurelius and to Epictetus. Their religious system is a complete materialism. It recognises only two principles, Matter, and an active Force eternally indwelling in matter and forming it. It knows of no incorporeal things, save as our own abstractions. God is the unity of a Force embracing the whole universe, penetrating all things, assuming all forms, and as such, a subtle Fluid, Fire, Æther, or Spirit, under which the Stoics understood a fifth element, to which the air served as a material basis. In this æthereal fiery force all modes of existence of the World-body animated by it are contained beforehand, and develop themselves regularly out of it: it lives and moves itself in everything, is the common source of all life and all desire. Now, as in this system God and necessity are one, everything ethical becomes physical. The soul of man is of like substance, and so is a breath or fire like the World-soul, of which it is a portion; but it manifests itself in man at the same time as the Force from which Knowledge and Action proceed, as Intelligence, Will, and Self-consciousness. Thus it is of nearer kin to the Divine Being, but at the same time a corporeal being, and so stands in reciprocal action with the human body. It is Heat-matter, communicating Life and movement, and tied to the blood. It is transitory, though it outlasts the body, perhaps so long as to the conflagration of the world. Accordingly it has in the most favourable circumstances the duration of the world-period; but with the running out of this period it must return into the universal æther or Godhead. Its individual existence and consciousness end.[1] In short, Marcus Aurelius and Epictetus know nothing not only of a future world, and of a moral or a personal God, but of morality itself as a work of free will. They preach the nothingness of every human action and affection, and under circumstances advocate suicide, as Zeno, Cleanthes, and Cato, their fellow Stoics, practised it. I think them, therefore, on the whole, inferior to another whom I shall choose, not because his personal character is unimpeachable, not because he has not many defects and weaknesses, not because he

[1] Drawn from the analysis of Stoical doctrine in Döllinger's *Heidenthum und Judenthum*, pp. 153, 159, 161. This will be found fully borne out by the *Meditations* of Marcus Aurelius, and the *Enchiridion* and *Discourses* of Epictetus.

is not even wanting in the religious mind. All this is true, and yet he is both nearer to the mass of men among whom he lived, and higher in his views upon morality and religion than those I have mentioned. Further, out of all the great men of antiquity I choose Cicero, partly because among the Romans it would be hard to find either a higher intelligence or a kindlier disposition; but more still on account of the time at which he lived. His life terminated about a generation before our Lord's advent; and when driven from his occupation as a Roman noble and statesman by the break-up of the Republic, he spent his last years in reviewing the systems of Greek philosophy, and in presenting abstracts of them to his countrymen. He had before him and was familiar with all the riches of the Greek mind from Plato down to his own time, so large a part of which has perished to us. Thus, though he has no pretensions to be a philosopher, or to have a philosophic system of his own—though no student of Aristotle can be satisfied with his vague eclecticism, or study it as a science—yet his sketches of moral and political philosophy and of theology, if it can be so termed, possess this special and, so far as I know, unique interest, that they are copies made in the very last period of ancient heathenism by a great Roman mind of what he considered most noticeable on the theory of life, morals, and human society, out of a vast number of Grecian originals which are otherwise lost. In the majesty of his own matchless style, and the undefinable rhythm of those perfect numbers which show us that prose as well as poetry possesses a hidden harmony of its own—for Cicero's felicity of diction and rhythm is as unattainable as Shakspere's, and more equable—he has transcribed for us the best, according to his judgment, which twelve generations of thinkers among the countrymen of Plato, Aristotle, Zeno, Carneades, and Panætius had to say upon man, society, government, and God. Of this great course of human thought during four hundred years we have but fragments: Cicero had not only the complete web of outward teaching, but the inner soul of living tradition. I remember being struck in a great French cathedral with the idea of a mediæval artist, who has placed in the windows the Evangelists on the shoulders of the four great Prophets. Now, that expresses Cicero's position with regard to the great lights of heathenism who went before him, and why I select him as the representative of the heathen mind.

There is no man whose writings are more thoroughly penetrated with his character: we will therefore consider his life and his doctrines together.

The son of a citizen of Arpinum, he began his public life at Rome just as the domination of Sylla portended the ruin which was to happen to the great commonwealth. In the interval of comparative tranquillity which ensued after Sylla's re-establishment of it, he, a new man, by the force of his great powers as an orator and lawyer, worked his way, between the twenty-seventh and the forty-fourth years of his life, through the great offices of State up to the crown of all, the consulship, which he attained in the last-mentioned year, the first in which he was legally capable of it—an honour so great and rare that a Metellus, an Æmilius, or a Claudius might have been proud of it; while in the maker of his own fortunes it was marvellous. Now, the new man, who became at forty-three Consul of Rome at the very height of her greatness, what does he set forth as the grand principle of human action? What else but glory; that is, the approval of his fellow-men; "the consentient praise of the good; the uncorrupt expression of those who judge rightly upon excellent virtue; that which is virtue's echo, and, as being generally an attendant upon upright actions, is not to be rejected by good men."[1] For indeed there was an object which filled and dilated his mind; there was a work which was the work of his life. The great fabric of the Roman commonwealth—that structure of ages, the visible home and embodiment of power, law, and dignity, on this his mind's eye loved to rest; and to hold his own in this, to be beloved and respected as a chief and influential citizen of it, this was the work of his life. In the year succeeding Cæsar's death, at the ripe age of sixty-three, he compiled a treatise on social duties, which is highly instructive, as giving us a view of the moral and intellectual world in which he lived. In this treatise man comes before us as endued with reason and speech, and thereby broadly distinguished from all classes of brute animals, which, like the sun, moon, and stars, and the revolution of the heavens, are made for his service. Thus he is capable of prudence, justice, temperance, and fortitude, virtues of the greatest importance for the maintenance of human society, which is the highest end contemplated by the writer. This human society, indeed, in one place he states to have been "constituted by the immortal

---

[1] *Tusc. Disp.* ii. 32. Compare Aristotle's character of the μεγαλόψυχος, Ethic. Nic. iv. 3, 15. τῆς ἀρετῆς γὰρ ἆθλον ἡ τιμή, καὶ ἀπονέμεται τοῖς ἀγαθοῖς: and just before, 9. εἰ δὲ δὴ μεγάλων ἑαυτὸν ἀξιοῖ ἄξιος ὤν, καὶ μάλιστα τῶν μεγίστων, περὶ ἓν μάλιστα ἂν εἴη. ἡ δ' ἀξία λέγεται πρὸς τὰ ἐκτὸς ἀγαθά. μέγιστον δὲ τοῦτ' ἂν θείημεν ὃ τοῖς θεοῖς ἀπονέμομεν, καὶ οὗ μάλιστ' ἐφίενται οἱ ἐν ἀξιώματι, καὶ τὸ ἐπὶ τοῖς καλλίστοις ἆθλον· τοιοῦτον δὲ ἡ τιμή· μέγιστον γὰρ δὴ τοῦτο τῶν ἐκτὸς ἀγαθῶν.

gods;"[1] and that they who destroy it, destroy with it beneficence, liberality, goodness, and justice; and are therefore to be deemed impious towards the gods: but this great fact remains barren in his hands. For the idea of God is singularly absent from the whole treatise: where his division of subjects would seem naturally to introduce it, it is not found. For instance: " Since, as Plato admirably wrote, we are born not for ourselves alone, and our country claims a part of us, a part our friends; and, as the Stoics say, all the earth's productions are created for the use of men; while men are generated for men's sake, to have a capacity of helping each other: in this we ought to follow nature for our guide, to throw into a common store what may be useful for all, by the interchange of kind offices, by giving and receiving, and so to make the arts of life, our labour, and our faculties, the bonds of man's society with man."[2] Observe here the absence of man's relation to God. The writer does not seem to be aware that he is a creature, at the moment that he uses the very word "creation" of the earth's products. Again, "the society and union of men will be best preserved if kindness be shown to each person in proportion to the nearness of his connection with us. But we must seek higher the source of the natural principles of human community and society. For the first is that which is discerned in the society of the whole human race. Now of this the bond is reason and speech, which, by teaching, learning, communicating, discussing, and judging, draws men together, and joins them in a certain natural society. Nor are we in anything further removed from the nature of brutes than in

[1] *De Officiis*, iii. 6.   [2] Id. i. 7.

this. Of them we often say that they have courage, as horses and lions; never that they have justice, equity, or goodness, for they are devoid of reason and speech."[1] He then proceeds to mark the various degrees of relationship: after the degree of humanity itself, that of tribe, nation, language; closer still, that of the same city; and yet closer, the ties of blood. From marriage springs the family, which is the principle of the city, and the seed-plot of a commonwealth. No union surpasses that of good men in friendship. "But," he adds, "when you have carefully surveyed all, no society is more effective or more affectionate than that which every one of us has with the commonwealth. Dear are our parents, dear our children, our relations, our friends; but our single country embraces all the tenderness we have for all. Where is the good man who would hesitate to die for it if he could serve it?"[2] Thus human society and our country are viewed as ultimate facts, beyond which the writer does not go. That they themselves exist for any further end does not occur to him. That they are made up of persons who have a good of their own distinct from the good of the local or general society in which they are placed, is a truth which he does not come upon: not one which he discusses and rejects, but which lies out of his field of vision. In the whole of this first book, treating specially on the cardinal virtues, the only glimpse which I can find of anything like personal religion, of anything discerned in the individual man to be superior to society itself, is in one sentence of the last section. "There are some things so foul, and partly so criminal, that the wise man would not do

[1] *De Officiis*, i. 16.   [2] Id. i. 17.

them even to preserve his country."[1] And a little further on he says, "In the community itself there are degrees of social duties, by which we may understand their order of precedency: first come those to the immortal gods; secondly, those to our country; thirdly, those to our parents; and so the rest." This is the only mention of the gods in the book. Of God as one ruling, ordering, preserving power, there is none. Of man's responsibility to such a being not a vestige. For though these duties to the immortal gods are mentioned as the first in order, there is not a word said of what they consist in. This is the only reference to any beings above man in the book; and with these two words it stops. But there is a passage in the second book which, more than any other I have met with, expresses the infinite distance of Cicero's mind from any true conception of the Godhead. It is the following: "Of those things which concern the maintenance of human life, part are inanimate, as gold, silver, the productions of the earth, and the like; part are animals, which have their impulses and appetites. Of these, some are without reason; some make use of it. Those without reason are horses, oxen, other cattle, bees, by whose work any effect is produced for man's use and life. Of those who have the use of reason, two kinds are given; one of gods, the other of men. Piety and sanctity will propitiate the gods; but next, and after the gods, men can be most useful to men. There is the like division of things hurtful and profitable; but as they do not believe the gods to hurt, excepting these, they consider that men are of the greatest advantage or detriment to each other."[2] From this expression,

---

[1] *De Officiis*, i. 45.   [2] Id. ii. 3.

that there are two classes of beings who have the use of reason, gods and men, it would seem that, in Cicero's thought, the former were a sort of men endued with immortal life and superior strength.[1] With regard at least to those for whom his stereotyped phrase is "the immortal gods," he would seem to be at infinite distance from any notion of attributing to them creative power. Perhaps he may have a nobler view of what in Stoical language he so often calls "nature," or the mind of the universe; but then this power would appear to be material, and most certainly impersonal. And the phrase "using reason," applied to gods and men alike, would seem to convey the notion that they both, in different degrees, participated in a common faculty; shared, that is, were portions of this so-called mind of the universe.

Now we should certainly expect to find in a treatise of moral philosophy the creature's obligation to the Creator; and, in fact, St. Ambrose, writing on the same subject, notes this absence of a reference to a supreme Ruler and a future life; and points out how the Holy Scripture, on the contrary, placed eternal life in two things, the knowledge of the Godhead and the fruit of good living; and refers to two psalms of David[2] as having plainly insisted on this long before the times of the heathen philosophers.[3] However, as Cicero has written a treatise professedly on the Nature of the Gods, which, too, belongs to the

---

[1] From Cicero's mode of quoting, it is often difficult to know whether what he says is his opinion, or that of others; here, I imagine, his own opinion agrees with that of the "summa auctoritate philosophi" whom he is citing.

[2] Psalms xciii. 12, and cxi. 1, 3, 5, 6.

[3] St. Ambrose, *De Officiis Ministrorum*, ii. 2. A friend has pointed out to me that this treatise is the Christian counterpart to that of Cicero.

same year of his life, let us see what light this throws upon his belief. And the first thing I should here remark is the total absence of anything like reverence in the position which he takes himself in his treatment of such a subject. He assumes the character of an Academic of the later school, with whom there is no such thing as certainty, but only probability. And the way in which he illustrates this is to put in the mouth of Velleius, as an Epicurean, in the first book, a scornful statement of all the ridiculous diversities of belief which existed as to the nature of the gods. This serves as a prelude to introduce the atheism of the speaker, whose own tenets are answered by Cotta. In the next book Balbus is used as the expositor of Stoic doctrine. And here, indeed, there is a long, eloquent, and seemingly serious statement of the argument from design, as indicating the world to have been arranged by one ordering mind. "For who would call him a man who, after beholding the exact certitude of the heavenly motions, and the fixed order of the stars, and the connection and adaptation of all these things with each other, should deny there to be any reason in these, and assert those things to happen by chance, when no wisdom of ours is equal to the task of measuring the wisdom by which they are governed?"[1] The demonstration is carried out through the physical world, and the bodily structure of man himself, and would seem to be complete. But in the third book Cotta is put up to refute this doctrine of the Stoics, as he had done that of the Epicureans. All this argument of the one ordering mind fails entirely to convince him. Nevertheless he is a priest, and highly conservative; and before he confutes Balbus he begins by

[1] *De Nat. Deor.* ii. 38.

assuring him: "I always will defend and always have defended the sacred rites and ceremonies delivered down to us concerning the immortal gods from our ancestors: nor will the speech of any one learned or unlearned move me from my ancestral opinion respecting the worship of the immortal gods. As to religion, I follow Coruncanius, Scipio, and Scævola, *pontifices maximi*, not Zeno, or Cleanthes, or Chrysippus."¹ We are reminded here of the answer of our own Scipio Africanus to a fervent spirit who invited him to join in prayer for the unity of all professing Christians. "I presume," he said, "you do not expect me, as her Majesty's adviser, to state to her that I do not consider the religion established by law to be true." Now this was just the case with the Romans whom Cicero puts on the stage, and with himself. Cicero the statesman would maintain the Roman religion "concerning the immortal gods" on the basis of tradition, for the sake of State policy: Cicero the philosopher thinks it more probable that there is a ruling mind in the universe than that there is not, though not a word is hinted as to that mind being personal: but Cicero the man remains untouched in all this. He is perfectly calm and impassive, balancing opposite opinions as to there being gods or not, with a preference for their existence; but to fall on his knees as a creature, and adore the God who made heaven and earth, whose life within supports him, whose gift is the body which he has elaborately described, and the mind which is his pride and delight: this is a thought which he never comes near. His writings are full of experience of social life, knowledge of the political world, appreciation of men and

¹ *De Nat. Deor.* iii. 2.

things, full of wit, liveliness, and observation. He had even in a sort of rhetorical way of his own run over a large part of the circle of human knowledge, and studied a great variety of philosophical systems, which comprehended the whole universe. But there are two ideas which simply never occurred to him: the idea of God as the Creator, Preserver, and Rewarder of men; and the idea of the soul of man as having a personal, enduring, responsible existence.

Such is the belief of the greatest orator and genius of Rome, the head of the conservative party, the Latiniser of Hellenic philosophy; of whom there is every reason to think that his disposition was more kindly and his life more moral than the disposition and the life of by far the greater number, at least of eminent public men, among his contemporaries.

But there are three critical points in his life at which we must glance in order to observe the effect which his belief had upon his conduct.

The first is his exile. Having by his consulship saved Rome, and taken the first rank in the Senate, he was felt to be an obstacle in the way of the man who was bent on ruling all. As Cicero was not prepared to become the tool of Cæsar, Clodius was set upon him. Betrayed by Pompey and by all his friends, he is driven from the city which he had saved. Forthwith that vision which made the sunshine of his life, "the consentient praise of the good, the uncorrupt expression of those who judge rightly upon excellent virtue, that which is virtue's echo," becomes overclouded. Driven back into himself, away from Rome, the contests and the triumphs of the forum and the senate-house, and reduced to the testimony of his own conscience, this man, proclaimed of late the father of his country, collapses utterly. He whines and begs for his soul's daily food a little human praise: nó smile of earth or sea in his enforced wandering, no caress of wife or child, can win from him an answering glance: until having been sufficiently humbled and broken for the purpose of those who had banished him, he is allowed to return, and to fancy himself again the first man in Rome.

Twelve eventful years succeed, in which Cicero is doomed to witness the growth of Cæsar's inordinate power: the flight, defeat, and death of Pompey, the final destruction of the Senate's authority. He has learnt to bend his neck to the conqueror, to abuse his dominion in private as the ruin of all honour and dignity, and extol him as the most clement of men in public, when the severest of domestic afflictions overtakes him—he loses his favourite daughter Tullia. Here was a trial requiring all the consolation which religion and piety could give. He threw himself upon books; his friends comforted him to their utmost. We have extant a letter from Servius Sulpicius, glowing with poetry and eloquence, but betraying the utter inanity of the friend's power to console, the utter hopelessness of the father's grief. "If there be any sense even in those under the earth, such was her love, such her affection to all her friends, that she would not desire you to mourn."[1] If there be any sense even in those under the earth—this was the measure of the comfort which Sulpicius could give and Cicero receive. Here is the practical value of those Platonic disquisitions on the immortality of the soul. Cicero is uncertain whether his daughter has any sense after death, and finally resolves to build a temple wherein he may

[1] Cic. *ad. Fam.* iv. 5.

worship her: in which he would only have exercised a liberty such as any heathen then possessed, and such as many used; "and thee," he cries, "O best and most learned of women, admitted into the assembly of the gods with their own consent, I will consecrate to the regard of all mortals."[1]

Once more. A few months pass: Julius, the noblest of tyrants, falls by the hands of conspirators, who dare not trust Cicero with their secret, but whose deed he applauds to the echo. Cicero looks round him, and beholds, in spite of Cæsar's disappearance, his temple of glory in ruins: his great model commonwealth, whose growth through ages, whose ancestral wisdom and long-descended piety he set forth with his utmost power, is gone for ever, irretrievably ruined by internal corruption. Antony the reveller seizes hold of it on one side, and the boy Octavius draped in Cæsar's cloak on the other; and before him looms a gigantic despotism steeped in blood. This is the third and crowning trial of his life. And what does it find in him to meet this brunt of fortune? This is the occasion when the inward man comes out; when Liberty, driven from her outward court of public life, retires and enshrines herself in the sanctuary of the conscience. Myriads of Christians have carried out all the sanctities of moral life, and exhibited a courage proof on the one hand against every form of death, and on the other against every seduction of worldliness, when they could not participate in political power, and when that power was wielded despotically either by friendly or unfriendly hands; but Cicero can only cry, "When

---

[1] Quoted by Lactantius from "The Consolation." See *Heid. und Jud.* p. 607, where other instances are given; especially of a Spartan lady named Epicteta, who deified herself beforehand, with her defunct husband and her children.

the Senate has been extinguished, and the tribunals swept away, what is there for us to do worthy of ourselves in the senate-house or the forum?"[1] So he retired to his country-houses, and sketched the camps of contending Stoics and Epicureans from his small academical watch-box, which he could shift as occasion served to all points of the compass. Yet this man did not want physical courage: once more he returned to Rome; he tried to breathe life and unity into those whose selfishness was too great for freedom; and when this failed, and his name was the first on the list of the proscribed, he looked his murderer in the face, and died without swerving. What he needed was, belief in a personal God, in whom he was to live, and for whom he was to die, and a will which would have rested secure upon that immutable truth.

Cicero lived in the agony of the Roman Republic: let us pass on four hundred and fifty years, until we come to one who lived in the agony of the Roman empire. The Senate's successor was the stern military monarchy of the Cæsars; the Cæsars' successors were the barbarians of the north. If the change from the first to the second was a great crisis in the world's affairs, assuredly the change from the second to the third was a greater still. The former change will be for ever one of the most instructive points in ancient history; from the latter, all Europe, and we ourselves as a portion of it, are sprung. We have seen how a great heathen Roman met the former change; what resources he found in society, in letters, in his own heart; how far, when a blight passed over his outward world, he was able to find a new world within. Now let us consider a great Christian Roman at the time

---

[1] *De Officiis*, ii. 1.

of the latter change: let us see what were his hopes and fears; what view he took of society and man, of the world and government; above all, what was his own inward life, the core and marrow of the man.

Augustine was born in the year 354 at Thagaste, a town of Africa, in which his father was a burgess of very moderate fortune. He completes his education at Carthage, and becomes a teacher of rhetoric, that is, one who made literature his profession, first at Thagaste, from his twenty-first to his twenty-fourth year; next at Carthage, from his twenty-fourth to his twenty-ninth year; thirdly, at Rome, for a short time, whence, in his thirtieth year, he moves to Milan, where for two years he holds a public professorship, and is, as he says himself, a "seller of words." A catechumen from his birth, through his mother's piety, and brought up in the Catholic faith, he fell at nineteen into the Manichean heresy, and remained in it during nine years. He has given us a picture of himself drawn to the life during these two years at Milan, listening with pleasure to St. Ambrose, first attracted by his eloquence, and gradually won over to the truth which he set forth. With infinite labour he disengages himself from one prejudice after another which the Manichean heresy had instilled into him against the Catholic faith. And now, indeed, he was no longer a Manichean, but he had fallen into Cicero's state of doubt, and could see truth and certainty nowhere; and he was bound as with an iron chain by the three concupiscences of the world. "I longed," he says, "after honours, wealth, and wedlock; and Thou," addressing God, "didst mock me. I suffered under these desires the bitterest difficulties, in which Thou wast the kinder by not permitting anything to become sweet to me which was not Thyself. See my heart, O Lord, whose will it was that I should remember this and confess it to Thee. Now let my soul lay firm hold of Thee, the soul which Thou didst extricate from the tenacious grasp of death. How wretched it was! and Thou didst prick my wound in order that, deserting everything, it might be converted to Thee, who art over all, without whom all else is nothing; might be converted and be healed." [1] And his friends Alypius and Nebridius were living with him: he calls himself and them "three hungry mouths gasping out to each other their wants, and waiting upon Thee to give them food in due season. And in all the bitterness which, through Thy mercy, followed our acts of worldliness, when we considered the end for which we were suffering this, dark phantoms met us, and we turned away groaning and saying, How long shall this last? And this we said very often, but did not desert the objects we were pursuing, because nothing distinct shone out before us which we could lay hold upon after relinquishing the other." [2] He was astonished at himself to think that for eleven years he had been in passionate pursuit of wisdom; and still for two years more he remained struggling to be free from every fetter of the world, "yet bound," he says, "by the closest chain of desire for female love, and the servitude of secular business." [3] For it must be added that, when only seventeen, he had attached himself, not in marriage, to a person with whom he had now lived thirteen years; that a marriage had been arranged for him, for which, however, on account of the bride's youth, it was requisite

---

[1] St. Aug. *Conf.* vi. 6. [2] Id. vi. 18.
[3] Id. viii. 15.

to wait two years. With a view to this he had discarded his mistress, who left him to return into Africa, and led evermore a single life; while he, unable, as he says, to imitate her, took another in the interval before his intended marriage. Thus torn asunder between the desire of truth, certainty, and peace, on the one side, and the tyranny of worldly passions on the other, he was approaching the end of his thirty-second year. A friend, by name Pontitianus, called upon him, and the conversation fell upon the Egyptian monks and the fathers of the desert. The subject was new to Augustine and Alypius: " We listened," he says, "in intense silence. He told us, then, how one afternoon at Treves, when the emperor was taken up with the circensian games, he and three others, his companions, went out to walk in gardens near the city walls; and there, as they happened to walk in pairs, one went apart with him, and the other two wandered by themselves; and these in their wanderings lighted upon a certain cottage inhabited by servants of Thine, poor in spirit, of whom is the kingdom of heaven, and there they found a little book containing the life of Antony. This one of them began to read, admire, and kindle at it; and as he read, to meditate on taking up such a life, and giving over his secular service to serve Thee. And these two were of those whom they style agents for the public affairs. Then suddenly filled with a holy love and a sober shame, in anger with himself he cast his eyes upon his friend, saying, 'Tell me, I pray thee, what seek we to attain by all these labours of ours? What aim we at? What serve we for? Can our hopes in court rise higher than to be the emperor's favourites? And in this what is there not frail and full of perils? And by how many perils arrive we at a greater peril? And when arrive we thither? But a friend of God, if I wish it, I become now at once.' So spake he; and in pain with the travail of a new life, he turned his eyes again upon the book and read on, and was changed inwardly, where Thou sawest, and his mind was stripped of the world, as soon appeared. For as he read, and rolled up and down the waves of his heart, he stormed at himself awhile, then discerned, and determined on a better course; and now, being Thine, said to his friend, ' Now have I broken loose from those our hopes, and am resolved to serve God; and this I enter upon, from this hour, in this place. If thou likest not to imitate me, yet oppose me not.' The other answered, that he would cleave to him to partake so glorious a reward, so glorious a service. Thus both, being now Thine, were building the tower at the necessary cost, the forsaking all that they had and following Thee. Then Pontitianus and the other with him, that had walked in other parts of the garden, came in search of them to the same place; and finding them, reminded them to return, for the day was now far spent. But they, relating their resolution and purpose, and how that will was begun and settled in them, begged their comrades, if they would not join, not to molest them. Then the others, though nothing altered from their former selves, did yet bewail themselves, as he affirmed, and piously congratulated them, recommending themselves to their prayers; and so, with hearts lingering on the earth, went away to the palace. But the former two, fixing their heart on heaven, remained in the cottage. And both had affianced brides, who, hearing of this, likewise dedicated their virginity to God."[1]

[1] St. Aug. *Conf.* viii. 15.

This was the bolt, shot seemingly at a venture by a chance hand, which reached Augustine's heart. When his acquaintance left, he went with Alypius into the garden of the house where they resided, and there followed that great conflict between the flesh and spirit which ended in his conversion. The wonderful pages of Augustine himself describing this are both too long and too well known for me to quote. At length he hears a voice, as of a boy or girl from a neighbouring house, chanting and oft repeating, "Take up and read, take up and read." " Returning to the place where Alypius was sitting, for there had I laid the volume of the Apostle when I arose thence, I seized, opened, and in silence read that section on which my eyes first fell : ' Not in revelling and drunkenness, not in chambering and wantonness, not in strife and emulation; but put on the Lord Jesus Christ, and make not provision for the flesh in its desires.' No further would I read, nor needed I : for instantly at the end of this sentence, by a light, as it were, of serenity infused into my heart, all the darkness of doubt vanished away."

From this time forth Augustine triumphs over that triple bondage of the world which hitherto had triumphed over him. Receiving baptism the next year, he declines marriage; he rejects all hope of wealth or honour from his profession. Cicero in riper years returned from his exile to seeming honour and consideration, in reality the humbled slave of the world which had trampled on him, waiting for his daily bread on its applause. Augustine, in the bloom of manhood, goes forth from his conversion into what seems a humble retirement and obscurity, but possessing inward liberty, a soul collected back into itself from the distraction of conflicting desires, but, above all, resting imperturbably on the Immutable One. There is in these two, upon the common foundation of human nature, great genius, a passion for knowledge, an ardent love of truth, as a liberal curiosity; but is it possible to conceive a completer revolution of the individual man than the one presents to the other? Who can express so well as Augustine the change which had passed over him? "Too late have I loved Thee, O Beauty, so old and yet so new. Too late have I loved Thee. And behold, Thou wast within and I without; and without I sought Thee, and rushed in my deformity on those fair forms which Thou hast created. Thou wast with me, and I was not with Thee. Things held me far from Thee, which would not be at all if they were not in Thee. Thou calledst; Thou utteredst Thy voice; Thou brokest through my deafness. Thy lightning flashed; Thy splendour shone; my darkness was scattered. Thy scent came forth, I drew my breath, and I pant for Thee. I tasted, and I hunger, and I thirst. Thy touch reached me, and I burnt after Thy peace."[1] This is the whole. Cicero and his world were without; Augustine and his world within. Cicero is the model of innumerable heathens; Augustine the type of myriads among Christians of both sexes, and of every age and condition of life. This is the change which had passed upon man in those four hundred and fifty years.

Take another scene in his life. He is returning, a year after his conversion, to Africa with that mother, of whose prayers and tears, continued through long, seemingly unhopeful years, he was the child, rather than of her natural throes. They are at Ostia, about to embark, and gazing down from a window over the

[1] *Conf.* x. 38.

garden of the house where they rested. "We were discoursing then together alone very sweetly, and, forgetting those things which are behind and reaching forth unto those things which are before, we were inquiring between ourselves, in the presence of the Truth which Thou art, of what sort the eternal life of the saints was to be, which eye hath not seen, nor ear heard, nor hath it entered into the heart of man. But yet we gasped with the mouth of our heart after those heavenly streams of Thy fountain, the fountain of life, which is with Thee; that being bedewed thence, according to our capacity, we might in some sort meditate upon so high a mystery. We were saying then: If to any the tumult of the flesh were hushed, hushed the images of earth and waters and air, hushed also the poles of heaven, yea, the very soul be hushed to herself, and by not thinking on self surmount self, hushed all dreams and imaginary revelations, every tongue and every sign, and whatsoever exists only in transition, since, if any could hear, all these say, We made not ourselves, but He made us who abideth for ever,—if then, having uttered this, they, too, should be hushed, having roused only our ears to Him who made them, and He alone speak, not by them but by Himself, that we may hear His Word not through any tongue of flesh nor angel's voice, nor sound of thunder, nor in the dark riddle of a similitude, but might hear Him whom in these things we love, might hear His very self without these (as we two now strained ourselves, and in swift thought touched on that eternal Wisdom which abideth over all); could this be continued on, and other visions of kind far unlike be withdrawn, and this one ravish and absorb and wrap up its beholder amid these inward joys, so that life might be for ever like that one moment of understanding which now we sighed after; were not this, Enter into the joy of thy Lord?"[1]

A few days after this conversation St. Monica sickens of a fever and dies: she dies full of hope, with one request: "Lay this body anywhere: let not the care for that any way disquiet you: this only I request, that you would remember me at the Lord's altar, wherever you be." And when she was asked whether she was not afraid to leave her body so far from her own city, she replied, "Nothing is far to God: nor is it to be feared lest, at the end of the world, He should not recognise whence He has to raise me up." You will not forget how bent Cicero was on building a temple to his daughter Tullia after her death, and how Sulpicius tried to soothe him by remarking that if there be any sense even in the dead, his daughter would not wish him to grieve over her. Augustine, too, had tears for the dead, and has recorded his prayers that her sins might be forgiven: "And I believe," he says (he was writing thirteen years after her death), "Thou hast already done what I ask; but accept, O Lord, the freewill offerings of my mouth. For she, the day of her dissolution now at hand, took no thought to have her body sumptuously wound up, nor desired she a choice monument, or to be buried in her own land. These things she enjoined us not; but desired only to have her name commemorated at Thy altar, which she had served without intermission of one day, whence she knew that holy Victim to be dispensed by which the handwriting that was against us is blotted out. May she rest, then, in peace, with the husband before and after whom she

[1] *Conf.* ix. 23, 25.

had never any, whom she obeyed, with patience bringing forth fruit unto Thee, that she might win him also unto Thee. And inspire, O Lord my God, inspire Thy servants my brethren, thy sons my masters, whom with voice and heart and pen I serve, that so many as shall read these Confessions may at Thy altar remember Monica thy handmaid, with Patricius her sometime husband, by whose bodies thou broughtest me into this life, how I know not. May they with devout affection remember my parents in this transitory light, my brethren under Thee our Father in our Catholic mother, and my fellow-citizens in that eternal Jerusalem which Thy pilgrim people sigheth after from their exodus unto their return. That so my mother's last request of me, through my Confessions more than through my prayers, be, through the prayers of many, more abundantly fulfilled to her."[1]

The conversion of Augustine was followed by forty-four years of almost unexampled mental activity. His life was based henceforth on the denial of those three concupiscences under the dominion of which he had groaned for fifteen years. He found it no longer impossible to carry out, together with friends minded like himself, a course of life made up of study, retirement, and meditation, which he had tried in vain with the same friends before. For the presence of women in their company then broke up this design.[2] With these friends, having given up his only property, a few paternal fields, he led a sort of cenobitic life. In a short time he was made a priest, and a few years

---

[1] *Conf.* ix. 36, 37.
[2] *Conf.* vi. 24. "Sed posteaquam cœpit cogitari utrum hoc munierculæ sinerent, quas et alii nostrum jam habebant, et nos habere volebamus, totum illud placitum quod bene formabamus, dissiluit in manibus, atque confractum et abjectum est."

later bishop. By far the greatest number of his works were produced during this episcopate, which lasted five-and-thirty years, while he became more and more eminent for a sanctity which increased as his genius unfolded itself. We have many thousand pages on a vast variety of subjects from his hand, of which I will only say that it is perhaps not possible to find one in which the writer does not show that he has steadily before him two objects—his own soul, and the immutable truth on which that soul rests and lives, the personal being of God. Exactly the two ideas which never occurred to Cicero make up Augustine's consciousness.

And here I cannot but admit the advantage which Augustine possessed over Cicero in natural genius as distinct from the gifts of divine grace. The contrast which he himself marks between Cicero and Varro, that they who loved words found their pleasure in the former, while they who loved things found instruction in the latter,[1] might serve to express the difference between the genius of the Roman rhetorician and the Christian thinker. Augustine's mind is every way deeper and larger than the mind of Cicero, more acute, and more accurate; and, what is marvellous, he works greater wonders with his old, refuse, worn-out Latin of the fifth century than the master and maker of Roman style did with the virgin ore of Latium, which he fused in the laboratory of his mind, and poured out tempered and wrought to express Grecian thought. For Augustine took up these half-defaced lumps of metal, which had served to express the

---

[1] *De Civ. Dei*, vi. 2. "Varro tametsi minus est suavis eloquio, doctrina tamen atque sententiis ita refertus est, ut in omni eruditione, quam nos sæcularem, illi autem liberalem vocant, studiosum rerum tantum iste doceat, quantum studiosum verborum Cicero delectat."

images of common things, and made them express metaphysical truths which never were disclosed to Cicero's eye. Cicero, indeed, philosophises; but Augustine is the parent of mental philosophy; in him our own ages seem to live and breathe, gazing inwards with intense introspection. Cicero is acquainted with outward society, is a man of wit, learning, and letters, but he never seems to break through the crust of human nature into the man; whereas it may be doubted whether any human eye saw deeper than St. Augustine into the soul's secrets, or exposed them more lucidly to view. Cicero's letters give us a faithful picture of a great man's petty weaknesses, vanity, and dissimulation, of all the falsehood and corruption which saddened Roman society at the time. Thanking Cæsar publicly in the Senate for the pardon of Marcellus, he cries, "Such gentleness, a clemency so unwonted and unheard of, so universal a moderation united with absolute power, wisdom so incredible and almost divine, it is impossible for me to pass over in silence."[1] This tyrant, who will not leave us even our thoughts free, he whispers to Atticus. But St. Augustine's letters and confessions, while they expose his natural weakness with a scalpel which uncovers the most secret fibres of our being, show the same man corrected and exalted, until he became a fountainhead of knowledge to every inquirer, an instructor in virtue to every wrestler with his own heart. There is scarcely a question of human or divine government of which he does not treat; and where he does not solve, because solution is impossible to man in his state of trial, he diffuses peace now in the reader's heart, as of old he did in the listener's, by the sublime,

[1] *Pro Marcello*, 1.

unfaltering resignation of a great intellect, and a still more loving heart resting upon God. Take as an instance of what I mean the following. What is the practical value in human conduct of the *probability* that there is a providence? Cicero the Academician thought it more probable that a divine mind ruled the affairs of the world than that things went by chance. And the effect of the probability on his life is, that his politics were a series of shifts and shufflings, a caressing in public of those at whom he sneered in private; and when great calamities, banishment, loss of child, loss of liberty, fell upon him, his very heathen friends are ashamed of his pusillanimity. St. Augustine sees the Roman world sinking into a chaos, in the midst of which his daily life is exact and unfaltering in the discharge of every duty, a continual sacrifice to fraternal charity, a holocaust to divine love. Now, in one of his letters he falls on one of those questions which lie in wait for us on every side : a question belonging to that curiosity of the eyes which is the proper temptation and continual cross of speculative minds : a question such as a child may ask, and no man living can answer. Why, he asks, does God give souls to those who, as He knows, will presently die? He suggests a reason, but adds, "We can likewise rightly leave these things to the rule of Him whom we know to bestow the most admirably beautiful and orderly arrangement upon all transitory things in time, among which are the springing up and the passing away of living creatures : while we know also that we are incapable of feeling that beauty and order, which, had we a sense to perceive them, would wrap us in unutterable delight. For it was not without a purpose said by the prophet, who learnt this by inspiration concerning God, 'that He bringeth forth His universe according to a preconceived harmony.'[1] And thus music, that is, the knowledge or the sense of correct modulation, was by God's bounty granted even to dying creatures who possess rational souls, to remind them of so great a fact. For if man, artificer of verse, knows the proper vocal intervals to be given to words, so that his composition, by a continual succession of emerging and departing sounds, may flow on in fairest order and pass away, how much more does God, whose wisdom, by which He made all things, is far superior to every art, in the case of natures which are born and pass away, allow no spaces of time, which stand in the position of syllables and words to the subordinate parts of this world, in this marvellous song of fleeting things, to pass with slower or longer pause than His foreknown and fore-established modulation requires? As this is true even of the tree's leaf, and the number of our hairs, how much more is it true of man's birth and death, whose temporal life endures not a shorter or longer time than God, the Disposer of all times, knows how to make to harmonise with the government of the universe."[2] This thought of the divine providence is in so complete possession of his mind that it starts up on the slightest occasion. In the sketch of his mother, he notices that when sent by her parents to draw wine in the cellar, she had got a habit of sipping a little from the brim of the jug. Whereupon the maid who went with her called her once, in a pet, a winebibber, which cured her for ever of that habit;

---

[1] Isa. xl. 26. "Qui profert numerose sæculum : secundum LXX., ὁ ἐκφέρων κατ' ἀριθμὸν τὸν κόσμον αὐτοῦ."
[2] St. Aug. *Ep.* 166.

and St. Augustine breaks out: "By one soul's madness didst Thou heal another, O Lord, the ruler of all in heaven and on earth, who turnest to Thy purpose the torrent in its rush, the flood of ages ordered in its very waywardness."[1] So again, in speaking of the different sacrifices appointed in the Old Testament and in the New, he says, "The sacrifice ordered by God was suitable to the first ages, but is not suitable now. For another suitable to the present age is enjoined now by Him who knows much better than man the proper medicine for every time; what and at what time He is to bestow, to add, to remove in whole or part, to increase or diminish, the unchangeable Creator alike and ruler of changing things, until the loveliness of this whole temporal dispensation, of which the subordinate parts are those which suit each their own times, run out like some grand composition of an unspeakably perfect artist, and from it those who even in the time of faith rightly worship God pass into the eternal contemplation of Him face to face."[2]

This perpetual vision of faith, this eye of the heart centred upon the Unchangeable One, is the great mark of St. Augustine. It was the character of him which impressed itself on the ages following him. And hence they found in his writings a special consolation amid the downfall of earthly things which tried them. The thought seems well expressed in a legend which I have somewhere seen. One had disclosed to him a vision of the blessed; and as he looked upon the great rose[3] of heaven, expanding all its

---

[1] "At Tu, Domine, rector cœlitum et terrenorum, ad usus tuos contorquens profunda torrentis, fluxum sæculorum ordinate turbulentum." *Conf.* ix. 18.
[2] *Ep.* cxxxviii. 5, p. 412.
[3] "In forma dunque di candida rosa," &c.—Dante, *Par.* xxxi. 1.

petals before him, resting for a moment on each leaf, and scenting each living odour, distinct and peculiar, and never repeated in that innumerable multitude, he cried, But where is St. Augustine? He is not here, replied a voice; he has been a thousand years in ecstasy, gazing on the Blessed Trinity.

Such is the force, upon human conduct, of doubt and of belief, as the element of our life. Cicero is the exponent of the one, and Augustine of the other.

I shall select but one more instance of contrast between them; and it is the most remarkable.

By the downfall of Roman liberty Cicero complained that all interest was taken from his life; he had nothing more to labour for; his leisure had lost all its dignity; his very thirst for knowledge satisfied itself with a review of the various mental systems, resting upon none. The world in which he had become consul, father of his country, augur, the first of lawyers, orators, and parliamentary debaters, was crumpled up in Cæsar's hand; and he felt crushed like a fly in the grasp of the conqueror. He possessed no inner world of freedom in his own mind: he had no hope for the race of men around him.[1] All the earth became to him dark; for the seven centuries of Rome's growth to universal empire were ending in her own servitude.

Now observe what happened to Augustine under like circumstances. While he had yet all the mental vigour of youth united with the ripeness of mature

---

[1] Since writing the above, I find the following statement of a good judge: "Cicero's writings may, I believe, be searched in vain for a single expression of reliance on the progressive improvement of mankind. The two poles of his philosophy, between which he wavers with perpetual oscillation, are, regret for the past, and resignation to the present." Merivale, *History of the Romans*, ii. 538.

age, he saw the frontiers of that vast empire, which had lasted now full four hundred and fifty years from Cæsar's death, broken in upon all sides; nay, the very heart of the empire was taken, and the immovable rock of the Capitol fell into the power of barbarians. The wail of the civilised world over the capture of Rome by Alaric struck through St. Jerome's heart, as he sat in sackcloth and ashes at Bethlehem: and St. Augustine heard on all sides the murmurs of half-converted pagans or weak believers[1]—the heathen gods guarded Rome and made her glorious, the God of the Christians has given her into captivity: Christianity has ruined the fairest civilisation which the world has yet seen: Christianity has broken up our empire of twelve hundred years.

And indeed the prospect of temporal things at that moment was wretched: Gaul and Spain were laid waste, Italy was open to the inroads of the Goths, and its capital sacked. The world seemed on the point of being delivered up to desolation and anarchy. Then it was that St. Augustine answered the denunciations of enemies and the anxious questionings of friends. Out of the very capture of the world's capital, and the impending fall of civilisation, the design arose in his mind to trace the origin, progress, and allotted course of the City of God. As all human powers, the armies of Rome, her acts of peace, her majestic municipal system, her matchless code of laws, and that crown of subject nations secure under her long-continued sway, which flourished like a rich garland round the Mediterranean, seemed dissolving visibly before him, his eyes fixed themselves more and more intently upon

---

[1] See the letters to Volusianus and Marcellinus, the germ of the work *De Civ. Dei.*

another vision, transitory indeed in one sense, in that it was passing in time, but springing from the counsel of God ordained before time, and flowing on till the full tide of its waves is gathered into eternity.[1] Starting from the basis of God, almighty in power, the supremely good Creator of all natures, who assists and rewards upright wills, who withdraws Himself from evil wills, and condemns them, but who is the orderer of both, he traces two commonwealths which emerge into mortality from the common door of Adam, and thence proceed and diverge to their own distinct and proper ends. Already the two races part asunder in the very children of the first parent; Cain stands at the head of one, and Seth at the head of the other. And their different tempers are apparent from the first. Cain begot Enoch, in whose name he built a city; a city of the earth, that is, not sojourning in this world, but resting in its temporal peace and prosperity, having here the end which it seeks. But the house of the men who live by faith looks for the promises which are future, but eternal; and uses temporal things as a pilgrim not to be taken captive by them, and turned aside from God to whom it tends, but in order to bear more easily the burden of the body weighing down the soul. And so the use of things necessary to this mortal life is common to both houses and races of men, while each has its own end in using them, and that end exceedingly diverse. Thus, even the earthly commonwealth, which does not live by faith, seeks earthly peace; and draws its citizens into agreement of command on the one side, and of obedience on the other, in order to produce

---

[1] Drawn from the following passages, *De Civ. Dei*, xiv. 26, xv. 21, 17, xiv. 28, tom. iv. 1544 B; *De Civ. Dei*, xix. 17, 26.

a certain harmony of human wills, in the things which concern mortal life. While the heavenly commonwealth, or rather that part of it which sojourns in this mortal state, and lives by faith, must likewise use that same earthly peace, until the mortal state requiring such a peace pass away. And therefore it is that while in the bosom of this earthly commonwealth it leads what is like a captive life of pilgrimage, having already received the promise of redemption, and the spiritual gift which is its pledge, it hesitates not to obey the laws of the earthly commonwealth, which administer what is necessary for sustaining mortal life, in order that, as this mortal state is common to both alike, in things which belong to this there may be concord between the two commonwealths. In fine, the city of the devil consists in the things of this world, where it is not a pilgrim, but a settled dweller, resting in temporal peace and happiness, and having here its chosen end. It has a self-love which reaches right up to the contempt of God; it boasts in itself; it seeks glory from men; it is swayed by the lust of empire; it loves its own virtue in its own great men; and its wise men, living according to the principles of human nature, pursue the goods either of the body or of the mind, or of both; it does not rejoice save over some temporal prosperity; it does not sorrow but for some temporal adversity. And the City of God lives in the hope of God, always enduring the earth, and hoping for heaven; it knows no evil, save offending God, and not reaching His promises; nor good, save meriting God, and obtaining them; it makes use of Babylon's peace, referring it to the peace of heaven, its proper good being the eternal and perfect peace, that is, the most well-ordered and harmonious society of those who enjoy God, and each other in God: its king is truth; its law is charity; its manner of being is eternity.[1] It has a love of God which it pushes even to the contempt of self; it glories in its Lord; in it by mutual charity are servants to each other, rulers who do good to their subjects, and subjects who obey their rulers. It cries, "I will love Thee, O Lord my virtue;" in it there is no wisdom of men save piety, waiting for this reward in the society of saints, angels as well as men, that God be all in all.

It was thus St. Augustine consoled his friends and expressed his own unshaken belief, as he stood between imperial Rome collapsing, and the northern flood bursting in upon her. This is the first Philosophy of History; and after fourteen centuries it remains the best, if not the only one. The whole mind of the Middle Ages for a thousand years after St. Augustine's departure lived upon it. This book was the delight of Alfred, the manual of Charlemagne and St. Louis, and of every Christian ruler and philosopher until men ceased to read history with the eyes of faith. To use his own image, it was like a magnificent piece of music sounding in their ears through the palace of time, and filling it with immortal harmonies. No writer seems to me to have grasped with so much force the idea that there is no moral evil save in the abuse of free will, nor to derive so continually the consequence how largely it enters into the design of God, not only to reward the good will, but to punish the evil will. And in this consists the completeness of his view, and its agreement with the course of events, where others fall short and are disproved by it.

[1] "Cujus rex veritas, cujus lex caritas, cujus modus æternitas." *Ep.* cxxxviii. 17.

But St. Augustine has himself supplied us with the key to his own life and writings, and as it gives touchingly and eloquently the cause of the whole change in individual man which I am here illustrating, I will quote the passage. It occurs in the last treatise which he wrote while yet a neophyte and a layman. He lived forty years after this to become the great voice of the Church, but nowhere has he set forth more lucidly the truth on which the Church lives.

"In all manners does God heal the mind according to the opportunity of times which are ordered by His marvellous wisdom; but most of all was His beneficence to the human race shown when the very Wisdom of God, the only Son consubstantial and coeternal with the Father, deigned to assume whole man, and the Word was made flesh and dwelt among us. For so He proved to the carnal, and to those who could not gaze upon the truth with the mind's eye, and to those who were given up to the body's senses, how lofty a place among creatures human nature holds, in that He appeared to men as a true man, and not merely in a visible form, which He might have shaped of air and tempered to our senses. For the nature which was to be freed was likewise to be assumed. And that neither sex might fancy itself to be despised by its Creator, while He took a woman for His mother, He assumed the Man.

"For nothing did He by force, but all by persuasion and exhortation. In fact, the old servitude was passed, the time of freedom had dawned, and it was seasonable and salutary for man to be persuaded with how free a will he had been created. By His miracles He obtained from man faith towards His divine Person; by His Passion, towards His human nature. Speaking to the multitude as God, when His Mother was announced to Him He admitted her not; and yet, as the Gospel says, He went down and was subject to His parents. For when teaching, He appeared as God; in the times of His life as man. When about to turn water into wine, as God He says, 'Woman, what have I to do with thee? Mine hour is not yet come.' But when the hour had come for Him to die as man, from the Cross He recognised His Mother, and intrusted her to the disciple whom He loved above all others. To their own destruction the nations were thirsting after riches as the ministers of pleasure; it was His will to be poor. They flung themselves upon honour and power; He refused to be a king. They thought children after the flesh a great good; He despised such wedlock and such offspring. In their utter pride they abhorred disgrace; He endured every kind of it. They considered injuries not to be borne; what greater injury than for the just and innocent to be condemned? They execrated bodily pain; He was scourged and tormented. They feared to die; He suffered death. They thought the cross the most ignominious kind of death; He was crucified. Everything through the desire of having which we lived amiss, He did without, and rendered worthless. Everything through avoiding which we shrunk from the truth, He endured, and made level to us. For it is impossible to commit any sin save by seeking for what He despised, or flying from what He endured. And therefore we have a perfect system of moral discipline in His whole life on earth through the Man whom He deigned to assume."[1]

[1] *De vera Religione*, 30, 31.

LECTURE IV

EFFECT OF THE CHRISTIAN PEOPLE ON THE WORLD

CICERO is a fair representative of human nature at the time he lived, of man such as heathenism had made him. We may sum up in him the thoughts, the principles, the motives of many generations. When the man who had sacrificed Cicero to Mark Antony surprised one of his grandchildren reading the works of his victim, he said, "My child, that was a great man." If Cicero looked to human renown as his reward; if his hope began and ended with his dignity as a citizen and senator of Rome; if he was unduly beaten down by adversity; if his private inner life was devoid of morality; and if the wide circle of his accomplishments excluded expressly the knowledge of a personal, all-seeing God, the rewarder and punisher of men, and of a responsible soul in himself, these were not peculiarities in him, but the very air of the atmosphere which he breathed. If one had searched through the Senate, the knights, and the commonalty of Rome in his day, the same results would have appeared in all. Amid the almost infinite varieties of individual character, these general lineaments would have been seen in each. Cicero's genius was his own, and raised him above most of his contemporaries; but these moral features were common to him with them all.

And in like manner the great genius of St. Augustine marks him out among all generations of men. His intellectual greatness was his own, and reached by few of any age; but the moral features of his life from the time of his conversion, the conquest which he achieved over the three master desires of man, the love of pleasure, of honour, and of wealth, with all "the curiosity of the eyes," these were common in him, not with all men, indeed, of his day, but with a certain number. And this number during four hundred years had been perpetually increasing. And those who, like him, presented these moral features were to be found in both sexes, in the very rich, in the middle class, and in the poor, in every tribe and people within the vast limits of the Roman dominion, and far beyond it, in the learned and the unlearned, in the free and the slave. No condition of human life was without them, and none was wholly composed of them. I have only taken St. Augustine as a specimen of a vast revolution which had occurred in the bosom of this effete Roman civilisation. It was a revolution unlike anything which had occurred before in the history of the human race. It was absolutely without a precedent. Just at the time that Tacitus, from the safe security of Trajan's reign, was uttering his sarcasms against Roman society, and expressing his hopelessness as to the world's course and the destiny of the human race; just as he was preferring the simplicity of the Germans in the depths of their woods to the gaudy but polluted brilliance of the world's capital, because "no one there smiled at vice, nor was it called fashion to corrupt and be corrupted;"[1] just at this time an author, whose very

---

[1] Tacitus, *Germania*, 19.

name is unknown, drew the following picture of a class of men who had lately sprung up.

"Christians are neither in country nor in language nor in customs distinguished from other men. For they nowhere inhabit cities which are entirely their own, nor do they use a language different from others, nor pursue a life marked by peculiarity. Nor was this discipline of life discovered by them through any invention or thought of curious men, nor do they represent any humanly-taught dogma as some do. Rather they inhabit both Greek and foreign cities, as the lot of each may be cast; and while they follow the habits of the country as to dress, food, and the rest, they exhibit a wonderful and confessedly strange citizenship among themselves. They dwell severally in their own country, but it is as sojourners. They take a share in everything as citizens, yet endure everything as strangers. Every strange land is a country to them, and every country a strange land. They marry like all others; they have children, but they may not expose them. With them the table is common to all, but never the bed. They are in the flesh, but do not live according to it. They dwell on the earth, but their citizenship is in heaven. They obey the laws which are in force, but surpass the laws in their own lives. They love all, and are persecuted by all. Men are ignorant of them and condemn them. They are put to death, and made alive. They are poor, and enrich many. They want all things, and abound in all things. They are dishonoured, and glory in dishonour. Men speak ill of them, and bear witness to their goodness. They are slandered, and bless; insulted, and show respect. They do good, and are punished as evil; and in this punishment they rejoice, as filled by it with life. The Jews wage war with them as foreigners, and the Greeks persecute them; and they who hate them cannot give the cause of their hatred. In a word, what the soul is in the body, that Christians are in the world. The soul is diffused over all limbs of the body; so are Christians through the cities of the world. The soul dwells in the body, but is not of the body; and Christians dwell in the world, but are not of the world. The soul invisible mounts guard in the visible body; and Christians are known as dwellers in the world, while their divine worship remains invisible. The flesh hates the soul; and though in nothing wronged by it, fights with it, because it is hindered in pursuing its pleasures; and the world too, in nothing wronged by them, hates Christians, because they set themselves against its pleasures. The soul loves the flesh and its limbs, while the flesh hates it; and Christians love those who hate them. The soul is imprisoned in the body, while it holds the body together; and Christians are imprisoned in the world, while they hold the world together. The soul immortal lodges in a mortal tent, and Christians dwell amid corruptible things, looking for incorruption in heaven. The soul is improved by reducing the body's food, and Christians are daily punished and abound the more. Such a post has God assigned them, which they may not decline. For, as I said before, this is not an earthly invention which has been handed down among them; nor is it a mortal device which they are minded to guard so carefully; nor are they human mysteries, with the dispensation of which they are charged. But the almighty, all-creating, invisible God Himself has implanted among them the Truth from heaven, and the holy Word incomprehensible, establishing it to abide in their hearts. Not, as any one might conjecture, that He sent to men some servant, an angel, or a prince, or one of those who administer the things of earth, or one of those intrusted with the dipensation of the heavens; but the Contriver and Artificer of all these; by whom He made the heavens; by whom He shut up the sea in its own boundaries; whose secret laws all the elements faithfully observe; from whom the sun has taken the measure of his daily course; whom the moon obeys when He bids her shine in the night, and the stars which accompany her course; by whom all things have been arranged, determined, and subordinated.—This was He whom God sent to them: but did He send Him, as any man might reason, to exercise tyranny, to inflict fear, and to amaze? Not so, but in gentleness and meekness. He sent Him as a king who sends his son a King; He sent Him as God; He sent Him as unto men; He sent Him to save them, to persuade and not to compel, for compulsion is abhorrent from God. He sent Him as loving, not as judging; for one day He will send Him to judge, and who shall abide His coming?—See you not that they are tossed before the wild beasts, in order that they may deny the Lord, and are not conquered? See you not, the more their punishers, the more they abound? Deeds like these seem not to be the deeds of man, but the power of God, and the signs of His presence.

"For out of all men what single one was there who knew what God is before He came Himself?—For God, the Lord and Framer of all things—being not only the lover of man, but full of long-suffering—conceived a mighty and ineffable design, which He communicated to His Son alone.—Then after having convicted in the previous period the inability of our nature to obtain life, He disclosed the Saviour, able to save even what was past salvation, and from both these things He intended that we should trust His goodness, and esteem Him Foster-father, Parent, Teacher, Counsellor, and Physician; our Intelligence, our Light, our Honour, our Glory, our Strength, and our Life.—And if you yearn after this faith, and receive it, first you will come to the knowledge of the Father.—And then with what joy will you be filled! How will you love Him who first so loved you! And loving Him, you will imitate His goodness. Nor be surprised that man can imitate God. He can, by God's will. For happiness consists not in ruling over others, nor in the wish to have more than the weak, nor in being wealthy and forcing inferiors to your will. Nor can any one imitate God in such things as these. They are external to His Majesty. But when one bears the burden of another, when one wishes to help an inferior out of the superiority which the bounty of God has given, such an one becomes a God to those who receive from him. He is an imitator of God. And so dwelling upon earth, you will see that God in heaven administers the human commonwealth; you will begin to speak the hidden things of God; you will love and you will admire those who are punished because they will not deny God; you will condemn the deceit and the error of the world when you come to the knowledge of true life in heaven, when you despise that which is but seeming death here, when you dread the true death which is kept in store for those who shall be condemned to the eternal fire that is to punish unto the end them who are delivered over unto it. Then you will admire those who endure for justice-sake a temporary fire, and in the knowledge of that other fire will hold them blessed."[1]

The writer of this admirable letter states that he was a disciple of the Apostles. And he was also an eye-witness of what he so vividly describes. His time is most probably placed in the first ten years of the second century: he may have seen St. Ignatius cast before the wild beasts in the Coliseum. But in these few words he has given us a perfect picture of Christianity as it presented itself during ten successive generations to the people of the Roman empire. Two such generations had preceded the writer; eight more were to follow him. In all these, Christians were like a seed sprinkled more or less sparingly, more or less abundantly, through all the cities of the civilised world from the Euphrates to Britain, growing up at first in silence and retirement, and escaping notice from their humility, but gradually emerging into air and light by the natural process of growth, and, moreover, multiplied with a fecundity which could not be concealed. Thus the grain sprung into the plant, and the plant became a tree; and the tree was everywhere, inexhaustible in life and fruitfulness. Or, to use another image employed by our Lord, the leaven of the Word incarnate was hidden in the lump of human nature, and was fermenting through the whole mass and changing it into itself.

Here, however, we must remark the order which it pursued. The restoration of the likeness of God in man was the work to be accomplished. It is evident that this work was to take place in the individual

[1] *Ep. to Diognetus*, 5-12.

man. On the individual soul of man the likeness had been originally impressed: in that same it had been defaced and obliterated; in the same it was to be restored. For this purpose every man by himself was a complete whole; every one therefore was approached individually. Never was the individual forgotten in the mass; never the mass approached but through the individual. The nature itself had been assumed in order that the nature itself might be restored; but the nature itself was whole and complete in every specimen of it. The progress therefore begun by the Christian faith took its start in the heart of each man. This was its unit, its pivot, its centre. To knit each particular man to God by the union of faith and love was the course it pursued. The grace—a communication of the divine nature—which it dispensed, and which was stored up in its sacraments, laid hold of each man by himself; for his spiritual birth, by baptism; for his adolescence, by confirmation; to remedy his lapse, by penance; to support him daily, by the holy Eucharist; to aid his last struggle, by anointing; in the natural union of the species, by marriage; in the propagation of the spiritual power, by order. Thus this restoring grace touched man at all points of contact, and possessed itself of his individual being. For man himself is of infinitely greater value than human society. This terminates with the present life, and is not reproduced; but he is eternal. Society is made for man's needs; but man is made for his Maker only. From this truth all Christian progress started, and it continues to be the measure and standard by which all Christian progress must be valued. It was through the individual and by multiplication of the individual that it laid hold of the world. The letter to Diognetus is especially valuable, because it marks the inward character of the process in the individual, and then its radiation from the individual to the mass. The invisible God, he says, has implanted in the heart the Truth from heaven, the incomprehensible Word; this is the first step: and then, what the soul is in the body, that Christians are in the world: here is the course and the work of the Church expressed in a line. At the same time, taking man in himself, not indeed as he came from his Maker's hand, in the dignity of an unfallen nature, but as he stood naked and degraded under a common fall, to be the subject of its operation, it did away simply and easily with the very groundwork of national distinctions, and of all superiority arising from the external gifts of rank, wealth, beauty, or talent, and that most grievous separation of all, which consisted in slavery. The most abject of Rome's "animated instruments" stood before it as complete a recipient of its regenerating power as a Fabius or a Lucullus. How was so prodigious a change as this impressed on the face of a society built on opposite principles? Let us trace some of the more remarkable points in the process.

Nothing is more striking in human society at the time of our Lord's appearance than the absolute disregard of man's life as man. Not that the citizen had not a certain political value, or that wealth was deprived of its natural influence. But I am speaking of the value attached to the life of man as a human being. In this light he was become, as we have seen, the vilest of all animals. The extinction of a belief in a future state of retribution was the main cause of this disregard; while the gladiatorial games, and the whole condition of the slaves of both sexes, were a striking exhibition of it. To measure the feeling of society as it was then and as it is now, let me remind you again of a single fact. In the servile war Crassus crucified ten thousand slaves in cold blood. Their bodies lined the road from Rome to Capua. No one blamed Crassus; but the general who should now put to death a single unarmed captive would not only deserve but meet with the world's execration. How was this change brought about? It was brought about by those who shed their blood like water for the sake of their belief. They who counted their life as nothing worth in comparison of the truth to which they bore witness, not only gained admission for that truth into the hearts of men, but gained for the life so sacrificed a value which it did not before possess. In the two hundred and eighty years which elapsed from the crucifixion of our Lord to Constantine's decree of toleration, there was probably no considerable city of the Roman empire which had not witnessed the spectacle of men, women, maidens, and even children, giving up their lives because they would not, by burning a few grains of incense on the altar of an idol, renounce their belief in one God the maker of all things, and cease to confess that the Son of God had become incarnate and suffered death to redeem man. One and all assigned the same reason for this conduct, that here they were in a state of banishment, and looked for their home elsewhere; that they who suffered in the present place of banishment would be crowned in the future place of reward. There was a disdain of the earth and of their human life, of all the comforts of civilisation, of all the enjoyments of wealth, in the profound yearning which they testified

for that other unseen life. To prince and people, the
ruler and the ruled alike, to the philosopher and the
illiterate, this disdain seemed an inconceivable folly.
But it prevailed. When St. Perpetua folded her
scanty robe around her in the amphitheatre of Carthage, anxious, not to protect her limbs from the gore
of the wild bull, but her nakedness from the eyes of
the spectators; when St. Cyprian, a man of credit
among the heathen, after renouncing the enjoyments
of wealth and talent in the world in order to become
a Christian, was further condemned to death for the
crime of being a bishop, when he heard the proconsul's
judgment, "Let Thascius Cyprian be executed with
the sword," and replied with tranquillity, "*Deo gratias;*"
when St. Laurence, lying on his bed of agony, said
to his tormentors, "Turn me on the other side, this
side is done enough;"—when this disregard of their
own life was repeated a thousand and a thousand times,
even by those who were in possession of youth, beauty,
health, and riches, that strange confidence in a future
life prevailed at last over the heathen. They learned
to value that which the martyrs threw away through
regard for the reward to which the martyrs aspired.
Not easily, not by appreciation of bodily comforts, not
by refinement of mental culture, not by the triumphs
of science, not by the appliances of wealth, or through
the love of renown, was the belief in a future world,
an unerring judgment, and an eternal reward, reim-
planted in the heart of man. It was a work of blood;
of bodily comforts rejected, of mental culture put
aside, of riches trampled upon, of fame scorned, of
science reckoned to be of no repute, of sufferings
freely accepted and borne unshrinkingly. It began
by the spectacle of One whose lacerated limbs were

stretched on the Cross for hours in the sight of a gazing multitude : it was accomplished in that passion repeated through centuries on a number which has passed beyond all human enumeration, but is stored up in unsleeping remembrance, to be produced one day in the most awful of assemblies. The suffering of the martyrs, as embraced by them voluntarily, had its only adequate motive in the sufferings of their Master; and by the suffering of the martyrs the heathen world reached at length to know the value of our human life as the seed-plot of eternity, after it had grown worthless in their eyes as an opportunity for sensual or intellectual enjoyment. It is strict truth to say that man learnt not to shed the blood of man, because the blood of the Son of God had been shed. Let us not suppose that regard for human life rests on any other basis than belief in man's future destiny, or would survive the extinction of that belief.

Again, in the age of Augustus Cæsar no virtue had become so rare and so little esteemed as the virtue of moral purity. In that large portion of mankind on which the ban of slavery lay, it was almost impossible to be exercised. That the slave of either sex could have any sense of chastity, was a thought that would seem never to have occurred to a Roman master. The slave's body was as much his master's property as his labour. But slavery was everywhere with all its consequences; and it must never be forgotten in the estimate of these consequences that this was a slavery of races equal to their masters in all physical qualities. The slave was not then first and chiefly a beast of burden, as he is in the production of cotton: Afra and Syra, Lyde and Citheris, were first of all instruments of licentiousness;

and Sporus is there as well. A heathen household is a sink of impurity into which we must not venture to enter. Suffice it to say, that with the dignity of man's soul that of his body was lost, when the Christian faith exalted the body as well as the soul to be the temple of the Spirit of God. But how was such a doctrine to pass into man's flesh and blood? Recur in thought a moment to ancient Rome when she sat a queen, and think how that poison of voluptuousness ran through every vein of her blood. The myriads of statues that crowned her public places, of pictures that coloured her halls and galleries, which of them did not breathe sensuality into the beholder? Her baths, which rose as palaces of the fine arts in every quarter, for what sensual enjoyment did they not offer the readiest means at the cheapest cost? Who could worship the Roman gods and be pure? For her gods in exhibiting consecrated every lust; and Jupiter, Venus, Mars, and Mercury surpassed even Tiberius, Nero, and Domitian in their sins against purity. Who could attempt to purify such a city? Who but one, the Son of the Virgin? Was it not a task worthy of Him who breathed into His Mother such a love of purity that she scrupled to accept the offer of a dignity before which the crowns of earth sink into nothing, until it was revealed to her that her virgin estate was compatible with that dignity? Yet even for the Virgin-born to bring a clean thing out of an unclean is a task of the greatest power. If this new virtue spring from His divine Person, which alone supports it adequately, and gives it a reason for being, yet to human nature, spoiled, impoverished, and degraded, it is an immense step from theory to practice. He is the King of Virgins as well as the King of martyrs; but who were to follow Him, and how? How was this flood of impurity to be rolled back, and the grace of chastity to appear the purest and the most radiant gem in the crown of a restored humanity? He chose the seemingly weakest and frailest to be fellow-workers with Him, by whose aid He would condescend to accomplish this result. I will quote three instances as specimens of a thousand others. In the city of Alexandria there was a female slave of remarkable beauty. As a matter of course the eye of her master fell on her; but she was a Christian, and all solicitations failed with her. Then he accused her to the prefect as a Christian, promising him a large bribe if he could induce her, through dread of punishment for her faith, to yield to his desires. But the threat, and even the application of torture, proved as ineffectual as had been the flattery of her master. At last the judge threatened to have her thrown into a caldron of boiling pitch unless she would obey her master. She replied, "God forbid that a judge should be so unjust as to order me to do what is unlawful!" Then the prefect in a rage bade her be stripped of her clothes and thrown into the pitch. But Potamiæna cried out, "I conjure you by the life of the emperor not to strip me naked; rather have me let down by degrees into the pitch with my dress, and you shall see what patience Jesus Christ, my God, whom you know not, gives me." This was done: she was let down inch by inch into the boiling pitch, and her martyrdom lasted three hours, until it reached her neck. Here, then, was a slave who ventured to be chaste; who sacrificed her life for purity's sake. But if Alexandria had her Potamiæna among slaves, Rome had her Agnes among the daughters of senators. Who does not know the story of the Divine Bridegroom preferred to the human, though he were the son of the prefect of Rome; the rage of the disappointed suitor; and the maiden of thirteen threatened in vain with tortures, and with worse, and the angel standing before her in the place of shame? The glory of Agnes, like that of Potamiæna, was the triumph of spotless virgin innocence; the unclouded preference of a youthful soul for the Divine Lover. But the annals of the Church, in the same persecution as that of Agnes, contain a victory not indeed more glorious, for that is impossible, but perhaps more touching— the victory of a soul once steeped in pollution, yet winning itself a place beside Agnes and Potamiæna. Afra had been devoted by her mother, a native of Cyprus, to the worship of Venus from her youth up, a worship which consisted in the utmost moral degradation. In a time of persecution the Bishop Narcissus with his deacon had entered her house, not knowing what her course of life was. By him she was converted, together with her mother and her three attendants, the partners of her sin. Like Rahab, she concealed her guests from the persecutors who sought them; and some time after, when leading a life of penance, she herself was arrested and brought before the judge. The judge, whose name was Gaius, knew who she was, and said, "Sacrifice to the gods; it is better to live than to die in torments." Afra replied, "I was a great sinner before I knew God, but I will not add new crimes, nor do what you command me." Gaius said, "Go to the temple and sacrifice." Afra answered, "My temple is Jesus Christ, whom I have always before my eyes. Every day I confess my sins; and because I am unworthy to offer Him any sacrifice, I desire to sacrifice myself for His name, that this body in which I have sinned may be purified and sacrificed to Him by torments." "I am informed," said Gaius, "that you are a prostitute. Sacrifice, therefore, as you are a stranger to the God of the Christians, and cannot be accepted by Him." Afra replied, "My Lord Jesus Christ said that He came down from heaven to save sinners. His gospels testify that an abandoned woman washed His feet with her tears and obtained pardon, and that He never rejected such women, nor the publicans, but suffered them to eat with Him." Gaius said, "Sacrifice, that your lovers may follow you still, and enrich you." Afra answered, "I will have no more of that execrable gain. I have thrown away, as so much filth, what I had by me of it. My brethren, the poor, would not have it, until I besought them with tears to take it, that they might pray for my sins." Gaius retorted, "Christ will not have you. It is in vain for you to acknowledge Him for your God. A prostitute can never be called a Christian." Afra replied, "It is true I am unworthy to bear the name of a Christian; but the mercy of God, who judges not after our merit, but His own goodness, has admitted me to be one." "And how know you that?" said Gaius. Afra answered, "I know that God has not rejected me from before His face, because He has permitted me to come to the glorious confession of His holy name, by which I hope to receive the pardon of all my sins." Gaius said, "These are tales; sacrifice to the gods, and they will save you." She replied, "My Saviour is Christ, who, hanging on the Cross, promised paradise to the penitent thief." "Sacrifice," said the judge, "or I will have you stripped and flogged in the presence of your lovers." "I am only ashamed," said Afra, "at the remembrance of my sins." The judge cried, "Sacrifice to the gods! I am ashamed to have disputed with you so long. If you will not you shall die." Afra said, "That is my desire, if only I am not unworthy to find rest by this confession." The judge answered, "Sacrifice, or I will order you to be tormented, and afterwards to be burnt alive." Afra said, "Let the body which hath sinned undergo torments; but I will not taint my soul by sacrificing to demons." Then the judge gave sentence, "We condemn Afra, a prostitute, who declares herself a Christian, to be burnt alive, because she has refused to offer sacrifice to the gods." Upon this the executioners seized her, and carried her into an island on the river Lech, upon which Augsburg stands. There they stripped her, and tied her to a stake. She lifted her eyes to heaven, and prayed with tears, saying, "O Lord Jesus Christ, Almighty God, who camest to call not the just, but sinners to repentance, and hast promised in Thy mercy that at whatsoever hour the sinner is converted, Thou wilt not remember his sins; accept in this hour the penance of my sufferings, and by this temporal fire which consumes my body, deliver me from the eternal fire which torments both soul and body." While the executioners were heaping a pile of vine-branches about her, and setting fire to them, she was heard to say, "I return Thee thanks, O Lord Jesus Christ, for the honour Thou hast done me in receiving me a holocaust for Thy name's sake; Thou who hast vouchsafed to offer Thyself upon the altar of the Cross a sacrifice for the sins of the whole world, the Just for the unjust and for sinners. I offer myself a victim to Thee, O my God, who livest and reignest with the Father and the Holy Ghost, world without end." Having spoken these words she expired, suffocated by the smoke.

And it was in the blood of thousands of virgins and penitents that the heathen world, if it was not baptized and new created unto the virtue of purity, learned at least to recognise what it could not imitate; and if the world has forgotten its benefactors, the Church forgets them not, presenting daily before the Divine remembrance the names of seven, as it were the first-fruits and standard-bearers of that bright band—Felicitas, Perpetua, Agatha, Lucy, Agnes, Cæcilia, and Anastasia, the first-named of whom was a slave.[1]

In what consisted the essence of heathenism? in what the force and hold which it exerted over men and women living in a stage of the most advanced civilisation, such as were the Romans of the first three centuries? At first sight, it would seem that the worship of more gods than one was an absurdity too great for man's reason to accept; and again, that the worship of such gods as those of Rome, Greece, Egypt, Syria, and Western Asia would be shocking to man's natural sense of right. But polytheism, idolatry, and the immoral worship of immoral gods were but symptoms and effects of the disease, manifestations of a universal permanent evil which lay much deeper. If we conceive of man as an animal endued with reason, having a body and no less a mind with certain needs

---

[1] They are named in the Canon of the Mass: "Nobis quoque peccatoribus, famulis tuis, de multitudine miserationum tuarum sperantibus, partem aliquam et societatem donare digneris cum tuis sanctis apostolis et martyribus: cum Joanne, Stephano, Matthia, Barnaba, Ignatio, Alexandro, Marcellino Petro, Felicitate, Perpetua, Agatha, Lucia, Agnete, Cæcilia, Anastasia, et omnibus sanctis tuis."

to be satisfied; a body which asks for perpetual support, replenishment, warmth, and clothing; a mind which has its own needs, affections, and craving for enjoyment; if we add that his time and place of life upon the earth make up the proper sphere in which he is to seek the satisfaction of all these needs, the attainment of all these enjoyments, which are the objects respectively of his bodily and mental desires; if we so conceive, and stop here in our conception of man, the result will be this: Man as an animal will give his body every indulgence in food and other animal pleasures which he can procure; and as an animal endued with mind will seek no less to satisfy the desires of the mind, such as consist in the cultivation of the affections, in acquiring knowledge, distinction among his fellow-men, power over them, whereby he may make them instruments of his pleasures. Perhaps such a state of things is most completely expressed in few words by the worship of wealth, because wealth commands naturally the possession of a large portion of such goods as are here contemplated. Money represents the value put by man upon such goods as are purchasable. Those, therefore, who place their end in the possession of such goods will worship money; and the more refined society has become, the more the bodily and mental needs and pleasures of man are multiplied, the more he is accustomed to satisfy mind and body therein, the more entire will that worship of wealth become. In such a state of things heathenism consists. Pericles and Alcibiades, as well as the Athenian demos; Augustus and Trajan, as well as the Roman plebs; Horace and Virgil, as well as the Mantuan or Calabrian peasant, were heathens in this sense. The worship of such deities as Jupiter, Apollo, Venus, and Cybele, and the deeds attributed to them, were invented in order to support and justify such heathenism. As long as it existed and flourished, so would they. Their worship rested upon it, not it upon them. When the Christians were brought before the Roman tribunals, and commanded to worship "the immortal gods," they replied by saying, that they would worship none but the one God, the Creator and Rewarder of men. "Cease your folly, and sacrifice," was the reply. And the conduct of the Christian *was* folly to the heathen, because he was resigning all the present and visible pleasures and goods of life for the sake of a future unseen good. But his act likewise tended to overthrow the very basis of heathenism; for it was proclaiming, by the sacrifice of all which the heathen held dear, that this heathenism was an utter mistake. His act said that man had not only a body and a mind, with their several needs and pleasures which claimed satisfaction in the earthly and visible life, but that he was the creature of a God who had made him for a higher end, and subordinated to that end both body and mind, with all their needs and all their enjoyments. Thus the true essence of heathenism consisted in cutting off man from his Maker, in prescinding the creature from the Creator; in other words, in giving to man a merely natural end to be worked out and accomplished in this life: and its force consisted in this idea being interlaced with all the habits of man from morning to night, and from the cradle to the grave. Society was formed upon it, and it was the secret thought of that empire into whose shape Julius and Augustus turned the old Roman life, and which by Diocletian's time had run out to its last results.

Now not merely the death of Christians in the last crowning act of martyrdom, but their whole life and worship were a protest against this idea. Their very outward mark was the denial of it in the most formal manner. For the mark of the Christian was the perpetual sign of the Cross upon the forehead and breast —an unceasing reminder to themselves and others of the act which struck at the heart of this heathenism. They thus showed themselves to be the disciples of One who, as far as this life was concerned, had undergone the most extreme humiliation and the most utter defeat. But by and in the act of suffering that humiliation and seeming defeat, He had placed the Creator of man in the new relation of Redeemer, and had become the Head and Father of a new race to be specially propagated from His divine Person. As the Father, such should be the children; as the Head of the race, such His descendants. And so this race of Christians, instead of eagerly desiring honour, pleasure, and wealth, the satisfaction of the mind and body, and the gratification of their several affections, looked with fear and distrust upon these things as dangerous to the higher life of their spiritual propagation. From the beginning the acquisition of any one or all of these things could never be the *end* of a Christian's life. That which expresses the dominion of these things in one word, worldliness, he recognised from the beginning as his greatest enemy. For several generations outward persecution of itself kept him in the continual practice of such principles. For he was liable to be stripped of all these things by the mere profession of Christianity. But even in the times of persecution Christians were seen to choose poverty instead of wealth, the unmarried state instead of the married; and this not for the reason which kept so many heathens in celibacy, that they might have more freely lawless enjoyments, but out of deliberate preference for the virgin state. They were seen to avoid positions of pre-eminence and rule with as much anxiety as others sought them; to live in privacy and great simplicity of food and dwelling; and further, to retire into deserts and lonely places, in order to carry out more uninterruptedly the worship of the unseen God, and their meditations upon an unseen future world. The root of all this was, that having the model of their Master impressed upon their whole character, they subordinated body and mind alike, the whole nature of man, to a superior, supernatural end. This character of theirs, which is ascetism, is contradictory of worldliness, and it made up the Christian character just as worldliness made up the heathen. It made up the Christian character, for it is the simply copying of the life and death of Christ, according to every man's several inward capabilities of spirit, and according to his proper position in the outward world. The copy would be more or less perfect, with almost infinite degrees and shadings; but if the resemblance to the divine Original glowed in apostles, martyrs, confessors, and virgin saints, it was also perceptible in the conflict which the weakest member of the Church underwent in order to maintain his daily life as a Christian. And as this conflict is perpetual, so the quality requisite to maintain it must be perpetual in the Christian; and the circumstances of his life which ensure this conflict vary as little as the divine Model whom in his degree he imitates.

There is another quality which was introduced by Christianity, and though distinct from asceticism or unworldliness, closely connected with it. If the one is the flower, the other may be termed the aroma breathing from it. The ancient Greeks and Romans, living for this world, lived an outward life; their tastes and enjoyments were external; their time spent in public. Their very cities bore witness to this, in that their magnificence in portico, agora, theatre, temple, circus, was external, made for those who lived in the open air and together. Family life was rudimental and scarcely developed; political and social life absorbed almost the whole man. Thus their literature, the reflex of their thought, is external. The soul of man, with all its infinite aspirations, seems not to exist for them. It is an unknown quantity which they do not come across. What interests the citizen or the statesman, what concerns the various arts and employments of life, is there; but little which interest *the man*. They deal with the outside of life, not with its inside. That which they lived for, they felt acutely and expressed vividly; but they lived for the outward relations of the world. On the contrary, the Christian's habitual thought was to consider these outward relations as the veil of the inward, present things as the path to future. "Every strange land," said the author quoted above, "is a country to them, and every country a strange land." "They dwell on the earth, but their citizenship is in heaven." Such a habit of mind drew the Christian from the outward to the inward; from the transitory to the eternal. He had something in him which he knew to be eternal; the whole of his consciousness was coloured by that thought. The perfecting that which in him was eternal was his work, while these outward relations of life were the circumstances in the midst of which this work was to be done. Such a thought dwelling in a man makes him do and say and write everything in a different way from what another who had it not would do, say, or write it. If any one will read a passage of a treatise of Cicero or one of his letters, or a page of Livy or Tacitus, and then read a page of St. Augustine's treatise on the City of God or of his Confessions, he will feel the force of what I say. This inwardness of character, then, if we may so call it, attended upon unworldliness; was its effluence. And so great was its force that it may be said to have thoroughly impregnated the modern mind. It constitutes a generic difference between heathen and Christian literature, taken in the mass; and even writers in no respect Christian in their lives and sentiments are far more inward than the Greek or Roman treating on such subjects would have been.

Cicero, as we have seen, in his treatment of moral virtues, excludes the relation of man to God. The relation of man to his fellow-men, to society, is given instead. But the basis of morals to a Christian was, that he was a creature of God, and further, a redeemed creature; and further yet, a redeemed creature intended to live for ever, his present sphere in time and sense being but the opening of his life. It followed, therefore, that all moral virtue was to him a matter between God and the soul. Two objects were continually before his mental consciousness—God and his own soul. It was in this sense that his Master had said to him, "The kingdom of God is within you." To the four moral virtues which comprehended the whole moral world to the heathen eye, and which have for their sphere of action the relations of men with each other—to prudence, temperance, fortitude, and justice, there had been added the three virtues, faith, hope, and charity, the object of which is God. That was a revolution of the whole man. It reunited the bond of the creature with the Creator, which heathenism had snapped asunder; it wound this bond all about the heart of man by showing him the Creator as at the same time Redeemer, with the cost of unspeakable suffering endured in His own Person. It proposed to him in an infinitely lovely object an infinite reward. The cardinal virtues were the highest reach of the heathen mind. But the fulfilment of them to the heathen was like the labour of the Israelites in Egypt, making bricks without straw, because the thought of God was detached from them. But with the theological virtues this object was restored to them also. The practice of the former became easy and cheerful under the eye, not of a taskmaster, but a loving sovereign; and the Christian building rose like the temple of Jerusalem, whose workmen felt not the toil because it was a labour of love, where every stone had been shaped to its place, and the whole design furnished by God, and the structure raised to His honour. Thus the cardinal virtues were transfigured by the relation towards God which was given them. And no less every part of Christian conduct was interpenetrated with this idea. The soul of the heathen, unconscious of itself, walked under a shadow; the soul of the Christian was warmed and illuminated with this abiding presence. Virtue had been to the heathen an outward thing, because dealing with outward relations, of which human law was the standard. But it became to the Christian the most inward thing, because its basis was laid in the inner realm of his thoughts. He prized himself exactly at what God prized him; and thus the individual man was the domain of which the kingdom of God took first possession.

I have hitherto considered four qualities as exhibited in the life of a multitude of men and women appearing in all parts of the Roman empire: that is, a contempt of death, even when accompanied with torments, in defence of their belief; a great preference for virginal purity; a disregard of worldly honour, wealth, and pleasure; and an inward character of virtue, which led them to place it entirely in the disposition of the heart towards God. In all these things they offered a very striking contrast to the mass of people among whom they lived; and in all of them they were imitators of a certain model which all had equally before their eyes, though the degree of imitation differed in each. Had these doctrines been merely contained in a book, had they been merely discussed in the Porch or Grove, they would probably have excited little more notice in the world than the doctrines of Grecian philosophy. Their force, their attractive and assimilating power, consisted in their being acted out by living examples. He whom they severally imitated had begun "to do and to teach;" and His followers in like manner taught because they first did. The life of their Master, His actions, and above all, His death, formed the great series of facts on which they rested; the cause of their life; and their own lives in like manner became the great instrument of persuasion to others. The propagation of their doctrine proceeded at the beginning from personal influence, and to personal influence its progress was likewise due. For they had always been a society. The revelation itself consisted in a change, a purification, a renovation of the individual man, taking rise altogether in the secret domain of his thoughts, and then exhibited in word and deed; and yet these individual men never acted as disconnected atoms, but as members of a society so close in its cohesion that the like had never been seen before. I will now draw attention to the influence which they exerted as a society on those around them; and to see this we must consider in what consisted their government.

Now this, again, like the virtue of the individual, emanated directly from the Person of their Founder. For the government of the Christian people existed before the people itself. The commission, "Feed My sheep," was given when as yet there were scarcely any sheep to feed. So little did this government proceed from the consent of the governed, or rest upon it, that it anticipated their very existence. The discipline was complete while the disciples were yet to be made. For all was a direct creation of the Founder—the *power* to govern a transmission from His person; the *fashion* of government an imitation of His conduct; the *qualities* of the governors transcripts of His qualities. I am now, then, to consider the one indivisible Sacerdotium of the Church in its action upon the heathen world around.

And first of all, it was one and indivisible, one in its source, indivisible in its exercise, the same in its character everywhere. There were Christians from Britain to Persia, from Morocco to India, in every country; but in every country, much as they might differ in language, social habits, political constitution, the Christian Sacerdotium was one and the same. Whatever forms of false worship it might encounter, and all these countries had diversified forms, whatever mixture of national temperament, and none could be more distinct than the Greek and Latin, the Persian, the Indian, the Semitic and Chamitic character, the Christian Sacerdotium remained, in and through all these, after intimate contact with them through centuries, true to itself, one, unchanged, uniform. No nation had been without a native priesthood of its own in some shape or other, entwined with its first roots of growth as a race; but these priesthoods differed widely according to the rites which they administered, the people which formed their material, the degree in which they had been faithful to the original tradition. On the contrary, the Christian Sacerdotium, springing from one seed, growing on one root, and developing into a tree, the branches of which came to overshadow the whole earth, had the same sap running through all its veins, and producing similar fruits over the whole. It met the Roman statesman in his disguise of Augur or Pontifex, declaring that religion was not a special statecraft intended to preserve and exalt the city of Romulus; it met the Greek hierophant, offering traditional sacrifices, or initiating into mystic rites, and told him that religion was not a worship of the deified powers of nature, nor of human passions endued with immortality, nor a secret discipline offering the few promises made in obscurity never to be realised; it met the Egyptian priest, darkly shrouding the secrets of the future world under fabulous histories of Isis and Osiris, with a full and clear revelation of eternal life and how it was to be obtained; it met the Phrygian victim of the mother of the gods with the teaching that religion is not the violation of nature, nor the revelling in secret lusts, but the subduing of the latter, and the sanctification of the former; it met the Persian worshipper of fire and the elements with the disclosure of a personal Creator; it met the monstrous confusion of the Hindoo Swerga, and the distortion of his imagined and antagonistic Trinity of Creator, Preserver, and Destroyer, with the one undivided Trinity of one power, wisdom, goodness, will, and godhead, the maker of His creatures and their Reward. But these are only specimens of an infinitely varied disease; the misgrowth of evil had the luxuriance of a tropical vegetation; the abortions of false religion were endlessly divergent, shapeless, monstrous, and contradictory. They everywhere found the same antagonist. The Christian Sacerdotium came forth among them stamped with the unity of God, whom it represented. I am considering it now as a whole. For the moment, and in order to obtain a clear and succinct view of a wonderful and unique creation, I consider it not in its degrees and distributions, but in its mass; I ascend to the fountain-head, and I take the stream as it came forth full and undivided from the Person of the Godman, as it passed from Him to St. Peter and the Apostolic College, and as it was communicated from them to unnumbered successors, that it may last to the end of the world. For this purpose I will view it under seven attributes, in which I think that its unity, its uniformity, and its universality will be found to consist. They rest upon seven divine aphorisms, dicta of sovereign power and wisdom, which are like nothing else in human language, identical with those elder ones, "Let there be light," "Let Us make man after Our own image and likeness," which ministered to the creation as these latter to the re-creation of man. They are such as these: the first, "Go and make disciples all nations;" the second, "Teach them to

observe whatsoever I have commanded you;" the
third, "Feed My sheep;" the fourth, "The Son of
man came not to be ministered unto, but to minister;"
the fifth, "I send you as lambs among wolves; if they
persecuted Me, they will also persecute you;" the
sixth, "Do this in remembrance of Me;" the seventh,
"It is enough for the disciple to be as his Master,
and the servant as his Lord."

1. First of all, it did not present itself as a work
of human reason, but as the message of a superior.
In this it was essentially distinguished from all the
systems of Grecian philosophy. These were, one and
all, reasonings upon the phenomena of nature, society,
the human mind, the beginning and end of man.
Infinitely varying in their development, they had one
source, one instrument, one standard, to the possession
of which all men might lay the same claim, the intellectual faculty in man. The Porch and the Grove
indicated what man could do of himself to unravel the
great problems of his own nature, of the world in
which he lived, of the issue to which he and it were
tending. Not so the Christian Sacerdotium. It spoke
in the name of another; it held out a commission; it
promulgated a law; it acted as a herald, an ambassador
as one sent. So far from professing to be an emanation of human reason, it pointedly abjured any such
title. It spoke of facts not contrary to reason, but
beyond and above its range. According to the word
of its Founder, it went forth and made disciples; and
the bond of their initiation was belief in a triune God,
that is, they received upon testimony an incomprehensible mystery. The testimony was the word of those
who heard it from their Founder. Thus the first root
of this Sacerdotium lay in an authority derived from

without. It ran up into the Person of Him from whom it came forth. And in accordance with this origin, from the beginning it was a society of living men, not an abstract doctrine. It came into the world to speak, to bear witness, to proclaim, to announce, to declare as a representative the terms of a prince to his subjects. All these are the actions of persons on persons, and therefore it was not contained in a book; it did not form a codex, nor lie upon a shelf, but lived, acted, persuaded, enrolled adherents, formed a body. A book is composed of disembodied thoughts, but this was thought embodied, incarnate. Human nature was its field. It laid hold on man in all countries and races, under all conditions of society, as its proper subject. Its Founder had written nothing; but He, the Eternal Word, had spoken, had used the word of man as His instrument; and His disciples had received that word committed to them to be spoken. Again, He had acted, and His acts contained the guarantee of His words, and their significance. So in like manner His disciples were to speak and to act. He founded a living society, resting upon His authority, derived from it in the beginning, but no less holding together in virtue of it throughout. His words and His acts were transfused into this society to be its life; and thus it was an extension and continuance of His own work on the earth. Thus from the beginning Christianity consisted in a Christian people. A certain number of men, believing and acting in a certain manner, made the religion. A mere doctrine is received by the individual reason and will, appropriated by them, and the man by his own act becomes possessed of it. But Christianity was never merely such a doctrine. Entrance into it was more than an act of a man's own will. It took place by a solemn initiation. Continuance in it was maintained by solemn rites, whose virtue came from without to the recipient. As men were admitted into it, so they might be excluded from it by acts and by actors independent of their own will. Those who followed a Grecian sect were masters of its doctrine, which they took, whole or in part, at their pleasure; took it when they pleased, left it when they pleased, mixed it with other doctrines as they pleased. The power of acceptance and rejection lay in the individual; but not so with that religion part of whose charter was, "Go and make disciples all nations." It was not only a law, but a kingdom.

2. Again, its office was to teach; but the volume, matter, compass of its teaching, were laid up within itself. Not, indeed, that these were arbitrary, but that the teaching was deposited in the breasts of living men, to be by them applied, unfolded, and set forth in action. The charter ran, "Make disciples all nations, teaching them to observe all things whatsoever I have commanded you." As the Founder's own ministry had been "to do and to teach," so He willed the ministry of those to be who were to carry on His work. It was a perpetual living chair of doctrine which He set up, and no mightier proof of His power did He leave. It was that in which the philosophers of Greece had utterly failed. The deepest thinkers had deplored the necessity of committing their thoughts to paper, when the living word could no more interpret them, no more answer the question, supply deficiencies, harmonise seeming contrarieties, bind the whole together. As soon as death had silenced the voice of their oral teaching, their disciples, following

the natural divergence of human thought, left their masters' traces, and struck out for themselves in various directions. Thus, in the region of thought, the four hundred years which followed after the teaching of Socrates were nothing but a conflict of the most contradictory systems of morality and religion. To set up, therefore, in the great Christian Sacerdotium one Cathedra of doctrine, which should be for ever the same, never contradict itself, but out of the sacred deposit committed to its charge bring forth for every occasion things old and new; which was to last not for a few years or a few generations, but for that undefined period in which the human race was to run its whole career in this stage of its being; this truly was a thing not only utterly unheard of in the heathen world, but so astonishing, that of and by itself it is a sufficient proof of divine power. A man had died by the most ignominious death reserved by the Roman law for the slave alone. At his death he had left not a single written word. Four hundred years after his death the Roman world beheld its whole surface covered with a network of churches in which the same solemn rite, exhibiting his death, was set forth by a body of ministers everywhere the same, preaching a vast system of doctrine which embraced within its range the highest mysteries of the unseen world, and the most trivial details concerning the duties of daily life; a doctrine one, accordant with itself in all parts of the world, and appealing for its authority back to the words uttered by this crucified slave. If this phenomenon was not worthy to arrest the attention of every thoughtful man, what does human life and history present which is like it? But how small a part of the truth is this! In those four hundred years the utmost power of the Roman emperors had been exerted to root out this doctrine; more than once they thought they had done it, and lying marbles survive which record their imagined triumphs, "*deleto nomine Christiano.*" What force, what fraud, what calumny, what outrage, what rending asunder of the ties of blood, friendship, and affection had been spared in order to overthrow this Cathedra of doctrine, to sweep away the spiritual building raised by the despised Jewish malefactor? Who can count the army of martyrs who in those four hundred years had died to defend it? Who can sum up their acts of heroism? What age was wanting, from that child of three years old who refused the caresses of the heathen judge, and crying out that he was a Christian, had his brains dashed out on the steps of the tribunal before his mother, St. Julitta, as she lay on the rack, to St. Simeon, who renewed the passion of his Lord at a hundred and twenty years of age; or St. Polycarp, crowning an episcopate of eighty years in the amphitheatre of Smyrna? Within that time miles upon miles beneath the soil of the imperial city had been hollowed out to witness and to protect the worship which that doctrine had established, and then to receive the bodies of those who had died to maintain it. This is in one city alone, the head and crown of heathenism, and therefore the chief seat and centre of the opposing doctrine. But every country, every city had its own witnesses; first its teachers, then its victims, and last its patrons. If the founder of Rome, who bathed its foundations in a brother's blood, yielded to those other brothers who shed their blood together for the maintenance of this doctrine, this example was repeated all over the earth. The cities forgot their heathen founders to put themselves under the patronage of those whose martyrdom they had witnessed. Augsburg did so with St. Afra, a foreign sojourner within her walls, once degraded by grossest sin, then converted and penitent, by-and-by sacrificed for her faith. Thus the proto-martyr of England, once an unknown heathen, taking at a single step the palm of a Christian witness, gave his name to the spot which had been consecrated by his blood. Thus in the valleys of Switzerland the city of Agaunum became St. Maurice, to recall that heroic legion and its commander who with arms in their hands suffered themselves to be mown down rather than offer sacrifice to the heathen gods, while the whole country passed under his patronage. Thus Cologne, mindless of its imperial foundation, throned in its shrine as heavenly defenders the three Kings of the East, once pilgrims to the royal Child, then preachers of His name. Thus at Alexandria the tomb of St. Mark, whose mangled body had been dragged through its streets, outshone the lustre of that which its founder, the world's conqueror, occupied, whence the sacred relic was only taken to become the guardian of Venice, as his name was the watchword of her armies. And to make the marvel greater, this one Cathedra of doctrine was assailed from within as well as from without. It first made itself a place and a name among the Greeks, to whom it was a folly, and the Jews, to whom it was an offence; it created its own atmosphere, in which to breathe, and move, and grow. It sprung up, no man could tell how, like seed planted by invisible hands beside rivers and watercourses; but forthwith, as it emerged and raised its head, a portion of those who had embraced began to alter and deface it. Some had a host of preconceived notions derived from the eastern or the Grecian philosophy or false worship, and these they would blend with the new doctrine. Some were aspiring speculative spirits impatient of check, and refusing obedience, and these would substitute their own reasonings for what it taught with authority. Some were imperfectly instructed, and their ignorance became to them and others a cause of error. It short, no sooner had the true doctrine appeared in life than heresies formed themselves around it, springing out with great force and vigour in opposite directions. Among all these it continued unchanged, or rather forming and defining itself more accurately as it was attacked, suffering perpetual loss among its adherents, but replacing them with others, and never deadened in its energy. Of these thirteen generations which had elapsed up to St. Augustine's time, every one had been fruitful in heresies. Some of these had dropped away and were extinct; others lingered on; others were in the first heat of their projection; but the doctrine they attacked held its course onward through them all. It was never merged in them, never obscured by them, never mixed with them; they were fluctuating, it was permanent; they contradictory, it consistent; they flattered a national peculiarity, a race's pride, or an imperial longing; but for it nations were provinces, races raw material, while emperors finished by espousing what they had sought in vain to corrupt. Fix the mind well upon this one object, for it is entirely unique in the history of man. The heresies gathering round the one Christian doctrine reproduce the course of the Grecian sects; they are human as these were; change, opposition, action, and reaction, incessant modification, the workings of vanity, self-love, pride, and curiosity, these are their marks. A man of great ability and powerful character arises; he forms a school; he dies, and his school breaks up; they call themselves still by his name, but his spirit is extinct, or it is passed through spiritual chemistry into new combinations. But this doctrine; friend and enemy know it well; the one calls it unchangeable in good, the other in evil. It has no counterpart; it stands alone. But consider its unity, its harmony, its completeness, its homogeneity. How it lays hold of human life, from the cradle to old age. How it has its own distinct principles in every possible question of morals or of politics that can arise. How it is bound by its own acts from generation to generation, so that once in the course of centuries to contradict itself would be fatal. When it appeared thus at the distance of four hundred years from its Founder to a mind of unsurpassed strength and breadth, St. Augustine exclaimed, "Securus judicat orbis terrarum." What all parts of the world bear witness to must be true. But we can now add fourteen hundred years of the most complex experience to the four hundred years whose witness he found so convincing, a world in comparison of which his world was a narrow space, a variety of circumstances to which those presented by history in his time were simple and uniform. If this power of teaching lodged in the Christian Sacerdotium, and exhibited in one consistent body of doctrine, was a sign of surpassing significance to him, if it converted the best of the heathen up to his time, what is it now to us? Men are carried away in these days by passionate love for the natural sciences. They are never wearied with examining the strata of the earth, the forms of animals, the derivation of their species; and since God is incomparably beautiful and unsearchably wise, even in His material works, I do not wonder that these things create a passion in the mind. But what is all this to the fabric of Christian doctrine, of which the Divine Word uttered the germ in oracular sentences, pregnant with inexhaustible meaning, and which He has built up in the hearts and lives of His disciples through so many centuries? Here is order, and classification, and fruitfulness, richness, beauty, variety, every delicacy of colour, every form of grandeur, not in the kneading out and parcelling of matter, but in a great spiritual creation, the object of which is to exalt man to a supernatural height of goodness and happiness. And they who have all eyes for matter and its forms have no eyes for this wonder-work of the Lord of Spirits. They who would pore over an unknown sea-weed, or worship a new shell-fish, are blind to the Word of God made Man, and to His operations in human nature, and to the truth to which He has given form and embodiment, through the operations of the human mind, using its own free will, but prompted, guided, strengthened, and supported throughout by the secret gift of His Spirit.

3. No less new to the world was the third attribute of this power, contained in the words, "Feed My sheep." Government of the body and oppression of the mind were indeed rife enough in the world; there was no liberty of the body or of the mind over which the Roman imperium did not exert control, or of which at times it did not claim the surrender. But it was reserved for the power which had given back to man the knowledge of his soul, which at the same

time had provided it with a doctrine worthy of its aspirations, to bestow likewise the culture, the guidance, the government fitting for it. Government of souls! We are familiar now with the word and with the idea. It conveys to us no doubtful image. But what meaning would it have conveyed to Plato or to Cicero, the masters of human thought, to Alexander or to Julius, the lords of human action, in those days? They would no more have understood the word "government of souls" than the word steam-engine or railway. For the priesthoods of the various heathen nations, as they were in possession of no moral doctrine giving life and human interest to their religion, were not moral teachers at all. The worship indeed whose rites they administered was often, if not always, immoral, and therefore, by the acts which they authorised and the example which they gave, they were instruments of demoralising those who regarded them as servants of a superior power. But properly they taught nothing, and as the government of souls deals with teaching, of course they could not govern that part of man which looks for moral guidance. But feeding and ruling are more than teaching, as secular government is more than legislation. This was a new charge enjoined by a Sovereign, and extending over that which was most precious to Him: "Feed My sheep." It was a character of which the conception itself was due to Him, for He said that nothing short of a triple gift of love would enable men to fulfil it. Or rather it never could have been conceived until He Himself had shown its reality, and given its perfect type. It was when He stood upon the sea-shore after His resurrection, with the marks of suffering on His hands and feet, that He gave this charge and invented this office, the reflex of His own. It was not only unexampled but unintelligible before the crucifixion. And now as we look back over the centuries of Christian history, the copies of that wonderful original rise before us. That of which there was no extant specimen is become a race moving through the world with a Christ-like character upon them; rulers of justice, rulers of peace, without father, without mother, without descent, having neither beginning of days nor end of life as to their civil condition; but whose flock are the tribes of all the earth, whose spiritual progeny the nations of Christendom. They have one law, the doctrine of their Founder; one charge, their share of the commission given by Him; but there is no part of the world which has not witnessed their labours, and seen its fruits; no class of society which they have not reached. From the first the poor—those who were forgotten of all men —found in them their comforters and defenders; but they have ruled the rich likewise, and their passport to them has been despising riches.

4. For another mark set on them by their Founder was that their rule should be a ministration, should consist not so much in commanding as in serving others. This was exactly what the world had never seen. Rulers had ruled for themselves; all men had laboured for themselves, and to enjoy the fruit of their own labours. Nay, success in life had been considered to be the appropriation of other men's labours and their fruits to oneself. And upon labour, as such, a mark of disgrace had been set. Among the castes of human society the least honourable was that of the tillers of the earth, whose work had this special honour given to it by Providence, that on it depends that

multiplication of human food upon which the race subsists and grows, while the labour employed in human art only shapes a pre-existing material. And in the institution of slavery, by which the whole of the slave's labour is reckoned the property of another, this scorn of work as the portion of man was summed up and intensified. Now all this the Founder of the Christian priesthood came to reverse. He did so by word, saying, "The Son of man came not to be ministered unto, but to minister." He did so by deed, making all His life a ministration to others, and carrying on this character upon those who should inherit His work. Thus the chief Apostle took as a title of honour the name "Slave of Christ;" and when the bishop of a great see assumed wrongfully the style of ecumenical patriarch, he was rebuked by the one who alone possessed that dignity, but who, standing in the chief Apostle's place, followed his guidance, and called himself in preference "Servant of the servants of God." But He who first gave this example made labour for ever honourable; His children carried out His example into all their life, the rulers the first and most eminently, until even the world has learnt to regard as its greatest men not those who command others, but those who labour for them.

5. Here, however, we are brought to the fifth attribute which attached to this Sacerdotium. Ruling carries with it the notion of power, greatness, eminence. As such it makes one of the master-passions of man. And if the soul be more precious than the body, the rule of it would seem to offer the subject of a higher and deeper ambition than that common rule of external things. No doubt it is so; and the Founder had already met this weakness of our nature by making

the rule which he established a ministration and service of others. But this likewise brings honour with it. He went further still: He attached to this rule a very peculiar condition indeed, and one which would effectually throw back human ambition from the desire of it. It was no imperfect or one-sided image of Himself, the chief Shepherd, which He was sending forth into the world. And therefore to this new rule, the persuading, teaching, gaining, and guiding of souls to their highest end, He attached the new condition of suffering. It did not carry wealth with it, but poverty; not the enjoyment of family affections, but the renunciation of them; not learned ease, but laborious self-denial; not the respect of the world, but its peculiar contempt. Its very essence consisted in unwearied patience, a great suffering in itself, since it is the sacrifice of the ruler's own time, tastes, faculties, his speech and his thought, all the wear and tear of mind and body, for the good of others. This when it was exercised in peace; but in persecution the first blows and the heaviest fell on the rulers, and the mark of the tenth, the last and fiercest persecution, was that it sought above all things to destroy the ruling order itself. Looking from St. Augustine's point of view over those four centuries, the distinguishing mark of Christian rulers had been suffering of every kind. The first sent to a country, as a rule, after a course of labours long or short, gave his life for it. Generally the new doctrine would not take root anywhere without being watered by blood, and those who carried it were the chief to shed theirs for it.

6. But all this was expressed and continually exhibited by the great central act which constituted the exercise of this Sacerdotium. All its title to speak

and to act, its very existence was derived direct from the person of Him who had fulfilled all typical sacrifices by that of Himself. Its work was to represent Him unceasingly, to prolong the three years of His public life through all time. But the culminating point of that teaching was in its final act, the giving up of His life. This act therefore was to be exhibited for ever in the public worship of the body which He founded. The heathen sacrifices had become mere external ceremonies, which had lost their meaning. No one saw what connection lay between shedding the blood of animals and appeasing the wrath of the gods. But here the meaning of sacrifice was disclosed. The highest worship, the deepest teaching, the sublimest love, the most perfect self-devotion, suffering, authority, and example, were joined together in that daily offering which made the Christian priesthood.

7. Thus in those four hundred years which followed our Lord's advent, and preceded the fall of the Roman empire, there was set before all the nations within its vast circuit an order of men scattered over its whole surface, but identical in their mode of life. They proclaimed with authority a new religion; they taught in what it consisted; they governed spiritually those who had voluntarily accepted it at their hands; yet their government was a perpetual service of body and of mind alike; and to it was attached the unceasing accompaniment of suffering; and finally, the central act of their priesthood set forth these things in a visible manner: it was an act of proclaiming, teaching, feeding, ministering, suffering, performed by their hands indeed, but in which the perpetual presence of their Founder made it His own, spoke and acted in them. But yet the doctrine of a religion would have done

little without the lives of those professing it. Had this order of men extolled obedience, and sought for command; had they praised poverty, and pursued riches; had they counselled the resistance to pleasure, and practised all the conveniences and enjoyments of life, we may be sure they would not have overthrown the dominion of idolatry, nor raised the Cross to adorn the diadem of kings. What we do find is, that while their religion honoured and sanctified marriage, they practised continence; while it allowed riches, they chose to be poor; while it sanctioned authority and rule in those to whom these belonged, they submitted themselves to a voluntarily chosen obedience. And for all this they alleged the Founder's example and His counsel. The society in the midst of which they lived and acted was desperately sick with the passion for enjoyment, the love of rule, and the worship of wealth. It was not to be cured by those who moderately indulged in these things, but by those who rose above them. The prefect of Rome demanded of St. Laurence the riches of the Church for the need of the emperor. He asked a delay of three days to collect them. On the third day he showed the prefect a crowd of poor, lame, halt, and blind. These, said he, are the riches of the Church. We know what was the barbarous vengeance of the prefect, and what the stronger endurance of the saint. But that day heathenism in Rome received a lesson which it never forgot; and from that day to this the very name of St. Laurence has been a power in the earth. And everywhere over the world the Christian Sacerdotium gave this lesson. It is the solid framework of the Church upon which the whole structure rises from the Rock which is its base. And being this in every age, it exhibited myriads of lives which rose far above the level of the world's practice, and so became types of a new virtue, and formed man after a new model.

I think that I have now shown that I was justified in taking Cicero as a type of heathen man under the civilisation which preceded Christianity, and Augustine as a type of man such as the Christian faith had made him. If we sum up what has been said above, we may thus state the moral progress made in the four centuries following the advent of Christ. The Christian faith had laid its hand upon the individual man, disclosing to him that he was a creature, whose end lay beyond the realm of the senses and the confines of the visible world in union with the invisible Creator. It thus recast his life, placing all virtue in the heart and inward affections, and setting before him a supreme model which had appeared in his own nature, as the Head of a new race, by virtue from whom it encompassed him with continual help, by means of sacraments supporting him from the cradle to the grave. Thus it bestowed a new, unheard-of value on man's transitory life, as the passage to an infinite good. And this faith found entrance into the heathen mind by the very prodigality with which this life and all its goods were sacrificed by unnumbered martyrs of both sexes and every condition of society, for the sake of a future unseen good. And further, such a faith produced types of the highest excellence, after this new pattern, throughout every land. And the intellectual basis for this excellence was found in its doctrine uniform and universal, which gave life and interest to its worship, and was embodied therein, and by its solid force gradually displaced the corrupt rites of heathenism, disjointed from moral teaching, and the contradictory opinions of philosophy in perpetual fluctuation. While in inseparable connection with its doctrine and its worship there rose before the eyes of men a new thing upon the earth, a perfect rule of spiritual government, which disarmed opposition, because it was rather the exercise of a perpetual ministration, and an exquisite charity spending itself for the needs of others, than a dominion after the fashion of Babylon, wherein the kings of the nations lorded it over them.

Thus then we find the unity of man's nature established, and with it a common morality for the whole race, which overrode the distinctions of conquering or subject nations, of freeman or slave. It was the first-fruit of the great Restorer's labour to make true the noblest words ever uttered by a heathen, in a sense far beyond what he imagined. What Cicero in some happy vision had sketched, men saw before their eyes. "The true law is indeed right reason, in harmony with nature, diffused over all, constant, everlasting; which by its commands invites to duty, by its prohibitions deters from wrong; whose commands and prohibitions, while they are not in vain to the upright, are without effect on the perverse. No right can amend this law; no privilege exempt from it; no force abrogate it as a whole. Neither by Senate nor by people can we be delivered from its obligation; nor anywhere else may we seek its explainer or interpreter. Nor will this law be one at Rome, another at Athens; one now, another hereafter; but being one, everlasting and unchangeable, it will enfold all nations for all time, and there will be one common teacher and absolute sovereign of all, God, by whom this law was invented, promulgated, and passed. And whoever will not obey Him shall fly from himself and, abhorring the nature of man, shall meet therein extremest punishment, though he were to escape all other imaginable penalties." [1]

So much for the first step, the restoration of man in himself. We have next to consider his restoration in his external relations; first of the family, and then of civil society.

[1] Cic. *de Rep.* 3, quoted by Lactantius, *Div. Ins.* vi. 8.

LECTURE V

NEW CREATION OF THE PRIMARY RELATION BETWEEN MAN AND WOMAN

THAT which in man is most divine, that wherein is placed his likeness to God, that which every man possesses, the least no less than the greatest, that, finally, which accompanies him through time into eternity, is his personality. It was the great revelation of the Christian Faith that this should be rewarded or punished everlastingly. Therefore it was that this faith laid its hold on the individual heart of man: of this it made its first conquest; from this it proceeded as its inmost fortress. It counted nothing worth but the possession of man's heart. In its eyes the outward work was mere hypocrisy without the inward intention. Such only could be a religion worthy of Him who made the heart. But the Christian Faith was intended to form a society; and it must therefore deal with man as a society. That it begins with the individual and makes him its unit of construction is quite compatible with its work being intended to create an organised whole. And much more than this. In the divine Idea, man—Adam—is a race, not merely an individual, nor a collection of individuals. In the first man the whole race was summed up; in him supernaturally endowed; in him as a race fell; and in one Man again, of whom he was the first copy, was as a race restored. The divine government, therefore, as being one of infinite perfection, deals with man at once as an individual and as a race. It is part of its perfection to bestow on him an exquisitely just and merciful retribution as an individual, and yet at the same time to deal with him as a society. In the divine plan the one does not contradict or exclude the other.

Nor, again, can we, in fact, detach man from his fellows. As he comes into the world he cannot stand a moment by himself. He is touched on all sides by his brethren. Of all animals the infant man is the most helpless and dependent on others, and of all he remains so the longest in proportion to his life. Dependent at his birth, in his nursing, in his education, in his marriage, and then again in his children, in his social, civil, and political life, this highest as a compound of matter and spirit among creatures in this visible world is the least able to stand alone. His very eminence surrounds him with relations, supports him with them, but fetters him too.

I. The first of all these relations is that between man and woman. It may be said to be the root of all the rest. It makes the family and all its affections. It is the fruitful germ of the larger society. Therefore, to estimate the condition of man at any given time it is of sovereign importance to examine the state of the relation between man and woman. On this the whole development of man in society depends.

But of what that relation was intended to be we possess an immutable record. As we have man portrayed for us as he came forth in perfect beauty, with the gifts of grace superadded to those of nature, from the divine hand, so we have the relation of woman to man at the same moment and under the same state set forth. The divine prophet, to intimate the fulness of knowledge concerning natural things which had been given by infusion to the first man, says that all the living creatures were brought before him, and that to each he gave the name proper to its habits, instincts, and purpose intended for it.[1] Here, then, was a wisdom and knowledge to which those of Solomon were as a drop to a fountain. But neither in these creatures made to be ruled by him, nor in the magnificent science which understood their several natures and relations, was there what would satisfy the natural needs and desires of the being so endowed. He was created for society, and it was not good for him to be alone. And, as it were, a second time a divine council was held.[2] The first had been concerning his nature, and ran, Let Us make man after Our image and likeness; and as if the second occasion was equal in importance and dignity to the first, since it was to give him society and help, it also ran similarly, Let Us make him a help like unto himself. Here, then, are two points in the original relation of woman to man: she was given that by means of her society might be formed, and she was given as a help to man, and that specially in the procreation of the race and all that is involved therein, companionship, sympathy, education of children. A third is, her subordination to man; for a state of innocence does not exclude inequality.[3] There is a

---

[1] Gen. ii. 19, 20.   [2] St. Chrys. *in Gen. Hom.* xiv. p. 112.
[3] St. Thomas, *Summa*, 1, q. 92, a. 1. "Duplex est subjectio, una servilis, secundum quam præsidens utitur subjecto ad sui ipsius utilitatem, et talis subjectio introducta est post peccatum. Est autem alia subjectio œconomica vel civilis, secundum quam præsidens utitur subjectis ad eorum utilitatem et bonum, et ista subjectio fuisset etiam ante peccatum. Defuisset enim bonum ordinis in humana multitudine si quidam per alios sapientiores gubernati non fuissent. Et sic ex tali

subjection of the house or state according to which the superior uses those subject to him for their own advantage and good, and this was the subjection according to which man was " the head of the woman " at the first; otherwise the good of order would have been wanting in human society if the wiser did not govern. But to show the nature of this subordination yet more, the order which had been followed in the creation of the other animals was not followed here. The sexes in them had been created simultaneously; but it was not so in man. As the head of the race, he was made alone, and from him so made his help was taken. This is the first reason given by St. Thomas in order that man after the likeness of God might be the beginning of all his species, as God is the beginning of the whole universe. A second reason was that his affection might be more perfect, and the union inseparable, when he saw that woman was formed from himself. A third, because beyond the ordinary tie which draws the sexes together, there is in man the society of the domestic life, wherein each has distinct works, but in which the headship belongs to the man. And fourthly, there was the reason of the great sacrament hidden under this formation.[1] But further than this, she was formed neither from the head of man, for in the social union between them her part is not rule; nor yet from his feet, because neither is her part servile subjection; but from his side nearest his heart.[2] "He built up," says the golden-tongued saint;[3] "it is no longer

---

subjectione naturaliter femina subjecta est viro, quia naturaliter in homine magis abundat discretio rationis. Nec inæqualitas hominum excluditur per innocentiæ statum."

[1] St. Thomas, *Summa*, 1, q. 92, a. 2. [2] Id. 1, q. 92, a. 3.
[3] St. Chrys. *Hom.* xv. *in Genes.* p. 118.

said, He moulded, but He took a portion of that already moulded, and built up a perfect creature, able by community of nature and of reason to support him for whose comfort she was made." In the richness of His wisdom the perfect Artist formed from the region of the heart this perfect creature in all things like to man, able to give him help at the points of crisis and trial in the events which hold his life together. Nor must we forget that in the special part from which she was formed lay deeper yet, closely veiled indeed, but fully intended, the great sacrament which was to be unfolded only when the most astonishing and affecting of all events had taken place. And when the divine Artist brought the last and best of His gifts to the man whom He had formed, that man spoke words which, as the greatest Authority tells us,[1] were the words of God Himself. They completed the union between man and woman by bestowing on it three qualities, indissolubility, unity, and inviolable sacredness. The union thus made could only be severed by death; it was between one and one; and it was to be held sacred and inviolate by both.

The original relation of woman to man consisted in these seven points. It was the source of the race's propagation, and so the starting-point of human society; it was made for man's help and support therein; it consisted in subordination to him, but a subordination tempered and exalted by perfect affection; it was a union indissoluble; a union between two only; a union to be respected and maintained by both alike, because it was not founded in mutual compact, but originated and consecrated by the act of God Himself.

[1] Matt. xix. 4-6.

It is in the most ancient of all existing books that we find this admirable and perfect picture of the primary human relation. Search through all which the wisest men of Greece and Rome, of Persia, India, Egypt, China, and if there be any other nations of the world which could compete with these, have said concerning the relation between man and woman, and you will find nothing worthy to be compared with the teaching which the great Hebrew prophet has here summed up in a dozen lines. And yet, which is much more, you will find in these very nations, and the more distinctly the farther you can trace them back, institutions maintained with more or less purity, but bearing witness, even in their debased and fragmentary state, that the nations to which they belonged possessed once the doctrine here set forth, inasmuch as their civil life in its very first origin was based upon it. It was not the elucubration of some greater wisdom, the reasoning of a Plato or an Aristotle, of a Zoroaster or a Confucius, but the original θεσμὸς of the tribe, created with it, and stamped upon it. I may cite as an instance the sacred marriage of the Romans *per confarreationem*, coming down from the cradle of the race as a patrician inheritance and a qualification for the higher priesthoods.

Thus God Himself is the author of human society, and establishes it upon a perfect law of marriage. As the first Man is the Father and Head of the race, so the first Woman is its Mother and Nurse. This will be the key to her position among all the nations, their descendants. Therein lay a rich gift indeed for the present, but a still richer prophecy of the future; for the relation so established is not merely an institution founding society, but a secret picture and pledge of the dealing of the Creator with the race created. From the beginning the natural covers and includes the supernatural, and what is last executed is first intended.

II. Let us now pass over an interval of several thousand years from the first foundation of human society, and having seen what it was in its origin, how it was constructed, and by whom, take a short review of the actual state of woman in the various countries of the western world during the last years of Augustus.

In Greek life the original position of woman was honourable.[1] The wife was man's companion, not, as in eastern countries of Asia, his slave. It was only because the Greeks had a true family life grounded upon monogamy that they possessed a sound and well-ordered political life. Polygamy was foreign to them; bigamy extremely rare. Polygamy only presents itself in the monarchs of the Macedonian kingdoms, who had been infected by eastern customs. In Greece woman was not kept under lock and key in harems; still less was she guarded by eunuchs. Her position was in many respects secured by law and custom, and provided with defined rights. Within her home she ruled as a mistress over slaves and children.

This was the fair side of the picture; but, on the other hand, the wife was looked upon not as the human creature, man's like and companion, but as means to an end, as an evil which could not be escaped, in order that there might be house and children. Her intellectual education was disregarded,

---

[1] Döllinger, *Heidenthum und Judenthum*, p. 679.

and so her influence over husband and children was slight; even the rich and noble were not brought up in accomplishments which might form the charm of a home. Thus we find Socrates admitting that the society of the wife was the last thing sought after by the husband. If he invited a guest, the wife did not dine with him. She was left to the solitude of her own apartments, never entered by a stranger. But with all this, there were accomplished women at Athens, whose society was sought after even by statesmen; remember only that these had lost the first ornament of their sex. Aspasia and Phryne represent a class which play a great part in Greek history, and lower prodigiously the standard of their domestic life. While with these the relation was free and intermittent, marriage, on the contrary, in Athens had to be made compulsory, as a duty to the State for the propagation of its citizens, a duty which, as Plato admits, was most unwillingly performed. This on the man's side; while on the woman's the condition of voluntary virginity was utterly without religious motive and competent position, and therefore unknown; but if involuntary, it was considered a great calamity. As for Sparta, marriage was there accounted a mere institution for producing healthy and vigorous citizens. Its moral sacredness was unknown; or the state of things which everywhere else was considered to be adultery was not there so considered. Wives were lent. The whole State was a breeding-place for human cattle.

But besides these defects in the relation of the sexes, the whole domestic life of the Greeks was eaten out by that fearful miasma of unnatural immorality which seemed like the curse of the race. The extent of this evil it is scarcely possible to exaggerate; on its details it is impossible to dwell.[1]

We have further the remarkable fact, that from the time of the Peloponnesian war a great moral deterioration sets in, which continues without a break down to the time of Plutarch. Families became extinct, through the desire to have few children. This was a result seen and deplored by Polybius a hundred and fifty years earlier. Speaking of the beginning of the Roman dominion over them, he says: "It is the accordant opinion of all that Greece now enjoys the greatest comfort of life, and yet there is want of men, desolation of cities, so that the land begins to lose its fruitfulness through want of cultivation. The reason is, out of softness, love of comfort and of ease, men, even if they live in the state of marriage, will bring up no children, or only one or two, in order to have a good inheritance. Thus the evil becomes ever greater, as if war or sickness takes away the one child, the family dies out."[2]

---

[1] For both of these, for the incredible state of public opinion and manners on the subject, for the conduct and judgment of the highest names in Grecian literature—Plato, Socrates, Aristotle, &c.—see Döllinger, *Heid. und Jud.*, pp. 684–691, sect. 32–40, especially sect. 33. "Bei den Griechen tritt das Phänomen mit allen Symptomen einer nationalen Krankheit, gleichsam eines ethischen Miasma auf; es zeigt sich als ein Gefühl, das stärker und heftiger wirkte, als die Weiberliebe bei andern Völkern, massloser, leidenschaftlicher in seinen Ausbrüchen war, &c.—In der ganzen Literatur der vorchristlichen Periode ist kaum ein Schriftsteller zu finden, der sich entschieden dagegen erklärt hätte.—So geschah es dass in zahlosen Stellen der Griechischen Dichter, Redner, Philosophen, wo von Liebe die Rede ist, an ein Weib nicht einmal gedacht wird, dass vor einem Gerichtshofe ein Liebeshandel mit einem Junglinge mit der selben Offenheit oder Schamlosigkeit verhandelt wurde, als ob von einer Hetäre die Rede wäre.—S. 34. Platon hatte unter dem Einflusse der Epidemie so sehr den Sinn für Frauenliebe verloren, dass er in seinen Schilderungen des Eros, des himmlischen wie des gemeinen, nur der Knabenliebe gedenkt.—S. 35. Den Sklaven hatte die Solonische Gesetzgebung die Männerliebe verboten, die also überdies noch als ein den Freien gestattetes Vorrecht erschien."

[2] Polybius, *Exc. Vatic.* ed. Geel, p. 105, quoted by Döllinger, p. 693.

Thus if we consider the wide-spread dislike of marriage, and even in those who married, of large families, the condition of the slave population, and the terrible prevalence of unnatural immorality, it would appear, says an historian, that no people in history had laboured more effectually for its own gradual extinction than the Greeks.[1]

The Romans possessed originally a domestic life of a yet higher standard than that of the Greeks. Not only was it based upon monogamy, but marriage had with them a certain sanctity, and the wife was taken into the communion of joys and sorrows for the whole life. She possessed all the goods of her husband, even to the participation with him in sacrifice; and the more solemn form of marriage was a quasi-sacramental rite confirmed with religious sanctions. If what is said be true, that even for five hundred years there was no instance of divorce at Rome, then the Romans would rank before any nation of antiquity in their estimation of the marriage bond. Their great strength would appear to have consisted for many ages in the force and purity of the domestic life, wherein the ideas of duty, obedience, and reciprocal respect were conspicuous. On these, first exercised within the family, the foundations of their civil polity seemed to rest. They were noble husbands and fathers before they became conquerors. But from the second Punic war at latest a great deterioration commences. It advances with the progress of external conquest. In the time of Augustus the very mention of the ancient Roman virtues in domestic life would seem a bitter satire upon the actual corruption. Conquest had inundated Rome with slaves, and the licence

[1] *Heid. und Jud.*, p. 691.

NEW CREATION OF MARRIAGE

engendered by slavery had infected every relation of the family. There was no pure and high religious belief to preserve the weaker sex from this contagion, and so all the evils which we have seen debasing Grecian life existed in full force here. Even the poor excuse presented by the sensitive and artistic temperament of the Greeks, and by their passion for physical beauty in all its forms, was wanting to the colder and sterner Romans, who sinned from fashion rather than from feeling. Suffice it to say that when the Roman empire had reached its height, as the virtues of the female sex were never so rare, so the respect for it had sunk to the lowest point.

In the great empire of the Persians, marriage had been debased by polygamy. Not only was the desire for numerous children general, but the law enjoined them; and in attaining this end, the intrinsic dignity and worth of woman were utterly disregarded. The Persian, according to his means, would have many wives and many concubines, and abhorred nothing so much as voluntary celibacy. A maiden of eighteen years of age who remained from choice unmarried was threatened with the heaviest punishments after death. Their domestic life was full of abominations.[1]

If we examine the position of woman in the domestic life of the Israelites, we find that, by virtue of their possessing the true religion, woman as well as man was recognised as made after the image of God, as intended to be man's companion, as, like him, destined to an eternal life, and as therefore needing a moral freedom for the free exertion of virtue. With the Israelite there had never been a *familia* in its original sense, wherein wife and children were merely slaves

[1] Döllinger, *Heid. und Jud.*, p. 376.

somewhat better maintained, but these made up his house and home; and woman with him is not a " bearer of children," as the Greek and Roman name signifies, but woman, another self. In like manner, the words by which he expressed son and daughter came from the same root, and again brother and sister, thus indicating an identity of nature, varied by sex.[1] In common with the man, she was to hear the public reading of the law, and so to be acquainted with the spirit of the sacred doctrine; she was to be honoured with the father, as the mother, and to instruct her children in the fear of God.[2] These great privileges made her social position among the Israelites higher than in any other ancient nation except the Germans.

But there were great drawbacks. At the time of the giving of the law, polygamy and divorce were already customs, and the former was tacitly allowed, the latter expressly regulated by it. Thus the great and pure idea of marriage contained in the book of Genesis itself was defaced, on account of the hardheartedness of the people. Down to the time of the Captivity, polygamy, brought into vogue by the practice of their kings, had grievously lowered the character of married life. It remained always lawful, even if rejected in fact, after that epoch, by the better-minded and more religious. But in the ages preceding our Lord's coming, and at the time of His ministry, the unlimited abuse of divorce had become the scourge of domestic life and threatened even the existence of the nation. No more pregnant sign of the temporary

---

[1] Rohrbacher, *Universal-geschichte*, Germ. ed. 7 B. 42. Γυνή from γείνω, femina from fecundus, fœtus; on the contrary, ish, isshah; ben, bath; ach, achoth.

[2] Deut. xxxi. 12; Exod. xx. 12; Prov. i. 8. See Molitor, *Philosophie der Geschichte*, iii. 73.

and provisional character of the Mosaic covenant could be given than this permission of divorce. The marriage given to Adam for the whole human race was one, sacred, and indissoluble: the covenant under the law was partial and provisional, and therefore admitted of repudiation in marriage. The effect was that between polygamy and divorce the position of woman among the Jews was greatly degraded from its original rank. It must be added that there was as yet no place for the higher meaning and rank of voluntary virginity.[1]

But when from the Greeks, the Romans, and the Hebrews, we turn to the bordering nations of the East and South, the heart is oppressed with a sense of the universal degradation into which the weaker sex had fallen. She had become the instrument of man's pleasures and his slave; wasting on him her youth and beauty, she appeared to exist but for his amusement; or she suffered, not with him, in life's alternate joy and woe, but in his stead; or she even laboured for him, like a beast of burden. Only in the far horizon of the North there is a streak of light, fitful indeed as the sunbeam amid those storm-regions. There a half-nomad race, fallen into a wild idolatry, and in perpetual feud with each other, yet have this single distinction above their personal bravery and freedom, that they honour woman. They have but their yoke of oxen, their caparisoned horse, and their arms; but what they have they give in marriage to the partner of their choice, as a token that she is to share with them every labour and danger of life, all its battle, but the glory and the suffering alike. They have, and they are almost alone among barbarians

[1] Döllinger, *Heid. und Jud.*, p. 784.

in having, but one wife, and they are faithful to her. No youth, no beauty, no wealth will make up in their eyes for the loss of virtue in woman. Fashion is powerless there to make vice merely ridiculous, says the admiring Roman.[1] This is the noble German race, hanging as yet on the outskirts of the Empire, beginning to invigorate its legions, but destined afterwards to supply the raw material of Christendom.

Now let us sum up the position of woman in the world in the last years of Augustus.

The law of marriage will indicate its highest point. But then the original divine institution had been infringed, specially in three particulars. First, the right of absolute divorce on the man's side was universal; and this right was exercised with the greatest abuse among the most civilised nations, the Greeks, the Romans, and the Jews. Among the Romans in later times the right was exercised by women also: the wife divorced her husband. Elsewhere, I believe, this was a supposed luxury jealously reserved by man to himself. Now divorce, followed by remarriage, destroyed the great safeguard of marriage, its indissoluble bond, its life-communion.

Secondly, adultery was only recognised on the woman's side. Husbands, even when they did not divorce their wives, assumed the liberty of bestowing on others the affection due only to the wife; and provided those others were not themselves married, they incurred no blame. Thus the sanctity of marriage was disregarded entirely on the man's side.

Thirdly, over a large portion of the world polygamy had completed the public degradation of marriage by destroying its unity. In nations where this was the

---

[1] Tacitus, *Germania*, 18, 19, 20.

practice woman had sunk fearfully; indeed it was the open proclamation that she was not the partner of man's life, but the instrument of his selfish pleasures; that if made at all from him, she was made not from the region of his heart, but from his feet.

There is one other very singular, and I believe, except among the Germans, universal rule, that woman was considered at all times of her life a minor. Thus in Rome she was first under her father, then under her husband; if she became a widow she fell under his relations. In Athens a widow upon the majority of her son came under his wardship. The meaning of this was that she might never be allowed to go by herself, to rule her house and children, or to rule herself. Generally she might not dispose of her property by will; sometimes of not more than a bushel of barley. By all these regulations man showed that he could not trust her.

But when we look at her in marriage, we look at her in her highest position. Except when so considered, the degradation was incomparably worse. Diminished as was her honour as wife and mother, all her honour lay in these two characters. Outside of them, that is, as a human being, she had none. Besides, the two great evils of human life, idolatry and slavery, had fallen with crushing weight upon her. Wherever there were male and female deities presiding over the propagation of the human race, and wherever there were licentious deities personifying human lusts, there the purity of woman was sacrificed as a religious offering. Wherever, again, slavery existed, and it was everywhere, this same virtue was in the hand of her master.

If we take, therefore, the condition of woman over the earth, at the best and under its fairest aspect, it might be expressed, with the utmost severity of philosophic truth, in those prophetic words : " I will multiply thy sorrows in thy conceptions; in sorrow shalt thou bring forth children ; and thou shalt be under thy husband's power, and he shall have dominion over thee."[1] So far, the gentle subordination under a lawful headship had as a penalty been altered to a severe rule. But there was far more than this. Human sin had further converted it into a servile subjection, a pitiless tyranny. Not only did the shadow of Eve rest on all her daughters, so that they might not go alone, and could not be trusted, since the fatal day of the first deceit; but to the divine sentence the hand of man had superadded such severity of degradation that the penance seemed turned into a curse.

Yet her degradation involved that of her children ; nor could man humiliate woman without proportionably desecrating his home, the seat of his tenderest and strongest affections. The dishonouring of woman, the depreciation of marriage, the avoidance of its obligations and of supporting children, out of selfishness and moral corruption, to which a series of hideous crimes ministered, the facility of divorce and remarriage, unnatural lusts, open shamelessness of life, and the degrading numerous classes of men to be the despised instruments of voluptuousness, these moral abominations, says the historian,[2] hung together, ruled far and wide, desolated whole provinces. For a thousand years at least, civilisation had been advancing with an ever unbroken tide in the East, the West, and the South. There had intervened no assault of darkness from without, no barbarism had burst in to break its

[1] Gen. iii. 16.
[2] Döllinger, *Christenthum und Kirche*, p. 384.

continuity. The three great empires of Assyria, Persia, and Macedonia had yielded up their stores of intellectual and material wealth unimpaired to the mightier Roman. All the arts which adorn life, and all which utilise it, had preserved their inventions for that majestic union of realms and races which the wise administrator Augustus in a rule of fifty years was welding cautiously into a world-wide dominion. He himself among all men who have wielded power may be said to personify civilisation. If in nothing else he had genius, his sagacity in gauging the spirit of the time, in measuring the power of wealth and the bond of prosperity as a hostage for the tranquil submission of men, amounts to this faculty. And when, in his later years, having secured personal supremacy, he looked round him and examined society, he acknowledged that its primary basis was fearfully shaken, and endeavoured at least to restore its solidity. Greek and Roman life had been founded on the sanctity of marriage and the careful rearing of children, and now at the highest point of civilisation men hated the bond of marriage, and cast away from them the burden of children. The very richest and noblest classes were dying out for want of heirs. No love of wife or children was so attractive to the Roman senator, knight, or freedman, as the humble deference, the perpetual court, paid to a childless rich old man. How was the emperor to restore purity and tenderness to the domestic affections? With infinite labour, against the wish of the higher classes, he caused laws to be passed fining the profligate celibacy of the times, rewarding and honouring marriage when accompanied with children, punishing adultery as a civil crime. These in his mature age and ripeness of judgment as a ruler were the acts of one who in his youth had torn Livia, just about to become a mother, from her husband, and in his middle age carried dishonour into numberless Roman households, his acts as the guardian of civilisation, the repairer of society. For how else could he deal with society but rudely and externally and with material force? How could he touch the secret springs of moral action? How could he neutralise the poison of a slavery which infected every vein of Roman life? If he ruled by making wealth secure, how could he lessen and regulate the homage paid to it by the sacrifice of domestic ties? His laws prove that he saw the greatness of the danger, and their ill success attests his impotence to meet it. But the example of the imperial house was more persuasive than law: his own acts bore fruit in his family; the taint breaks out in his own blood, and his only child, beautiful, accomplished, intellectual, once the cynosure of Roman society, calls down at length from him the bitter wish that he had never been a parent, is denounced by name to the Senate as an ignominy to her sex, is banished by her father in dishonour to a barren rock, where at last she dies by her husband's judgment, yet had lived long enough to be Agrippina's ancestress and Messalina's precursor.

Vain, no doubt, was the attempt to restore the chastity and honour of woman, the sanctity of marriage, the love of offspring, the gentle, sweet rule of home, by penal laws. But what was Augustus to do? The evil was instant and universal, striking at once every individual family and the whole empire in the first springs of life. Let us put ourselves in his place, and take a sketch of his resources.

Now the Greek mind stood before him, representing human reason in all its force. There a matchless language, which, compared with the rough railroad iron of our English idiom, seems like purest gold, fit to enchase the diamond and ruby, served to give adequate expression to a philosophic intellect ever ceaselessly discussing all the problems of moral and social life. But what was the tangible result after these four centuries of incessant thought? What deposit had human reason stored up and presented to the accomplished ruler and guardian of society? The philosophers in their lives had been the vilest of men. Their names, far from being associated with honour to women or reverence to children, were connected with the most depraved excesses of immorality. A careful father kept his son specially from contact with philosophers. In fact, with all their genius, in the enjoyment of unbroken peace, wealth, and law, under the radiant climate of Ionia, earth's paradise, uttering ever wise sayings in their golden language, the countrymen of Socrates were dwindling away into self-inflicted extinction. Not from human reason could Augustus hope that the restoration of the family might come.

Turn to Rome, the centre of his power, whose history had been the embodiment of practical good sense, unbending perseverance of will, perfect discipline. Civilisation had struck with a mortal blight the old Roman domestic virtues. The poor Etruscan, Sabine, or Latin tribe had reverenced female chastity, and guarded its hearth as the most precious of earthly goods, the fire which was never to be extinguished. In those days woman could die rather than survive the infringement of the single marriage. But now when the Roman emperors furnish us with many a Truquin, the Roman matrons of the empire yield no Lucretia.

None had tested the matter closer than Augustus himself. How was he to recover what had perished? How to reverse the sentence of his own courtier-poet?

> " Ætas parentum pejor avis tulit
> Nos nequiores, mox daturos
> Progeniem vitiosiorem."

If the emperor tried to improve morality by imposing fines, he knew probably better than any one else what was likely to act on Roman minds.

But Spain and Gaul, Libya and Egypt, Syria and Asia, was there anything in their laws or manners inspiring hope for the future? In the West, Roman civilisation was spreading its own immorality. As to the East, it was doubtful whether the gods or the vices of these nations were the most dangerous to the well-being of society. To Rome, as to the central point of empire, streamed all their corruptions; and its rulers strove in vain to keep out Isis and Cybele, and the hideous forms of men and women which lurked behind their darkness-loving shrines. Hear the poet:

> " I cannot rule my spleen and calmly see
> A Grecian capital in Italy:
> Grecian! ah no; with this vast sewer compared
> The dregs of Greece are scarcely worth regard.
> Long since the stream that wanton Syria laves
> Has disembogued its filth in Tiber's waves,
> Its language, arts, o'erwhelm'd us with the scum
> Of Antioch's streets, its minstrel, harp, and drum.
> Hie to the circus, ye who want to prove
> A barbarous mistress, an outlandish love.
> Hie to the circus! there in crowds they stand,
> Tires on their head, and timbrels in their hand.
> . . . . . While every land,
> Sicyon, and Amydos, and Alaband,
> Tralles, and Samos, and a thousand more,
> Thrive on our indolence, and daily pour

> Their starving myriads forth ; hither they come,
> And batten on the genial soil of Rome,
> Minions, then lords, of every princely dome." [1]

There was no moral strength in these dissolving nations of which the utmost foresight could avail itself to reinvigorate a corrupt people.

But what if Augustus ever turned his glance on those outlying barbarians of the North, who, amid their uncivilised virtues, had retained from the ancient heirloom of man regard and respect for the female sex ? Probably Augustus did not even know the peculiarity which Tacitus pointed out. They acted on his empire only as a threatening war-cloud, calling ever for the utmost diligence of Roman military discipline to meet its descent. But no Roman eye could discern the power which could detach that single constituent of domestic life from the surrounding cruelty and idolatry, and refine it to be the staple of our modern Christian home.

Let us further add, to aid Augustus in his search, all the minds which have left us a record of themselves from Cicero to Tacitus. There is not one who does not look upon the world's course as a rapid descent. They feel an immense moral corruption breaking in on all sides, which wealth, convenience of life, prosperity, only enhance. They have no hope for humanity; for they have no faith in it, nor in any power encompassing and directing it. Their ancient republican freedom is irrecoverably lost, because the virtues which supported it were gone before. Of anything higher they have no glimpse. Where were the elements of life in that loveless prospect of power which respected no sanctuary of manhood

[1] Juvenal, iii. 95–115, Gifford's translation.

—of manhood which resisted no temptation of wealth?

But it might seem that we have omitted the one nation from which something might be hoped. The Jew, believing in the one God, the belief in whom was the sanction of all morality, was everywhere scattered as a commercial settler over the whole East and West, ready to be the missionary of a new religion, the upholder of a pure morality. Yes; but on the other hand, he was bitterly unsocial; his married life was scandalous by the licence of polygamy and the practice of divorce. Even a century later, St. Justin tells us that he was notorious for carrying off a handsome wife wherever he could find her,[1] unrestricted by the one he had already. His master passion would seem to the Roman then, as now, the love of wealth; his marked feature a concentrated national pride. His country was an obscure province, the prey of one foreign conqueror after another, before Augustus had contemptuously left it in Herod's stewardship, until he chose to confiscate it for his own use. The last place in all his empire to which probably Augustus would have looked for means to turn aside that moral ruin which he yet wished to stem, was that distant and very subordinate province; and the last spot in it a deserted cave, sometimes frequented by stray shepherds as a stable, the cave of Bethlehem.

III. Yet from the birth in that cave sprang the great social revolution which reversed the servitude of woman, and enabled her to share in equal degree the restoration of man. The basis of that restoration,

[1] Dialog. cum Tryphone, s. 141. εἰ συνεχωρεῖτο ἣν βούλεταί τις, καὶ ὡς βούλεται, καὶ ὅσας βούλεται λαμβάνειν γυναῖκας, ὁποῖον πράττουσιν οἱ ἀπὸ τοῦ γένους ὑμῶν ἄνθρωποι, κατὰ πᾶσαν γῆν, ἔνθα ἂν ἐπιδημήσωσιν ἢ προσπεμφθῶσιν, ἀγόμενοι ὀνόματι γάμου γυναῖκας, κ.τ.λ.

as we have seen, was the making known to him afresh his true position as a creature, and the end for which he was intended, and the bestowing on him adequate means to reach that end. The knowledge and the means were both the gift of the Child there born. But as originally woman had been made not independent of man, but his partner, and subordinate to him, so the loss of his position as a creature of God intended for a noble end had told doubly on her. If he had become degraded in his own opinion to the rank of a merely rational animal, without a future, she had become not the partner but the instrument of such an animal's natural wants and desires. The revolution which opened out to him a new and boundless future made her likewise the sharer of it. In the Greek, the Roman, the Persian civilisation, in all the half-civilised races surrounding the empire, whatever rank and consideration woman still retained, she held as wife and as mother, that is, relatively to man, not absolutely. This indeed was a necessary result of man's own degradation, who ranked himself as a freeman, or a citizen, or a master, or a conqueror, but not as a human being. Among all these nations, therefore, the idea of woman, not as the mother of his family or the companion of his home, but as the human being, was lost. But when man as such recovered his rank, when the Creator and Redeémer, coming in man's own likeness, living and dying, teaching and suffering for him, claimed him as His own, and disclosed to him his inheritance, woman recovered her rank too. When he had been discrowned, she had been enslaved; for the discrowning had been in some sense her special work, and she had been the mother, by her own fault, of a degraded race. But now that the time of forfeiture had run out, and the estate been recovered, and a Prince of unimaginable rank had been born in the disinherited line, and had raised it to his own degree, her servitude determined likewise; for the Prince was born of her alone, and her work in the recovery was as special as it had been in the descent. In virtue of that birth in the cave of Bethlehem, and of that Child who was Man Himself, but Son of woman alone, the Christian woman at once took a rank no longer merely relative and dependent, but absolute, and her own, as co-heiress with man in all Christian rights and promises. At the beginning of man's history there stood a woman surpassingly fair in body, fairer yet in mind, to whom it was given to bear in her single hands the destiny of man. Evil approached her from without, feebly and insidiously; for it had no hold on the inner sanctuary of her mind; she could have repelled it with one effort, in virtue of the magnificent grace with which she was dowered; but she listened to it, yielded to it, and persuaded man to yield also; and she carried his race and hers with her in the fall. Thenceforth sorrow upon sorrow, in what seemed a never-ending flood, fell upon man's life; but how much more upon woman's, for the first seduction had been hers. At length, when the history of many thousand years had shown but a series of failures on man's part, when his last and most elaborate civilisation had made his life the most valueless in his own eyes, and the slave and the gladiator had become the measure of the rank which he assigned to his own nature, there stood in the most secret path of the humblest life another Woman to whom likewise it was given to bear in her single hands the whole destiny of man. As the messenger of darkness had appeared to that first woman, and she yielded in the trial, severing the bond which united her race with its Maker, so the messenger of light appeared to that second Woman; once more the whole lot of man hung upon a creature; but she did not sink under the burden; rather, armed with incomparable humility, she bore the destiny of the race entrusted to her up to the very throne of God; a divine Person became her Son, and she, by accepting the rank of Virgin-Mother, restored to her sex, so long a byword for weakness and untrustedness, far more than the honour it had lost. As Eve, the occasion of her husband's disinheritance and her children's fall, marks the position held by woman through all the centuries preceding Christ, which are simply the carrying out of the fall in its consequences; so Mary, the Virgin-Mother of the Redeemer, establishes through all generations of her children the absolute rank and place of woman. In the society founded by Mary's Son woman takes equal rank with man, as a human being joint partaker with him of the promises made and the inheritance bequeathed. Her rank relative to man, in the first society of home, is neither taken away nor altered, but is made secondary to the former. This place, unknown to the heathen, feebly and intermittently acknowledged by the Jew, is first of all her Christian place; and the subsequent relations are not done away with, but ennobled and consecrated by it. When she is ennobled in herself, how should she not be nobler in her virginal purity, or in her special relations of wife and mother?

Man and woman then being first restored in themselves, marriage, the primary relation of society, is restored in them. That absolute restoration was the glorious work of the Child born in the cave of

Bethlehem, not only had its source in His Incarnation, but subsisted by virtue of perpetual union with it. Now the same union was applied to the basis of social life. Marriage in its first idea was not a civil contract, the work of man naturally yearning for society, but the institution of God created in view of the Incarnation as future in time, but predetermined before all things: so that the words spoken by Adam under divine inspiration when first beholding his wife as brought to him by his Creator, had a secret but a certain reference to the act of that Creator in Himself espousing human nature. And the seven attributes which belong to its original institution, as we have numbered them above, that is, society, help and support in forming it by the bearing and rearing of children, subordination in it of woman to man, which is tempered by affection, indissolubility, unity, and sanctity, were given to it as an image of the Incarnation yet future and undisclosed. For the restoration of marriage it only needed to unfold the latent sacrament.[1] Every one of these parts in the original institution was in Christian teaching supported by a divine counterpart. Thus the natural society of man and woman was viewed as the germ of the sacred society of men redeemed; the natural propagation and education of the race became the nursery for the corporeal increase of the Church; for how should it profit the offspring to be born unless it be reborn, since, in the words of St. Augustine, it is born unto punishment unless it be reborn unto life?[2] The

---

[1] "Quamvis enim matrimonio, quatenus naturæ est officium, conveniat, ut dissolvi non possit, tamen id maxime fit quatenus est sacramentum; qua ex re etiam in omnibus, quæ naturæ lege ejus propria sunt, summam perfectionem consequitur." *Cat. Conc. Trid.* 2, c. xi.

[2] *De Nuptiis et Concupiscentia*, lib. i. c. 19.

subordination of woman to man is consecrated by the relation which the former bears to the Church, and the latter to Christ; and so their mutual affection represents that which the mystical Bridegroom and Bride bear to each other. The bond of marriage is indissoluble, because the Church is the Spouse for ever, who may never be repudiated; it is one, because there cannot be two Churches or two Christs; it is holy, because holiness is the end of the whole union between Christ and His Church. In all these the natural relation becomes supported by supernatural assistance, and is the image of a divine original; and so all the qualities of marriage as it exists in the law of nature obtain by virtue of the sacrament their highest perfection. This is that great sacrament of marriage which the Church first set forth to the world at its age of utmost moral impotence and incontinence, under Tiberius and Nero, the wife-murderers; which it impressed on all the divine society in the face of the degenerate heathen and luxurious carnal Jew; which it guarded against the wild force and untamed passions of the northern barbarians when they broke in on the civil polity of the empire; which the Sovereign Pontiffs at the first creation of modern society made the public law of Europe; which they maintained unbroken and respected against reluctant kings ever ready to use their power for the rejection of a yoke which bound them to an equality with the weaker sex, and repelled every caprice of passion and appetite of change.

Thus the restored society of man with woman rested for its basis on the Incarnation itself, and was in all its parts a copy of that great fact. It was not enough that man and woman as creatures were restored and exalted by it in themselves, but the condition of their living together was for ever linked to it, associated with it, consecrated by it. This is the transition-point from man as an individual to man as a race, as a society, and therefore the seal of the Incarnation is set upon it. This meaning the ancient Fathers saw in the presence of our Lord at the marriage-feast of Cana. He came thither, says St. Cyril, to bless the beginning of human life, and being the joy and delight of all men to reverse the former punishment of woman that she should bear children in sorrow.[1] We may add to St. Cyril's remark, that thus it was most fitting that He should perform that first miracle at the intercession of a Virgin-Mother, whose own child-bearing had introduced the blessing in virtue of which her sex was henceforth to have joy instead of sorrow in the production of the race, and to be saved in that wherein it had suffered.

To set forth a doctrine in theory and to carry it out in practice are things as widely different as precept and example. Had these statements concerning marriage been merely written in the sacred records of the Church, they might have served to gain the admiration of the student and the praise of the philosopher, but they would not have been imprinted on the minds and actions of men, nor have formed the tissue of everyday life. But this was what had to be done. Marriage is an act, and its laws and conditions affect not only the State as a whole, but every family, every individual in it. Any change in these touches the most universal condition of social life. The grafting, therefore, the natural properties of marriage upon a divine sacrament could only be carried out by the Church as a society. It was a direct matter of spiritual rule to lay down

[1] Τετίμηκε τῇ παρουσίᾳ τὸν γάμον, ἡ πάντων εὐθυμία καὶ χαρὰ, ἵνα τῆς τεκνογονίας τὴν ἀρχαίαν ἐξελάσῃ κατήφειαν. *In Joan.* c. ii. 1, tom. iv. 135.

that the marriage of Christians was indissoluble. It brought the Church at once into *collision* with the habits of society in the Roman empire, under which wives might be repudiated, and even husbands. For whilst the Roman civil life was rigidly built upon monogamy, so that the taking two wives at once brought with it the civil punishment of infamy, it was open both to husband and wife to repudiate the marriage-bond; and it was the most ordinary occurrence to do so. And the unity of marriage was broken in another way by the universal licence practised at least by the stronger sex with slaves and others; a licence which did not offend a heathen. In these two points then the Christian society had to impress on all its members a rule of life at variance with the civil law and the universal custom. It had to subdue therein and tame and bring under obedience the most powerful appetite of man, in races which had long yielded to it unrestrained indulgence. During three centuries it had to do this, while scattered, concealed, oppressed, under a persecution always possible by the mere application of standing laws, often actual. It had to control its members in matters most sensitively felt, which occurred not exceptionally, not intermittingly, but entered into almost every man's life every day. Public opinion, universal custom, degraded nature, the most powerful of human passions, rose up in force against it. I think it is impossible to imagine any stronger test of a society's power and influence than this. It attempted this task, and it succeeded. When it began this great work, not only was the unity of marriage broken by repudiation of the bond, and perpetual violation of its sanctity, but in the background of all civilised life lurked a host of abominations, all tending to diminish the fertility of the human race, and to destroy life in its beginning or in its progress. Of course, the power which guarded the unity of marriage protected it likewise from this still worse desolation. Let us take the sum of that long engagement with civilised heathenism, and calculating only the result of the battle, judge thereby of the force put forth in it, a moral force alone, exerted against the utmost possible preponderance of material power, wealth, and authority. That destructive superstition, the members of which Tacitus[1] described, at the end of the first century, as detested for their domestic crimes, and convicted of hating the human race, had succeeded not only in rolling back the tide of pollution, but in establishing the basis of all social life, the unity and indissolubility of marriage. And this work, so far beyond the power of Augustus and the imagination of Tacitus, had been done, as it were, without hands, by taking each soul in the secret of its conscience, holding up before it a divine original, making it love an uncreated beauty, and imitate a transcendent example. The power of a sacrament had silently been insinuated into the decayed, the almost pulverised foundations of social life, and built them up with the solidity of a rock, which would bear the whole superstructure of the City of God. Three centuries after Tacitus had denounced Christians, and despaired of Rome's moral life, St. Augustine tells us: "A marriage once entered upon in the City of our God, where, even from the first union of two human beings, nuptials carry a sacrament, can in no way be dissolved, save by the death of one." And again: "The good of marriage consists, among all

---

[1] Tacitus, *Annals*, xv. 44.

nations and all men, in the generation of children as its cause, and in the fidelity of chastity; but as respects the people of God likewise in the sanctity of the sacrament, by virtue of which it is a crime even for a repudiated woman to marry another whilst her husband lives, though it were done only to have offspring; for this being the only object of marriage, yet even if it do not ensue, the nuptial bond is not dissolved save by the death of the spouse."[1]

Let us now vary the scene of trial. One of the contending forces has changed, the other remains the same. The Roman empire has been broken up; but the divine society lies unbroken amid its ruins. In Gaul, Spain, Germany, and Italy, the invading northern tribes and the old population, formed and trained in the civil rights of Rome, are struggling together, surging up and down in a ceaseless conflict. The long-haired kings appear, not only disregarding the sanctity of marriage, but with strong leanings to polygamy. At least everything is full of the crimes and violence of a half-civilised life among perpetual warfare. All things are in fluctuation save the Church's divine hierarchy, her teaching, and her sacraments. Not only has the majesty of the "Roman peace" departed for ever, but a great part of the Roman civilisation. Races mix, languages change, Europe is in the throes of birth, and cries in her travail; literature and the fine arts almost perish amid the struggle for hearth and field. It is a period as long, or longer, than the last; no one can trace its details, but we have its issue. These long-haired kings, once raised on the shields of their soldiers, whose sovereignty is only on the field of battle, have come to wear Christian

[1] St. Aug. *de Bono Conjugii*, 17 and 32.

crowns, and to be anointed within cathedrals; and in spite of their savage instincts and passions of conquerors, they have stooped likewise to the gentle sacrament of marriage; they have acknowledged the nuptial bond as one, holy, and indissoluble, out of reverence to that of which it is a copy, as they date the years of their reign from the Incarnation; for amid war, conquest, and all its interminable train of violences on one side, and of suffering on the other, the nuptial bond has been ever held before their eyes by Rome, the great centre of moral light, from which the Christian law radiates, whose Pontiffs have so protected the feeble, and so charmed the strong, through those centuries of strife, that alike in the halls of these kings, now become Spanish, French, English, or German, from the countries which they have occupied, and in the cottage of their serfs, one wife alone is recognised, in rank her husband's equal, whose place cannot be taken by another during her life.

Then comes a period of full five hundred years wherein these new-formed monarchies have entered into a stable alliance with the Church older than themselves, whose missionaries have converted them, whose bishops sit as their hereditary counsellors, building up their realms as bees their hive. The law of the State runs parallel, as it were, with the law of the Church. They are kings in the nation, but likewise most favoured sons in the house of God; as temporal benefactors, defenders, patrons, they have special power and influence with the common Father; and more than once they have used the utmost power which their sovereignty and its alliance with the Church could exert, in order, if it might be, to corrupt the judgment of that Father in the affairs of their domestic life reserved to his cognisance. A queen slighted without cause by her husband flies for restitution of her conjugal rights to the chair of universal justice at Rome; another, wrongfully divorced, fears to be supplanted by a younger and fairer rival; a third has to defend the sterility of her marriage against a husband greedy for heirs: but in all such instances, repeated again and again, never do the Sovereign Pontiffs consent to sacrifice the indissoluble bond of marriage for fear or for reward. It stands recorded to their honour that they preferred to suffer a powerful kingdom, and still more powerful race destined to dominion, to break from their obedience, rather than they would surrender the right of one deserted wife; for in her right lay the right of all wives, and the sanctity of all marriage.

And this period, too, has passed, and another ensued, far different in all its tendencies. It is not now that Christian kings only, or only the rich and noble, seek for privileges in their own case incompatible with Christian law, but society as such strives to emancipate itself from obedience to any law but one self-imposed; and that not a law of Christ, but a law of its own, which it would make for itself—a law with parts gathered from Paganism, with parts retained from Christianity, the end of which, as it conceives, would be social ease and comfort, material wealth, and worldly prosperity. It is the age of humanity rising up in its own strength, with the resources bestowed on it by centuries of Christian faith and practice, against anything which is above itself, when what it calls law is but the expression of general will, neither the command of One reverenced as superior, nor the choice of One loved as good. Before this spirit of self-will, which assumes the guise of liberty, and sweeps over modern nations as the flame over the prairies, the Church maintains still the self-same law of marriage, as the last defence of the weak against the strong, the last rampart of the family and of society against their invaders. What nobler instance of her defence could be found than when, sixty years ago, the man who embraced in his single person the power and genius and more than the will of Cæsar and Alexander, who was, besides, the symbol and embodiment of his age, called upon the Sovereign Pontiff to annul a marriage made by his brother, as too humble for his own soaring ambition? In the face of all that power, genius, and self-will, Pius VII. himself examined the circumstances of the marriage, and declared that it was impossible for him to annul it. The Sovereign Pontiff was once more seen proclaiming that no seduction and no threat could induce him to dissolve a legitimate marriage, though the mightiest ruler on earth was the postulant, and a Protestant of humble degree the wife assailed.[1]

We have now passed rapidly over a period of more than eighteen hundred years, through four entirely different states of society, and we have seen the Church equally maintaining the sacrament of marriage, its unity, sanctity, and indissoluble bond, in the face of the Roman despotism, under an often crushing persecution, in the face of northern conquerors, amid the ruin of civil institutions, the licence and anarchy of violent change, before her own Christian sovereigns, her sons,

[1] See the Letter of Pius VII. to the Emperor Napoleon, June 27, 1805, summing up the doctrine of the Church on marriage, the occasion being the marriage of Prince Jerome with Miss Paterson. Rohrbacher, *Histoire de l'Eglise*, xxviii. 54–58.

patrons, and defenders, and before a civilised Europe, half hostile and half alienated. We saw that when she began to do this, society, by the confession of its ablest representatives, the rulers and thinkers of Rome, had no help in itself, no device or wisdom whereby to restore a ruined morality, and all the broken affections of the family. To complete the demonstration, look around, and outside of the one Church you will find no civilised nation, no uncivilised tribe of man, in possession of the complete Christian marriage, in its unity, sanctity, and indissoluble bond. The Turkish Mahometan is a polygamist. Is he an affectionate husband, a tender father, or a faithful brother? Do not the cities which he found rich and populous dwindle into villages, and the villages become deserts; and have not the most fertile countries been struck with barrenness beneath his feet? Is not the beautiful Ionian climate itself a desolation under his rule? And is not this the first generation in four hundred years, if indeed it be the first, when his reigning family has not been polluted with its own blood? The Hindoo, the Chinese, both in possession of a most ancient civilisation, are polygamists. Can any one look into their domestic life without horror? The Jew is settled in all the countries of the world, and wherever the law of the land in which he sojourns will permit it, he may be, as far as his own law is concerned, a polygamist and a divorcer. So much for civilised man who is not Christian. If we go to the uncivilised, we find the old heathen abominations still prevailing. But the proof does not stop here. Take nations who consider themselves to be in the van of civilisation, to be marching onwards at its front to all the conquests of science and art, whose boast is self-government, whose pride is freedom, but who have rejected the gentle rule of the Church. What do we see? We see them one and all incapable of maintaining the perfect Christian marriage, its unity, sanctity, and indissolubility. Already three centuries ago the very patriarchs of the revolt met in council in order to allow a princely adherent, who dutifully laid before them the confession of his incontinence, the privilege of a second wife. And now the growing power of self-will has extended everywhere in Protestant countries what was once reserved as a privilege for birth and rank to a general permission under the name of divorce from the nuptial bond. Even the Greek and Russian communions allow this; and there is no marriage sacred and indissoluble upon earth, save where; to use again St. Augustine's words, "from the first union of two human beings nuptials carry a sacrament, in the city, among the people, of our God." As the ancient civilisation was powerless to prevent unspeakable immoralities, so the modern—forthwith when it leaves the sanctuary of the Church—becomes unable to sustain the idea and practice of Christian marriage; and only the one, the holy, the perpetual Spouse of Christ can uphold the nuptial bond, of which she bears the mystery in herself.

Thus the Church of God succeeded in a task too great for any power but hers, that of basing natural society upon the Incarnation. Let us observe two consequences of the utmost importance which resulted from this.

I. First, she thereby created a fresh family life. In that great apostacy from primitive truth and corruption of original institutions to which we give the collective name of heathenism, though man could never so far degenerate as to be born without the natural affections, yet the family, which is, as it were, the form which receives and sustains them and holds them together, had been broken up by the force of idolatry, slavery, and moral corruption. These affections, instead of being tenderly cultivated and nurtured in their native bed, grew wild and were debased. Strongly as the human family had been marked with a divine likeness at the beginning, it had ceased to be the picture of any divine relation, or to be associated with any divine hope. Such was its state when our Lord entered into the world, borne witness to in numberless writings of Greek and Roman philosophers, historians, poets, and orators. Let us see how the remedy was applied.

What was the spring of the whole divine impulse given to man by the Christian religion? It was that act of boundless love which moved God Himself to take man's nature, and in that nature by suffering to redeem it. Now He chose for the visible sign, the ever-present picture, of that act the marriage relation.[1] This is the point wherein human affection is naturally deepest and tenderest, and this therefore He selected to be the image of an incomparably greater, deeper, and tenderer love, His own love for the race of man. Marriage viewed only as a natural institution is the germ of the human society; but in virtue of the sacrament enfolding and supporting it, every Christian household became a picture of the fact by which Christians were redeemed and made a people. The natural and supernatural society were joined together

---

[1] "Quum enim Christus Dominus vellet arctissimæ illius necessitudinis, quæ ei cum Ecclesia intercedit, suæque erga nos immensæ charitatis certum aliquod signum dare; tanti mysterii dignitatem hac potissimum maris et fæminæ sancta conjunctione declaravit," &c. *Cat. Conc. Trid.*, pars 2, c. viii. q. 15.

at the root, and so the natural affections, the love of husband and wife, the love of parent and child, the love of brother and sister, grew up and flourished upon a supernatural stock. Thus the wild olive-tree of human nature came to bear the richest and most delicate fruit.

For instance. How do Plato, the ideal legislator, and Augustus, the actual ruler, regard marriage? As a duty which every citizen owes to the state for the rearing of citizens. And to this duty the polished Athenian and Roman must be urged by fines; and when the whole possible system of rewards and punishments has been exhausted, it remains a burden so reluctantly taken up and so inadequately fulfilled, that the population, instead of its natural increase, wastes and dwindles away. But the Apostle,[1] in strongest contrast, sets the self-denying, the purifying, and sanctifying love of Christ before the husband as his model; and before the wife, the love of the Church for her Bridegroom. The Roman husband had for many ages the power of life and death over his wife: as a contrast, the Christian husband is the head who is to cherish the wife as his own body; and this not simply, lest even that image might be scarcely worthy of the tenderness of the relationship, but after the pattern of the divine original, as Christ is the Head of the Body. Over this primary relation of man, this germ of all human society, the perpetual operation of a sacrament is diffused, and that so great a sacrament that it represents the very greatest of all God's works.

Was not this a mould fit for the new creation of the family? And from it accordingly sprang husbands

[1] Ephes. v. 25–27.

and wives, parents and children, brothers and sisters, such as the world had never seen before. Are these the fruits of temporal peace, of commerce, industry, art, and science ? Not so : such things were at their height—a height which in many points we have not yet reached—when the family was decayed and almost destroyed. And such things that very people was obliged to sacrifice during ten generations, in the bosom of which this restoration of the family took place.

What was the school in which Christian parents taught their children obedience ? Was it that old Roman school of force, in which the father had power of life and death over the child, as the husband over the wife? This lay at the bottom of Roman life, as the paternal power did of Chinese ; but it was able to preserve neither from degradation. Instead of this, another example lay before the Christian child. There was a vision, fairest of all created things in heaven or earth, on which his imagination and memory ever loved to dwell—the vision of One performing, from childhood up to the full strength and age of manhood, the meanest tasks of the most ordinary life with undeviating obedience, but with how much tenderer affection. There was One on whom he loved to think as sitting at His Mother's feet, or bearing water for her from the well, sharing a foster-father's toil, or ministering to His parents at their meal. The house of Nazareth was the model of all Christian households : those who dwelt in it, examples of father and mother, husband and wife, parent and child, which all generations were to retrace. There the sacrament of marriage found its highest specimen, for there its purity was untouched by the faintest breath of earthly soiling ; there the love of Mother and Child shone before every mother and child with a glorifying halo; there the loving obedience of the Christian Son received a consecration which should last to the end of time, the fruitful source of imitations innumerable.

Four natural affections surround man's birthplace, cradle, and home—the conjugal, parental, filial, and fraternal. Not only are these distinct from each other, but they are further modified in themselves by the difference of sex. Loves which are reciprocal are not identical, as that of husband and wife, brother and sister; and the father's love for his children of the two sexes differs, and so the mother's, the children's love of the two sexes towards their parents in like manner, and towards each other. Thus in a complete household of six persons, three of each sex, the four species yield fourteen varieties,[1] to all of which the Creator, in His affluence has given their own distinctive hue and fragrance. And these are themselves each and severally the copies of something divine. For creative love, inasmuch as through the infirmity of the creature it could not represent itself adequately in one, produced in all things a numberless variety and inequality, so that multitude might make up for some of the creature's defects, and the good of order, the fairest good of all, might reflect the Maker's beauty in His universe. Nor can there be any doubt that the God, who into His own absolute unity admits the relations of Father and Son, and proceeding from these a third, their mutual

---

[1] The varieties will run thus:—two conjugal—1. the love of husband to wife; 2. the love of wife to husband; four parental—3. of father to son; 4. of father to daughter; 5. of mother to son; 6. of mother to daughter; four filial—7. of son to father; 8. of son to mother; 9. of daughter to father; 10. of daughter to mother; and four fraternal—11. of brother to brother; 12. of brother to sister; 13. of sister to brother; 14. of sister to sister.

Love, has created the human family to be a special representative of Himself. Has He not called its head and ruler by His own dearest name and title of Father? We know besides that the first institution by which He formed the family was a copy of that great act by which He intended to redeem the race. But under the debasing influence of Paganism the family had lost all its divine significations. The human father no longer represented the heavenly. Only when the Son of God, made Man, Himself became a member of a human family, He touched all these affections with His life-giving power, bearing them all in His own Person, either naturally or mystically. The affections of husband and wife, father and mother, son and daughter, brother and sister, so touched by Christ, while they lost none of their original variety, had the virtue of the Incarnation communicated to them, by which they might bloom in a supernatural perfection. Richly, then, as the family was originally dowered, as the seat of human affections, the Son of Mary reserved to Himself, when it had degenerated and seemed ready to disappear, the privilege of bestowing on it its crown. This sacrament of marriage is His special gift, which, by guarding under a divine sanction the unity, sanctity and indissolubility of the bond, secured for the human family the soil, as it were, in which every flower of its various affections might be produced. Take away either of these three conditions, as by polygamy its unity, by divorce its continuity, by licence of either sex its sanctity, and the family becomes fatally impaired. We know that under polygamy the conjugal, parental, filial, and fraternal affections almost wither away. We know that remarriage after divorce, while it announces the dissolution of the conjugal bond, the tie of all the rest, sacrifices the children, distracts and dissipates their love. It is needless to dwell on the desecration produced by licence on either side.

The mode, therefore, by which family life was restored and perfected was by making the members of it, husband and wife, parent and child, first and before all things Christian. The flood of impiety which had assailed its foundations and almost swept them away was thus arrested at its source. The most powerful impulse of our nature was checked in its excess and brought under control. Thus it was that in nations where chastity had been rarest, and human life vilest, Christian marriage was seen to produce every grace and ornament of social life. The noble German barbarian, retaining the idea of purity, unity, and companionship for life in the nuptial bond, bestowed on his bride his horse, his arms, his oxen, the goods of his own life, but could not give her that which he had not—the court of heaven for the Valhalla, the City of God for the City of Odin. His marriage therefore might reach the level of his own life, but could not rise above it. It was only when his race had received the strong graft of Christian faith that it became fruitful in all the sanctities of home.

II. The second great work of Christian marriage as the basis of human society is education. The Greek with all his artistic genius, the Roman with all his practical good sense, had nothing of the kind. They both had schools in abundance wherein grammar and rhetoric, all that we now understand by literature, were taught, wherein the arts of life and the existing sciences were communicated; but as to the meaning of life itself, and the object for which it was given, they were ignorant. The state of marriage alone gave to Christian parents an infinitely higher knowledge concerning this than the wisest and the best among them possessed. For the mother, however poor and ignorant she might be, knew that the children she was bringing into the world would not only belong by birth to an earthly State, but were to be made citizens of an eternal kingdom. She possessed and would communicate a definite knowledge of this, of which Plato, Aristotle, and Cicero had not dreamed in their highest flights. Take the example of Horace, who in a beautiful passage records with tender gratitude his father's care of him; how, being a poor provincial clerk, he would not send his son to a country-school, but took him to Rome to learn the arts which the knight or senator taught his children, watched as the most incorruptible of guardians over his purity, and so was the cause, he says, of whatever virtue and goodness he had. Yet this most elegant of poets, this bosom friend of Mæcenas and Augustus, free from all taint of avarice and meanness, and beloved by his friends, was, in his own words, "a hog of the herd of Epicurus." He has bequeathed to posterity his specific disbelief in providence on God's side, responsibility on man's; for him the gods "lie beside their nectar careless of mankind." His creed, expressed in most harmonious verse, and faithfully carried out in his life, was, "Let us eat and drink, for to-morrow we die." Now, let us translate Horace somewhat magnified into our own world. Or rather let us conceive one possessing the full mastery of mind, as the organ of thought and reflection, passionately fond of the natural sciences, keen in the perception of art, an eloquent speaker, a finished linguist, full of worldly wisdom, energy, consideration. Such a man will possess the highest amount of instruction; but in virtue of all this he will not possess the lowest degree of education. For all these accomplishments do not touch the human being, the possessor of the soul, at all. All these things the age of Augustus possessed, and it was what we have seen; man was without value, woman without honour, society without a stay, breaking through and falling in amidst the accumulated wealth of ages. Could one have given to Plato the Child's First Catechism, he would have recognised therein the basis which he wanted for his ideal city. For to what end are the arts and sciences of life if life itself be without value? And what value can that have which is simply transitory and leads to nothing permanent? But the solid point on which the whole social progress of the race could be built, which was wanting to the Greek and Roman world, was possessed by every Christian household. There the mother became an educator; because the first lessons bestowed by maternal love unfolded to the child the highest relation in which he stood, the relation which ruled all the rest—his relation as a responsible creature to a rewarding Creator. It was a species of priestly office [1] which the state of marriage thus fulfilled throughout the wide extent of the Christian Church; it was a rank created for the bodily multiplication of the divine kingdom, as the proper priestly order was for its spiritual government and increase;[2] and thus it was

---

[1] Döllinger, *Christenthum und Kirche*, b. iii. s. 105.
[2] "Quantum ad communem Ecclesiæ utilitatem ordinantur duo sacramenta, scilicet ordo et matrimonium. Nam per ordinem Ecclesia gubernatur et multiplicatur spiritualiter, et per matrimonium multiplicatur corporaliter." St. Thomas.

at once the material germ of the Church, and the miniature copy of its work.

Let not the commonness of this idea at present disguise from us its infinite value. The mother in the place given to her by Christian marriage begins the children's education, plants in their minds the first and most precious principles of duty; when the mind is most plastic and receptive, "wax to receive, and marble to retain," she forms and moulds their disposition. It seems like a truism. But the Church's institution has made that common which was before unknown, which outside of its influence is unknown still. The Christian mother alone does this, does it in virtue of the sacramental power of her marriage, and of the position which it bestows on her. The mother in polygamy has never done it, can never do it. The mother where divorce dissolves the nuptial bond can never do it. There the band of the house is broken, there is enmity where there should be love, and the children are the first victims of the parents' guilt. The entire purity of the sacrament is required for the education of the child, as distinct from its instruction, to take effect. It is as a sacrament, not as a civil institution, that marriage is the relation which builds up human society.

Now, to comprehend what has been done by the teaching and action of the Church with regard to this primary relation between man and woman, let us briefly sum up what we have said.

The position of woman has been restored in four great points: first, as she is in herself a human creature, wherein she has taken a rank by man's side unknown to the Greek, the Persian, the Roman, the co-inheritrix of all his hopes, of all the divine promises;

secondly, in her great and primary relation to man as the companion of his life, wherein her subordination has been preserved, while the impress of a glorious likeness, full at once of exaltation and tenderness, has been set upon it; thirdly, as the mother of the family, the creatrix of that home which is almost too dear to man, since it sometimes in its sweetness beguiles him of his promised heaven, that home which Athens in the greatness of her science, and Rome in the glory of her empire, did not possess; and fourthly, as the nurse and nurturer of her race and man's, in that primary and most precious education which moulds the yet ductile disposition, and infuses principles growing with man's growth and serving for the whole framework of his subsequent thought and action. To know what in these four points the teaching of the Church has done, we must call up the state of things which existed before it began; and I am convinced that whoever does so will come to the conclusion that in these four things the Church has re-established the very basis of human society; that in maintaining them she is maintaining it; that no degree of material wealth and power would preserve it from falling into decay without them, as the Rome of Augustus was falling.

Again, marriage is the germ of the human society: the family, tribe, nation, are but expansions of it in one line; in another, the village, the town, the city, the league, the empire, are but aggregations of it. It is the spring of man's social growth, the point at which individuals combine to make the race. Accordingly a false idea of it corrupts the whole social structure. Never was there a people great or good in which the marriage-bond was defective.

Further, the inspired records of the Church declare that the union of man with woman was the act of God Himself at the first creation of the race, not a work of society, or a social compact, or in any way the result of man's forethought. And the original institutions of all nations bear witness to this fact; the marriage-tie becomes the purer and stronger the further it can be traced back. It stands on the first page of historical nations complete and distinct. It is defaced and decayed only when they are perishing. This being so, a dissolution of the marriage-bond by human enactment is a rejection of the divine government of the world in that relation which is the basis of all society. It is the alteration and destruction by man of that which he did not create; the proclamation specifically that he is the maker of society, whose law is thus made to derive its sanction from his consent, not from the will of a superior.

On the contrary, the Church took up the original attributes of marriage, and without addition or alteration, revealed the sacrament which supported and consecrated them. And by this her work, carried out in history amid unnumbered difficulties, the foundation of social life in man became visibly a copy of the great master-work of God, which exalts man to union with God. In this work of Christian marriage the Creator and Redeemer were revealed together; the same who established it in innocence restored it after the long night of the Fall as part of His organism for the renewal of all things. Therefore when a nation repudiates the indissolubility of marriage, it repudiates the basis of human society as given to man before the Fall, the basis of human society as restored by God when He became Man. So far as it can it removes the foundation-stone of Christian civilisation, and resumes the errors and immorality of the heathen as to the two sexes. There is but one security against this; and it is found "in the city, among the people, of our God," in whose ears the voice of its legislator is ever sounding, repeating from age to age, "What God has joined together, let not man put asunder."

LECTURE VI

CREATION OF THE VIRGINAL LIFE

Ἐκ παρθένου γεννᾶται, παρθενίαν νομοθετῶν.[1]
Χριστὸς ἐκ παρθένου· γυναῖκες παρθενεύετε, ἵνα Χριστοῦ γένησθε μητέρες.[2]

THAT on which the eyes of Christian men were fixed with undeviating gaze, after the coming of the Author of Christianity, was His personal character. His revelation, with all its long-descending consequences, was contained in Himself. The earth could not be after His coming what it had been before it; and this simply because He had come. On the eve of His dying on the Cross an executed criminal, the scorn and outcast of the human race, He declared that He had finished the work given Him to do. For, indeed, He had lived a man upon the earth, and had set up before all nations that surpassing type of humanity by which, crowned with His death and completed in His death, He was to draw all men to Himself. Other lawgivers have promulgated an external law; other teachers disseminated a doctrine derived from a source outside of themselves. But because He was God the Word made flesh, His law and His doctrine were contained in Himself, His life, and His death. For

---

[1] St. Greg. Naz. *Orat.* xliii. 62.
[2] Id. *Orat.* xxxviii. 1, on Christmas-day 380.

many ages His people summed up their whole belief in a symbol[1] indicating merely His Name, His Natures, His Person, and His Office, in five words, Jesus Christ, Son of God, Saviour; and each individual Christian called himself by a mystical title drawn from the five letters beginning these words, and conveying the conviction that their new life and being were derived from Him and contained in Him. We have under our eyes a process going on, which may give us some notion how after this manner Christendom was formed. Civilisation is day by day impressing upon society a certain model. The daily press is herein its great moulding power, which by a thousand organs in many lands embodies a certain number of principles representing human life, its objects, trials, rewards, and punishments in a particular light. For instance, peace and order, the increase of wealth, the discoveries of art and science applied in manifold ways to the improvement and refinement of life, the softening or removal of bodily pain, all things which concern the ease, well-being, progress of man in his present state—the circle of ideas herein comprised constitutes something real in the minds of men, up to which they are educated, whose commands they are taught to obey, to deflect widely from which is to become a social outcast. The ideal thus set up is confined to no one nation or region: rather its empire is becoming wider day by day. Representative men, ministers of State, rulers even clothed with despotic power, invoke a certain superior power which they call public opinion, and

[1] The word 'Ιχθύς, comprehending the initial letters of 'Ιησοῦς Χριστὸς Θεοῦ Υἱὸς Σωτήρ, and indicating that each Christian was a fish drawn by Him out of the sea of this life, with a reference also to baptism.

themselves profess the allegiance of vassals to a world-wide empire termed civilisation.

The model thus set before men has without doubt a certain consistency, force, and assimilative power, abstraction though it be, and not person. But how much more was the Christian people formed after a certain likeness! Their religion consisted in following its Author: but to follow is to imitate.[1] They had before them a most definite picture, which each one strove to reproduce in himself. The life of Christ was an inexhaustible study, extending its lessons over the whole range of every human life, from which a likeness was to be taken off by each individual for himself. The likeness indeed would vary infinitely in the degree of similitude; but the model was perfect for all.

We have now to consider a particular feature in the character of the Author of the Christian faith, which had the most wonderful influence on His disciples, by calling forth their tenderest love in the imitation of it, and which, through their imitation, has brought about a moral revolution, whose waves, moving on through all the eighteen centuries which have as yet elapsed, will roll forwards to the end with undiminished force, refreshing and restoring human society.

I. It required no less than the Virgin Son of a Virgin Mother to create upon the earth a thing so new and strange as the Virginal Life. And first of all, Christianity itself was based upon a miracle which expressed the high honour belonging to that life. The whole religion lay in His Person who, while

---

[1] St. Aug. *de sancta Virginitate*, s. 27, on the words "Sequi Agnum quocunque ierit," quid est enim sequi, nisi imitari? Tom. vi. 354 A.

He condescended to have an earthly mother, chose not to have an earthly father. The course of all the preceding ages had run upon the divine command, Increase and multiply.[1] But when this blessing had taken effect, the true Head of the race, on His appearing, brought in another order of things, by being born of a Virgin. Thus the human birth of Christ, on which the Christian mind rested with the tenderest love and adoration, touched with an ineffable consecration the Virginal Life, so hallowed by Him in the very spring of His earthly being. He who was enshrined in the innermost sanctuary of Christian thought chose to be Virgin-born. Nor only so; but She[2] by whom He was to touch the whole human race, yet unconscious of that maternity to come, had chosen for herself the Virginal Life, notwithstanding the universal spirit and practice of the chosen people avoided and indeed abhorred such a life. She met the announcement of her singular maternity by declaring to the angel as her intention the choice of that life in which no creature should share the undivided gift of her love to the Creator. In the deepest heart of the Christian people was stored up the virginal choice of Mary and the virginal conception of her Son. And to this we must add the emphatic consecration of

---

[1] This view is set forth at length by St. Greg. Naz. in his poem on *Virginity*.

[2] St. August. *de s. Virgin.* 4. "Quomodo fiet istud, quoniam virum non cognosco? Quod profecto non diceret, nisi Deo virginem se ante vovisset.—Exemplo sanctis futura virginibus, ne putaretur sola virgo esse debuisse, qui prolem etiam sine concubitu concipere meruisset, virginitatem Deo dicavit, cum adhuc quid esset conceptura nesciret, ut in terreno mortalique corpore cœlestis vitæ imitatio voto fieret non præcepto, amore deligendi, non necessitate serviendi. Ita Christus, nascendo de Virgine, quæ antequam sciret quis de illa fuerat nasciturus virgo statuerat permanere, virginitatem sanctam approbare maluit, quam imperare."

spotless purity contained in His own choice of a virginal life.[1] His doing was, above and more than all, His teaching: of greater force even than His words were His acts; and this act especially, being, as it were, the summary of His life, had the most constraining, the most attractive power on Christian thought and feeling. Every word that He uttered was to be diligently gathered up and pondered on by His people, and wrought into their life in all succeeding ages. How much more then should this act of virginal purity, extending over all His life, be the seed of countless similar acts in His people? On this triple fact, accordingly, of Mary's virginal choice, of her Son's virginal conception, and of His own virginal life, rested the honour which was to belong to the Virginal Estate among the Christian people for ever.

It was entirely a new honour. To have children, to have many children, to be renowned for the multitude issuing from them, was the honour which had hitherto been coveted by man. And especially among the chosen race was this feeling strong; for there to be unmarried, not to carry on the house of Israel, to exclude oneself from the possible parentage of "Him that was to come," was a reproach. When Mary "raised the standard of Virginity,"[2] it was a new ensign, which the Father of the age to come was

[1] "Gaudium virginum Christi de Christo, in Christo, cum Christo, post Christum, per Christum, propter Christum. Gaudia propria virginum Christi, non sunt eadem non virginum, quamvis Christi. Nam sunt aliis alia, sed nullis talia. Ite in hæc, sequimini Agnum, quia et Agni caro utique virgo. Hoc enim in se retinuit auctus, quod matri non abstulit conceptus et natus. Merito eum sequimini virginitate cordis et carnis, quocunque ierit. Quid est enim sequi nisi imitari?" Id. s. 27.

[2] St. Ambrose, *de institutione Virginis*, 35. "Egregia igitur Maria, quæ signum sacræ virginitatis extulit, et intemeratæ integritatis pium Christo vexillum erexit."

Himself to bear aloft, as the oriflamme denoting the presence of His own sacred Person, around which His body-guard was to rally for ever, in the long battle which He would inaugurate.

But when from the people of Israel we cast our eyes on the civilised nations surrounding the Mediterranean, and first and chief upon the Hellenic and the Latin races, nothing can be imagined which was in greater antagonism to their practice and their habits of mind than the virtue which lies at the root of the Virginal Life.[1] The tide of human sensuality had far over-flooded the confining banks of marriage: it was like an inundation sweeping down on the race of mankind, spurning all restraint, and revelling in gratification of itself to the degree of wasting away the very springs of life. The most civilised, as we have seen, were in this respect the most corrupted. In Greece and Rome the annual increase of the population did not supply the vacancies produced by death, at a time when moral purity was almost unknown. Idolatrous worship was in almost every case linked with degrading and unblushing sensuality: nay, sensuality itself became not merely an imitation of the recorded life of these false gods, but an act of worship to them.

At such a time, in the midst of such races of men, acting upon populations enervated by centuries of refined effeminacy or savage passion, appears the wonder we are noting. "He is born of a Virgin, and becomes the Legislator of Virginity."[2]

How did this legislation, which was to plant its

---

[1] In the Vestal Virgins at Rome, in certain Greek priestesses, in praises of Virginity scattered here and there among the poets, we see the traces of a higher feeling, and of a tradition connecting unsullied purity of life with the service of God.

[2] St. Greg. Naz. *Orat.* xliii. 62, tom. i. p. 816 D.

law in the innermost freedom of the human will, take effect? After this manner.

All Christian thought and feeling were concentrated upon His Person. His coming was an era which made all things new. All motives of action started from a new basis in Him, and tended to a new result. But He Himself was not only the Virgin Son of the Virgin Mother. More than that; His virginal birth belonged to His office of Saviour: it was the mode of His assuming the nature which He saved by taking without its sin. It was by human generation that the sin had descended from father to son: it was by a virginal birth that deliverance from it should come to man. Thus it was from the Annunciation itself, the starting-point of our Lord's human history, that an indescribable glory was shed on the virginal life of Her who bore Him. But when to this was added the whole course of His own life on earth, the example which He gave in this, and which was imitable,[1] we see at once how Christians from the beginning discerned a special likeness to our Lord and to His Mother in the virginal life. This special likeness was the source of their veneration towards it: this, and nothing else, the spring of their own free choice of it.

It will be well to collect together in a few words the view which all the ancient writers of the Church give us as to the Virginal Life; a view not embraced by one and rejected by others, but universally diffused

---

[1] "Christus pro nobis passus est, relinquens nobis exemplum, ut sequamur vestigia ejus. Hunc in eo quisque sequitur, in quo imitatur: non in quantum ille Filius Dei est unus, per quem facta sunt omnia; sed in quantum Filius hominis, quæ oportebat, in se præbuit imitanda: et multa in illo ad imitandum omnibus proponuntur, virginitas autem carnis non omnibus." St. Aug. tom. vi. 354 B.

among them with a perfect harmony of principles and even identity of expression.¹

First of all, and as the root of all, they see in it a special imitation of Christ. And here a martyr in the last of the ten persecutions, St. Methodius, may stand simply as a mouthpiece for the twelve generations of men from the Ascension to St. Augustine. "It may be asked," says he, "why, when many prophets and just men have taught and done so much that was admirable, did no one either praise or choose virginity? It seems that this mode of life was reserved to be sanctioned by the Lord alone, since by His advent alone He taught men to pass unto God. For it was fitting that One who was Arch-priest, Arch-prophet, and Lord of Angels, should also be called Arch-virgin. In the ancient times man was not yet perfect, and therefore had not strength to receive the perfect thing, Virginity. Though he had by birth the image of God, he still needed to recover God's resemblance. And this the Word was sent down into the world to accomplish, and first took upon Him the form of man, punctured as it had been all over by multitudinous sin, in order that we for whom He bore it might be enabled again to take the divine form. And how can a perfect resemblance to God be attained?

---

¹ Virginity is viewed specially as an imitation of Christ by
St. Clement of Rome, *Ep.* i. *ad Virgines*, s. 6.
St. Ignatius of Antioch, *Ep. ad. Polyc.* 5.
St. Cyprian, *de habitu Virginum*, c. 4.
St. Methodius, *Convivium decem Virginum*, i. 4, 5.
St. Athanasius, Letter to Constantius, 33; *de Incarnatione Verbi*, 51.
St. Gregory of Nazianzus, in his poem on *Virginity*, 189-214, 592-606, 527-564, and *Orations* 38 and 43.
St. Ambrose, *de institutione Virginis*, ch. 17 and 5; and *de Virginibus*, lib. ii. c. 2, and lib. i. c. 3.
St. Jerome, *contra Jovin.* i. 19; *Ep. ad. Eustochium*, 18 and 21.
St. Augustine, *de sancta Virginitate*, 27-30, 35, 37, 38.

Only like skilful portrait-painters by drawing on the easels of our own minds the very lineaments of His human life, pursuing as disciples the path which He opened. It was precisely that we might have before our eyes as drawn upon a tablet a divine ensample of life, in which we might imitate the Artist that He chose, being God, to put on human flesh. For He did not say one thing and do another, nor give an ideal standard of excellence without teaching it as imitable, but at once taught and did what was useful and beautiful. What then did the Lord, the Light, and the Truth, when He came down into the world, actually carry out? He maintained His flesh in incorruptible virginity, in order that, if we would be like Him, we should honour that life."[1]

It is but drawing out this principal feature of imitation when we go on to say that they considered the Virginal Life to be a dedication of the whole creature to the Creator; and again, a continual sacrifice offered to Him of that which is most precious in man; and again, the soul's espousal of the heavenly Bridegroom; or again, as compassing and involving the whole range of sanctity; or again, as an anticipation of the angelic life, and that the more wonderful, because maintained amid a conflict to which that life is not exposed; or again, as the cutting-off of all human cares and anxieties, and so possessing a simple self-sufficiency resting upon God. It is a new form of expressing all the above, but a very striking one, when St. Chrysostom says that self-denial, or to use his own word, the crucified life, is at once the root

[1] St. Methodius, *Symposium decem Virginum*, i. 4, 5. Gallandi, iii. 677, 678.

and the fruit of Virginity.[1] We must add two points to complete the picture. This life is not a command, but a choice, and so the more dear and precious to Him for whose sake it is chosen;[2] and the value of it lies in its being consciously chosen, and chosen irrevocably;[3] and lastly, it is not the mere result of human election, but at once man's freest choice and a special divine gift.

What has been here summed up in a few words might be illustrated at endless length from the writings of the first five centuries. Two contemporaries of the Apostles express it very strongly when they say, St. Ignatius of Antioch, that virginal purity is maintained "in honour of the Lord's flesh,"[4] and St. Clement of Rome, that our Lord "put on the body in which He bore the conflict of the world from a holy Virgin, by which we may understand the majesty and glory of virginity."[5]

---

[1] For the above citations, see
St. Chrysostom, περὶ παρθενίας, 68, tom. i. 323.
St. Augustine, *de s. Virginitate*, 30. "Tollite hostias quisque suas et introite in atria Domini."
St. Athanas. *ad Constantium*, s. 33. τὰς γοῦν ταύτην ἐχούσας τὴν ἀρετὴν νύμφας τοῦ Χριστοῦ καλεῖν εἴωθε ἡ καθολικὴ Ἐκκλησία. ταύτας δὲ Ἕλληνες ὁρῶντες ὡς ναὸν οὔσας τοῦ Λόγου θαυμάζουσι.
St. Clemens Rom. *Ep.* i. *de Virginitate*, 3. "Quicunque enim profitetur coram Domino se servaturum castitatem, debet cingi omni virtute sancta Dei," &c. Gallandi, tom. i. iv.
St. Chrysost. ut sup. 79, 80. μᾶλλον δὲ καὶ ῥίζα καὶ καρπὸς παρθενίας ὁ ἐσταυρωμένος βίος ἐστίν.
St. Ambrose, *exhort. Virginit.* 31. "Nullis in hoc saeculo curarum anfractibus reflectitur."

[2] St. Chrysost. ut sup. 41. περὶ τούτου φανερῶς ὁ Χριστὸς διετάξατο, κωλύων εἰς ἐπιτάγματος ἀνάγκην ἐλθεῖν τὸ πρᾶγμα. And St. Aug. ut supra, 30.

[3] St. Aug. *de sancta Virginitate*, s. 11. "Nec nos hoc in virginibus praedicamus quod virgines sunt, sed quod Deo dicatae pia continentia virgines." And s. 42.

[4] St. Ignat. *Ep. ad Polyc.* 5. εἴ τις δύναται ἐν ἁγνείᾳ μένειν, εἰς τιμὴν τῆς σαρκὸς τοῦ Κυρίου, ἐν ἀκαυχησίᾳ μενέτω· ἐὰν καυχήσηται, ἀπώλετο.

[5] St. Clem. Rom. *Ep.* i. *de Virginit.* 6. "Uterus virginitatis sanctae

This tradition springs without a break from our Lord through St. Paul and St. John, and diffuses itself into all lands and all times without an exception. And what the Christian writers teach, the Christian people executes.

For if this were but a matter of sentiment, a merely theoretical preference of an ideal condition, if it were but a Platonic Eutopia, or piece of Aristotelian reasoning, how little would it have counted! As I have already remarked with regard to the Christian doctrine of marriage, so I may repeat with regard to this doctrine likewise, that the world would have been as slightly affected by such words, had they been unaccompanied by deeds, as it actually was by the sects of Grecian philosophy. But in this new people which had sprung up from east to west and from north to south, which was found in all the cities of the Roman dominion, there was likewise, from the date of our Lord's ascension onwards, found to be a certain portion which cultivated this new and unheard-of life. In the sex which had known no other duties than those of the mother, had possessed no other hold on man than the charm which belongs to the union of the sexes, there appeared suddenly young maidens who disregarded the joys of marriage, and the condition which up to that time had seemed to be the only hope of woman's life. Then first the young and beautiful were found to disdain what had hitherto been the prize of youth and beauty. And whereas among men the unmarried state of adults had only been a mark of presumed profligacy, there were now

gestavit Dominum nostrum Jesum Christum filium Dei, et corpus quod gestavit Dominus noster et in eo agonem in hoc mundo fecit, ex virgine sancta induit. Hinc ergo intellige majestatem et gloriam virginitatis." Gallandi, tom. i. vi.

seen those who renounced for ever the bond of marriage, and with it the engagements, the ambition, and the success of the world, in order to give themselves to a life either of contemplative piety or of active charity, the one and the other previously unknown. During the ten generations of intermittent persecution which marked the first planting and youth of the Church, such a resolve could only be practised by man and woman in the secrecy of private life. There could not be public and avowed associations of those who sought to carry out a common purpose by mutual assistance. The virgin remained with a secret dedication in her father's house, and the youth, most generally giving himself to the special service of the sanctuary, did the like. But from the beginning both these classes existed. In the middle of the third century, after one of the longest periods of tranquillity which occur in these three hundred years, and when peace and security had produced a considerable relaxation of Christian spirit, St. Cyprian addresses this class among women: "We are now," says he, "speaking to virgins, for whom our solicitude must be greater in the proportion that their glory is more exalted. They are the flower of the Church's growth; the grace of the Spirit has in them its beauty and delicacy; they are our pride and bloom; in them praise and honour have their perfect and uncorrupt work; they are God's image reflecting the Lord's sanctity; the more illustrious portion of Christ's flock. In them exults, in them beauteously flowers the glorious fecundity of our mother the Church, and the more Virginity adds to its number, the more that mother's joy increases."[1] A hundred years later St.

---

[1] St. Cyprian, *de habitu Virginum*, 4.

Athanasius, addressing the Emperor Constantius, said: "The Son of God, our Lord and Saviour Jesus Christ, after becoming man for us, and annulling death, and freeing our race from the bondage of corruption, in addition to all His other gifts bestowed on us this, to have upon earth the image of angelic sanctity, the Virginal Life. At least, those who possess this virtue, the Catholic Church is wont to call the Brides[1] of Christ. When the heathens round us behold these, they look up to them with admiration as a shrine of the Word. For, in real truth, nowhere is this sacred and heavenly profession carried out save among us Christians alone. And this is above all a very great proof that real and genuine piety exists among us only."[2] Fifty years later St. Augustine tells us: "Undoubtedly the chief lesson and example of virginal purity must be contemplated in Christ Himself;" and then turning himself, as it were, to that Saviour to bestow on them the gift of humility, whose deep foundation was the more needed because of the height of the building to be raised upon it, he cries: "Look upon these troops of virgins, of holy youths and maidens. In Thy Church this race was brought up: for Thee burst forth its vigorous bloom from the mother's breast: there it lisped its first accents into Thy name, Thy name which it drank in as the milk of its infancy. Of this number no one can say, I who was first a blasphemer, a persecutor, an evil-doer, but I obtained mercy because I did it ignorantly in unbelief: nay, rather what Thou didst not command

---

[1] I am aware of the abuse of the συνείσακτοι, and of what may be said upon it; but neither those who fail to keep such a life of perfection as is indicated by St. Athanasius, nor those who falsely imitate it, do away with the merit of such as are true to it.

[2] St. Athanas. *ad Constantium*, s. 33.

but only propose as the prize of a willing violence in those words, 'Let him that can receive, receive,' these made their prize, offered their vow, and for the kingdom of heaven shut themselves off from marriage, not through dread of Thy threats, but through love of Thy promises."[1]

Now these great writers here give what may be termed simply the logical ground and basis of a great historical fact, beginning with our Lord's ascension, and repeated through eighteen centuries in every climate under every condition of society. Let us weigh well the gravity of this fact: its incompatibility with any merely natural principles of human society, its perpetual recurrence and continuity. It is not the result of race, for the most different races, sterile before, produce it as soon as they become Christian; not of climate, for it flowers alike in scorching Egypt and the frozen north; not of national temperament, for the speculative East and the practical West give it forth in equal abundance; not of riches, for poverty is usually its accompanying mark; not of poverty, for multitudes of the rich embrace it; not of learning, for the simple unlearned form the great mass of its professors; not of ignorance, for among them the Church has ever had its reserves of wisdom, learning, and all human accomplishments, from which have gone forth the maintainers, restorers, and promoters of all learning; not of a barbarous or incipient state of society, for like a flower amid ruins it forces its way to the surface through the middle ages of struggle and warfare, while it blooms no less in the Sybaritic atmosphere of imperial Rome, and among the softest conveniences of modern life.

[1] *De sancta Virginitate*, 35-37.

For such a production, so difficult, so unearthly, so precarious, yet so constant, there is but one mother soil, the Church's bosom. And the never-dying root of this flower of all Christian ages and climates is imitation of the Virginal Son of the Virginal Mother, an imitation which can only be fully carried out by itself.

For with one mouth all the ancient Christian writers proclaim the Virginal Life to be the *condition* of all perfect following of our Lord. This truth both lies in the nature of things, and is deduced directly from the words of Scripture. Thus the Apostle[1] bids the chief teacher to whom he is writing to labour and endure like a good soldier of his Lord, adding immediately that no one in military service entangles himself in secular business, in order that he may please the commander to whom he has engaged himself. But the most usual image of Christian life represents it as a warfare. And the most complete as well as the most inextricable entanglement in secular business is that which results from marriage and its attendant cares. It is emphatically the dividing of the heart. The thorns which choke the seed in the parable are the cares of this life and the deceitfulness of riches. But the very portion of married life are these cares. Its work lies amid anxieties for this very deceitfulness. On the other hand, the price to be paid for deliverance from these secular cares was a high one, no less than the renunciation of all for which man naturally lives—wife, children, wealth, prosperity, the prizes and the human loveliness of life; in one word, that word of mightiest power over man's heart, of fascination all but irresistible, the world. And for

[1] 2 Tim. ii. 3, 4.

what? To make the absolute surrender of body as well as soul to the unseen love of a spiritual object. The youth and the maiden who made this choice rested from that time, and entirely, on the soul's secret espousal with God. The world as a tie, as an enthralment, as a heart-dividing power, was taken away, and for it the Lord of the world in His naked majesty, His supreme loveliness, was substituted. It was a choice which before it was made was perhaps inconceivable to human flesh and blood, to the weakness of the heart, its craving for human sympathy and yearning for human affection. To the heart still filled with these objects it remains inconceivable, an unsolved secret ever misinterpreted, as the love of a heavenly vision which entrances the eye beholding it appears gazing on vacuity or madness to the eye which sees it not. But it was a choice created by the greatest of all wonders, the Incarnation: it was the answer of man's heart to God becoming Man; the answer of human love to the excess of divine love, an earthly copy of creation's Masterpiece. In that very world which had been for ages a prey to all sensual indulgence, among races the most enervated slaves of pleasure, it became a fact of no infrequent occurrence. A great multitude of both sexes renounced that which no Christian precept called upon them to renounce, the state of marriage, and with it all the merely human and natural interests of life, in order to be like their Redeemer and His Mother in their virginal purity which they had introduced. His example and hers, His as the Maker and Spouse of Virgins, hers as their Queen, the plant which had brought forth the Virginal Flower, shone before the two sexes, and produced then, and have produced since, unnumbered imitators. "To follow is to imitate;" and to them is reserved the singular privilege "of following their Lord whithersoever He goes."[1] In this passage of the Apocalypse, St. Methodius[2] sees a proof of the great rank and estimation which the virginal life possesses, and of its being a new thing upon the earth. The whole assembly of the redeemed, he says, was a multitude which no man could number. But amongst them was a certain determinate number of the highest dignity and without spot, the first-fruits of the earth, those twelve times twelve thousand, the number which indicates created perfection. And they sang a new song before the throne, our Lord appearing as the Leader of the choir. The rest, says St. Augustine,[3] may follow their Lord in the seven beatitudes: here the married may at least pursue His traces, walking in the same path, though they set not their feet perfectly in His very steps: the rest of that multitude may follow Him everywhere, except when He walks in the beauty of Virginity; but these follow Him even then. They sing a song in His praise, which the rest may hear, but they alone can utter. Thus, as He is the fountain of prophecy, and the giver of pastoral mission, He is the Leader of the Virginal Band; the Chief Prophet and Chief Shepherd is Chief Virgin.

Such a belief and such alone is competent to produce the fact to which history bears witness. As soon as our Lord had preceded, and drawn in His life the perfect lineaments of virginity, a crowd of

---

[1] Apocalypse, xiv. 4.
[2] St. Method. *Conv. dic. Virg.* i. 5. Gallandi, iii. 678.
[3] St. Aug. *de s. Virg.* 28.

souls betrothed and espoused to Him arise all over the earth. It is not a temporary or partial phenomenon, not one to be accounted for by any natural cause. But wherever in time or space the wave of the Christian people spreads itself, in periods of persecution or of tranquillity, of decaying or advancing civilisation, of barbarous violence or the quiet peace of social wealth and strength, here a portion of this people is found on whom the example of its Lord and His Mother acts as a magnet, drawing them to itself, severing them from the world, giving them supernatural instead of natural aims, heavenly instead of earthly affections. Before our Lord's Incarnation [1] no race on earth, whatever its natural gifts, had produced such a phenomenon. After it even the weakest of Asiatic races can exhibit these choosers of a self-denying life, these affianced lovers of an unseen beauty; and the strongest offspring of the North, the men whose wills have gained kingdoms, and founded the freest and most self-relying polities, have bent no small portion of their sinew, and rendered up the very flower of their beauty to this humble following of a Crucified Love. Norman nobles, the stoutest of the earth, and Annamite youths the weakest, heirs of Roman greatness, the long-descended line of Scipio, whose possessions were provinces, whose

[1] This does not exclude such rare types of our Lord amid the Jewish Prophets as Elias, Daniel, Jeremiah, and others. I imagine that the precepts of the Essenes were derived from a study of the lives of these prophets by a sort of anticipation of Christian feeling. At any rate, they did not continue, nor propagate themselves. Upon the Oriental Virgin and Child, and certain Buddhist institutions, we require further information, as to the time of their arising, and as to what the institutions in practice really are. There is every reason to believe that the Christian religion was once widely spread in these regions. I know not whether it can be proved, but certainly it may be surmised, unless contradictory proof be alleged, that these appearances were posterior to our Lord's advent.

halls were crowded with busts of consular ancestors, and the daughters of Syrian mothers, who wept " in amorous ditties all a summer day" for "Thammuz yearly wounded;" the chancellors and ministers of wise and politic kings, who each in their day thought to make the Church their vassal, and the slaves of Roman matrons, who made a pastime of human suffering; all these, and every variety of earthly race and station, will be found hereafter in that mystical number of twelve times twelve thousand, who represent these special attendants, because they have been special imitators of a God made Man.

II. We have seen how the natural propagation of the race was put under the guard and shadow of the Incarnation in the original marriage which was its image, for the words of Adam describing his union with his wife, " This now is bone from my bones, and flesh from my flesh; she shall be called woman, because she has been taken from man. For this cause a man shall leave his father and his mother, and shall cleave to his wife, and they shall be two in one flesh " —are interpreted by St. Paul[1] to indicate a great mystery, that is, the whole work of the Incarnation, and the union of Christ with His Church. By this interpretation of the Apostle the following principles are laid down.

The Incarnation is a remaking of the very same Adam, or human nature, spoilt at the Fall, the flesh assumed being that identical flesh which the Creator moulded from the clay, and animated with His breath.

The ecstasy of Christ in His passion is the truth of which Adam's ecstasy when Eve was formed is the shadow.

[1] Ephes. v. 25-32.

The formation of the Church from the side of Christ sleeping on the Cross is the truth of which Eve's formation from Adam sleeping is the shadow.

The spiritual generation of Christ's members from the Church is the truth of which Adam's words to Eve represent the shadow.

The man who shall leave his father and his mother and be joined to the wife is Christ.

The manner of the joining is that virginal espousal by which the soul is first made the bride of Christ, and then bears to Him other souls as the fruit of that espousal.

And lastly, in the spiritual generation Virginity corresponds to marriage in the natural. It is as much the means of propagating the spiritual race as marriage is of propagating the natural.[1]

Thus, on the one hand, marriage was consecrated from the very first as being an image of the Incarnation. But, on the other hand, the Incarnation itself was to be achieved by Virginity. And so this was a special imitation of our Lord's life and of His Mother's. And further, in accordance with its origin, and with this imitation, a special work is assigned to it, the propagation of the supernatural life and of its peculiar works. Virginity, with the virtue of continence, subordinate to it, is found to be the condition of the Church's fecundity. The prophecy of the Gospel times is, "The Virgin shall conceive and bear a Son," which is true first in our Lord's Person, and then in His mystical Body.

Let us proceed here, as before, to interrogate the

---

[1] The principles of interpretation here laid down may be found in St. Methodius, *Convivium decem Virginum*, *Thalia*, 8. Gallandi tom. iii. 688, 689.

witness of history, and to see whether it accords with the dogmatic basis just laid down.

For not only is the virginal life beautiful and admirable in itself, whether we consider it as a peculiar imitation of our Lord and His Mother, or as a dedication of the whole creature to God, or as a continual sacrifice offered to Him, or as an espousal of the heavenly Bridegroom, or as an anticipation of the angelic life, and that in a body beset by earthly desires, or not as a command, but as the freest of free choices; but it seems to be likewise the almost necessary preliminary condition of other things which are not commands but counsels, not enjoined on the whole multitude, but reserved for the most devoted and loving. Without it how can either the possession of worldly goods be disregarded, or voluntary obedience of the will practised? The portion of marriage, as I have already said, is worldly cares, the pursuit of riches, the conflict for the material prizes of life. The very best of men, so involved, become in spite of themselves slaves of the outward world, unwilling and murmuring slaves it may be, but still slaves. The spring of their actions is their advancement in temporal goods, a motive coloured by them with the love of wife and children, but which is in itself a proscription of all liberty and independence. Poverty of spirit and desire of prosperity are the negations of each other. The family life becomes a sort of closed and sacred circle, within which the strongest affections of the human mind are nurtured and developed, for which men and women live, while all else is exterior to them, and almost indifferent, except as an object to be gained and used for the former's sake.

Over and against such a life the Virginal Estate,

looking to God alone, and content with Him for its portion, stands in the strongest contrast. If it be not itself a perfect self-sacrifice, it is at least alone compatible with it. If it be not itself an exercise of the highest freedom of the will, of the most complete independence of external things, it alone makes its possessor capable of such freedom and independence. If it be not itself the completest form of voluntary obedience, it alone makes such an obedience possible. All great works undertaken for the supernatural life and its propagation in the world, such as the government of souls, the conversion of the heathen, the reformation of great evils, demand the sacrifice to them of the entire man, and often of life itself. They are therefore incompatible with the domestic life, which has its reserves jealously maintained; which will give to duty a certain portion of the man, of his time, his labour, and his health; but keeps back another portion as belonging to others, the nearest and dearest to him.

From the certain operation of these principles, rather than from any outwardly-imposed law, arose the exhibition of the Virginal Life in two great institutions which run through the whole history of Christianity, the secular Clergy, and the Religious Orders of men and women.

The creation of the Clergy must be considered a work of the Holy Spirit in the Church. It was not formed by human policy: it did not spring from secular motives, nor lean upon temporal support. On the contrary, it was the prolongation of the Good Shepherd's office, whose characteristic it was to give His life for His sheep. Accordingly the devotion of the whole man to this one work, the pastoral charge, was its first necessity. To evangelise the world was the work; and it could only be attained by complete simplicity of purpose, by absolute surrender of the whole man. No half-service, no mixture of secular motives and worldly success, was allowable here. But such a mixture was infallibly introduced by the married state. The moment a man had a wife and children, it became his duty to support these, since not to provide for one's own household is to be worse than an infidel. But to provide for one's household, and to give one's life for the sheep, are duties which clash. They cannot proceed together, for they interfere with each other. The bond of marriage accordingly would have made the clerical office a profession, that is, a mode of gaining a secular livelihood, which is foreign to its nature. Its nature is to carry on the office of Christ the great Shepherd. Thus by an internal necessity from the beginning a deliverance from the bond of marriage was sought after. But this could only be gradual. When the Apostles were chosen, the institution of Virginity did not exist in the world. It had to grow up out of the example of our Lord and of His Mother. What could be done was done. First, to be the husband of but one wife [1] was given as the rule for the pastoral office, because the Christian society afforded among its converts examples of those who had never divorced their wives, or who, becoming widowers, had never married again. Presently we find the rule prescribed, continence in the married life itself to the clergy. As time went on, and Christian principles had taken root and borne fruit, the choice became restricted to the unmarried, or at least widower; and finally, long before the cessation of the great

---

[1] 1 Tim. iii. 2. δεῖ τὸν ἐπίσκοπον εἶναι μιᾶς γυναικὸς ἄνδρα· and Tit. i. 6.

persecutions in the first three centuries, a profession of virginal or continent life is found established as the rule among the clergy. Now the more it is examined, the clearer will be the conviction that this profession marks the line between the simply human life of natural affections, a life permitted among Christians, a life sanctioned, the life ever of the vast majority, and that higher life, the voluntary choice of the few, which rests simply on superhuman affections, supports, and rewards; which at once and for ever sacrifices all thought and aim of temporal prosperity, and takes for its portion God alone. How could the clergy—the very meaning of whose name signified God's lot— choose any other portion than this? And while the Church was still considered by the Roman empire as its great and deadly enemy; while the empire was still doing its utmost to destroy that enemy, this choice was made by the clergy. It grew up everywhere as an instinct of the spiritual nature, an aspiration of the Christian heart; and so it came to be considered as a condition for those who were to guide and govern the Christian flock, and bear the brunt of the world's enmity against it. This profession of virginity or continence, therefore, which had had no existence before our Lord's coming, which was abhorrent from Jewish nature, and seemed to the whole Gentile world, while still in its unbelief, a renunciation of man's task to subdue the earth unto his use and to multiply his race, became a reality, an institution, a power all over the earth. Nay, more; it seemed the special consecration of those who were to carry on their Lord's work; the condition and the token of their victory over the world, and of their success in His work; the condition of their independence, endurance, courage, and self-sacrifice; the token of their worthiness to lead others, and to be the example of those whom they should govern. So it must always be; for the principles here involved are independent of time, and lie in the nature of things. Those only can efficiently resist the world who care not for its frown, and do not solicit its rewards. And all spiritual government implies sacrifice; when severed from sacrifice, it is false to its Original, and so bereft of His power. Those who represent Him in His work of governing souls must follow Him; and "to follow is to imitate;" and it is precisely this imitation which marks the limit between the worldly and the unworldly, the natural and the supernatural.

When we pass from theory to fact, it is not without an effort that any mind can rise to the force of this phenomenon. In age after age through eighteen hundred years in all countries a certain portion of the human race is found to make the voluntary sacrifice of the heart's strongest affections to the service of God.[1] In all that innumerable multitude who have done so in these long centuries there was not one who could have continued this sacrifice to the end by force of any natural energy of character and his own determinate choice alone. Mere human

[1] I do not touch upon corruption existing at particular times and places, whether in the clergy or the monastic institute. This may be conceded,
"As in this bad world below
Noblest things find vilest using;"
but not only do I believe that the amount of corruption has been small in comparison with the whole mass; but, likewise, the abuse is no argument against the merit of those who "to noblest things give noblest using." And if the abuse of a thing were an argument against its use, what institution in the world could stand? *e.g.* marriage, or civil government. Think of the sufferings of wives from bad husbands, and of subjects from bad rulers, from the beginning of the world.

nature sinks under any such trial. Yet it has been done. The oblation of the heart made by him who lay on the Lord's breast, and was intrusted with His Virgin Mother, has been repeated in unnumbered instances down to him who died yesterday, bearing before the judgment-seat of the Virgin Son of the Virgin the imperishable lustre of his own virginal crown, the spotless raiment won for an eternity. One single such instance is a proof of the reality of a religion which no argument can gainsay; for it is a proof utterly beyond man's power, which triumphs over all the forces and dwarfs all the results of the richest civilisation. But the Christian Church possesses not one instance, but countless thousands of them in her long probation; nay, has been bold enough to count on the permanence of this spirit of sacrifice in her bosom, and to trust to it for nothing less than the propagation of her faith and influence among men; for she chooses this condition as a chief test of aptitude in her ministers for the execution of her functions, and so depends on it for a supply of those without whom she would cease to be.

And looking at this institution as adopted by the Clergy, who are charged with a supernatural work, we cannot but note the correspondence of the means with the end. Their work is the edification of believers, the conversion of unbelievers, the maintenance of the Christian faith. But herein nothing rests upon temporal motives or supports. These are objects not to be gained by a calculation of temporal rewards, and accordingly they are pursued by those who have on them the mark and seal of what is above nature.

But the Virginal Life runs naturally out into the

contempt of wealth and of ambition, into the renunciation of temporal goods, and of the pride which their attainment and enjoyment foster. And thus it appears complete and perfect in the institution of the religious life, which rests upon this triple sacrifice, and becomes thereby an offering to God of the whole man without reserve. The profession of virginity or continence having become the mark and distinction of the clergy,[1] not only continues with them, but passes on and is incorporated with these two cognate sacrifices, and so becomes the root of the associated religious life. The greatest teachers and bishops of the fourth century, St. Athanasius, St. Basil, his friend St. Gregory, in the East; St. Ambrose, St. Martin, and St. Augustine, in the West, themselves introduce this life by their example as well as by their precepts. No sooner had St. Augustine, upon his conversion, renounced the intention of marriage, than he drew together a number of like-minded friends, who with him also gave up the possession of private goods, and the pursuit of every object of temporal ambition. St. Basil and his friend St. Gregory had a generation before done this, with an earlier and more perfect choice, inasmuch as they had not first tasted the pleasures of the world. St. Athanasius, driven by persecution to Treves and to Rome, publishes a life of St. Anthony, and spreads throughout the West an admiration of the marvellous virtues which he had witnessed in the Fathers of the desert. By and by the great legislator of the monastic life in the West, St. Benedict, arises, who systematises for

---

[1] St. Jerome, *liv. Ep. ad Furiam*, tom. i. 283 A. "Quasi et ipsi aliud sint quam Monachi; et non quicquid in Monachos dicitur redundet in Clericos, qui patres sunt Monachorum."

all succeeding ages the religious institute, as based upon the three vows of continence, poverty, and obedience.

Let us state in the simplest and fewest words why the religious life rests upon these three vows.

It is a state of men who aim at Christian perfection. But this perfection consists in charity. Now there are four degrees of charity; the first is to love God as much as He is lovable, that is, with a love as infinite as Himself. This degree of charity belongs only to the three Persons of the Blessed Trinity. The second is to love Him not as much as He is lovable but as much as the creature can love Him; and in this consists the happiness of the Blessed, whether angels or men. The third degree is to love Him neither so much as He is lovable, nor so much as the creature absolutely is capable of loving Him, but so much as a mortal creature can love Him, who removes every impediment in the way of that love, and surrenders himself wholly to it. This is the perfection aimed at by the religious life. The fourth degree is to love Him less indeed than this, but yet so much as to love nothing more than Him, and nothing equally with Him. And this degree is enjoined upon all men.[1] The distinction between this degree and the former one is shown in that answer of our Lord to the young man who stated that he had kept all the commandments from his youth, and who asked what yet was wanting? To which the reply was, prefaced by the words that our Lord looked upon and loved him, confirming thereby the truth of his statement, that he had kept the commandments, "If thou wilt

---

[1] See St. Thomas, *opusc.* xviii. p. 115, and *opusc.* xix. p. 128; and Bellarmine, *de Monachis*, lib. ii. c. 2 and 3.

be perfect, go, sell all that thou hast, and give it to the poor, and thou shalt have treasure in heaven, and come, follow Me."

Now the fittest means for attaining this third degree of charity, the highest attainable in this life, are those three virtues of Continence, Poverty, and Obedience. For it consists in two things—the total surrender of the creature to God, and the removal of all obstacles in the way of this surrender. The surrender consists in giving Him the mind by means of obedience, the body and all its affections by means of continence, and outward things by means of poverty. And these virtues remove likewise the obstacles to this surrender, for they are all summed up in that cupidity which has its triple growth in the three concupiscences —the desire of the body, the desire of the eyes, and the pride of the world—which these virtues severally cut off and extinguish.

And inasmuch as this perfection aimed at is not a fleeting or changeable thing, but a durable state, which moreover derives its special value and excellence from its being a dedication of the creature to the Creator, and of he redeemed to the Redeemer, all these three virtues must be consecrated and ratified by a vow.

This is the permanent basis of the religious life, which then spreads itself out into three broad currents, subdivided into countless streams. For God can be loved in three ways—by contemplating Him, and the union arising from this; by serving Him in His members; and by the mixed life which joins the contemplation and the action of charity together.[1]

The contemplative life may be divided into many

---

[1] Bellarmine, *de Monachis*, lib. ii. c. 3, who gives the partitions of Orders assigned in the text.

forms: such were those of St. Anthony, St. Pachomius, St. Benedict, St. Basil, St. Romuald, St. Bruno.

The active life is plainly divisible into as many forms as there are works of charity, such as are the care of the sick, whether in hospitals, or from house to house; the visiting of prisoners, the redeeming of captives, the burial of the dead.

The mixed life may be equally varied, as we see it in the great Orders of St. Francis, St. Dominic, St. Ignatius, and so many others. These in particular have given themselves up with a most steadfast self-denial to the manifold work of education, becoming ever more complex and difficult with the advancing refinement of society, and demanding the more complete unselfishness as the empire of the world prevails.

Thus the particular institutions of the religious life may be as diverse as the natural bent of men, one to solitude, one to active life, one to study, one to labour, one to soothing the pains of the mind, another those of the body, and so on; but one and all rest, and rest necessarily, on the triple vow of Continence, Poverty, and Obedience. And of these the root,[1] that which makes the other two feasible in the conditions of human society, is the Virginal Life, which is a special imitation of our Lord and of His Mother.

The human soul surrendered up to its Maker, on the one hand, as these three virtues alone can surrender it, and delivered, on the other, from the anxieties of wealth, the care of a family, the turmoil of secular

---

[1] "Igitur per votum religionis abrenuntiatur illis quibus humanus animus maxime occupari consuevit, et a divinis obsequiis impediri. Quorum primum et principale est conjugium. Secundum est possessio divitiarum terrenarum. Tertium est propria voluntas, quia qui suæ voluntatis est arbiter solicitudinem habet de vitæ suæ gubernatione." St. Thomas, *opusc.* xix. p. 128.

ambition, can throw itself into works of charity for the good of others in forms as various as the needs of human misery, or its own natural bias and inclination. There is not a single work of mercy conceivable for the execution of which a religious institute may not be formed,[1] and very few indeed are there for which such institutes do not actually exist. But remove the tie of charity which encloses these hearts together in its triple bond, remove the vow which consecrates their condition, and makes it stable and permanent, remove the sacrifice which joins to God and severs from the world, then, even were it possible for the heart to remain the same, yet the efforts of each would be desultory, unconnected, often conflicting; the benefit of association and co-operation would be lost; continuity of action and singleness of aim would depart. But there is something beyond this. Who has not seen the Sisters of St. Vincent, as if vested with an unseen robe of mail bestowed by their religious consecration, pass among the other sex in the continual work of charity, with eyes and hearts so simply fixed upon that work that the very thought of danger comes not near them, as the thought of profanation comes not to those who meet them? And this spiritual independence, which is here so striking, because it rests upon those who mix largely with the world, belongs to the religious consecration as such and to all its various rules. Take it away, and woman would relapse into her natural condition of her sex's dependence; but with it, as Mary stood by the side of the Cross, so she stands in virtue of " the crucified life,"

[1] " Nec est aliquod opus misericordiæ ad cujus executionem religio institui non possit, etsi non sit hactenus instituta." St. Thomas, ut supra.

the tenderness of her sex unchanged, but a superhuman power supporting it within and guarding it without. If the heart therefore could remain the same, without the religious consecration, the place and work would be far different. But we know how far short of the truth this would be. It is impossible for the heart to remain the same without the bracing of this triple bond. The innate selfishness of man would resume its sway when the power of the three concupiscences should be set free, and that total surrender to God withdrawn. The law of civilisation is that each one labour for himself; it is the effect of Christian charity alone to labour for others without reward and at the cost of self.

Then consider how wonderful is the wide-spread and continuous fecundity of the religious life. It is not a transient ardour of devotion springing up and then dying away, but a fountain perpetually welling forth in all ages and countries. Take one instance as a specimen. St. Benedict lived in the middle of the sixth century. There are said to have been already thirty-seven thousand religious houses which own him as their remote or immediate patriarch. But the Benedictine sap is not yet dried up, and hundreds of these houses counted each a life of centuries, and how many souls in each who lived and died under that rule. Yet the spiritual progeny of St. Augustine may almost vie with that of St. Benedict in number, since it has counted as many as one hundred and fifty different variations of his rule,[1] fighting under his standard; and the children of St. Francis, St. Dominic, and St. Ignatius, perhaps exceed it in the prodigious influence which they have exercised upon the world around. It

[1] Helyot, tom. ii. p. 1.

required eight large volumes more than a century since to give some account of the Religious Orders; and the mere catalogue of the different rules, their names, and descent, would confound with its multitude and intricacy. The internal life of each rule is a world by itself; the mass of the rules a universe, with its clusters of distinct stars; and in each star a crowd of souls, a crowd in number, yet every one distinct in its own grace and beauty, and because of this distinction rendering to the Sovereign a homage yielded by no other, who have all gone through life on the strength of that triple vow, giving their hearts to the King fair in form above the sons of men, despising the world because they were enamoured of the beauty of Him who made and redeemed the world, yet giving out to that world the fragrance of unceasing works of charity. More than fourteen centuries ago St. Augustine wrote a treatise upon holy Virginity. It may be termed in strictest truth a manual of history setting forth the principles illustrated in the lives of a vast, innumerable multitude since his time: a manual of a history which is not yet closed, nor shall ever be closed while man lives upon the earth. So permanent in its marvellous beauty and its unrivalled fecundity is that superhuman love, reflected by Him who was despised by man for man's sake upon the souls who choose Him for their own portion instead of earthly wealth, affection, and honour. Such the multitudinous variety of those virginal choirs whose song St. Ambrose described as attuned by Mary at their head, the song of triumph that they had passed over the flood of the world without being tossed by its billows. How, he cries, will She embrace each one, and lead them before the Lord, exclaiming, Here is one who has kept her nuptial faith with my Son!¹

We can now recur to the rule of Virginity or Continence as manifested through all the centuries of the Christian Church in two great permanent institutions, manifested as a condition of the clerical life, as the basis of the religious life. Its own character, its intrinsic excellence, we have touched upon; its source, in the conduct of our Lord and of His Mother; its special consecration as a following of their example. Now let us view it in another light, and note its correspondence in the spiritual order to marriage in the natural order. Exactly as marriage provides for the animal increase of the race, the Virginal Life, with its subordinate form the Life of Continence, provides for the propagation of the Christian society. For this depends on the work of the Clergy and the Religious Orders. Of the latter the Virginal Life is simply the basis; of the former it is the necessary condition for all freedom from worldly ties, for zeal, for energy, for endurance, for independence of wealth, for deliverance from ambition; for all, in short, which makes it a divine and not a human institution, an office representing Christ, not a profession of life. Let us consult history again, and the witness of eighteen centuries. By whom was the Christian faith first spread over the Roman empire in the three quarters of the world which border on the Mediterranean Sea? Who made Europe, and Asia, and Northern Africa Christian? Missionaries who lived in continence, whether they were Apostles, Evangelists, Bishops, or

---

[1] "O quantis illa virginibus occurret, quantas complexa ad Dominum trahet, dicens, Hæc torum Filii mei, Hæc talamos nuptiales immaculato servavit pudore." *De Virg.* lib. ii. 2, 16.

Priests; and men in religion who added the sacrifice of individual wealth and a strict profession of obedience to the life of continence. Who went forth from age to age to enlarge the bounds of the Christian society? Who ruled the Christian flock of believers at home? Who were eminent for the defence of the Faith against a series of emergent heresies? Whose writings, labours, and sufferings edified the faithful and converted the unbelieving? These, and these alone: an unmarried Clergy and Religious Orders of men and women. One was their sharp weapon for conflict with the world: one the power of their Lord in them: one the seed which should spring up, but scarcely ever before it had been watered by their blood, into endless harvests, ever new: that complete surrender of themselves of which the Virginal Life is the mark and seal. Thus alone souls have been governed and directed; thus alone the Christian Faith preserved intact; thus alone heathen men converted. And this is the triple work of propagation, the maintenance of the Christian people, their extension, and the safe guardianship of that by which they live, their Faith, the body of divine truth which they inherit and bear on.

In this work of propagation evils are to be overcome and obstacles removed which continually demand the sacrifice of wealth, whether in the form of not possessing it or not aiming at it, or of surrendering it when possessed, in which is included the giving up of that ease and comfort which belong to the placid enjoyment of wealth; and not this only, but the sacrifice of bodily health and strength, and of the heart's affections; the sacrifice again of the will, by submitting it to labours of every kind, to which it is naturally repugnant; and lastly, the sacrifice of life itself by exposing it to manifold risks beyond the measure of a man's natural lot. But these are the very goods for which in the natural constitution of the world men labour. To obtain independence, wealth, rank, distinction, and honour; to preserve health and strength; to gratify the domestic affections; to found and maintain a family; to crown our human life with its natural circle of joys; these are the motives by which society is kept together and impelled. What power is there that can ask it to sacrifice these things, or what can be substituted for them? The Christian Faith alone in the history of the world has asked for this sacrifice, and alone has received it. And the preliminary condition of it is, that solemn profession of the life of continence which is exhibited in the Clergy and the Religious Orders.

If we examine, we shall find that the human society has one motive power for its actions—the love of money; and the divine society another—the love of God. For instance, how will the human society deal with the teachers of religion? It will consider them as engaged in a profession; one demanding indeed certain intellectual and moral qualifications, but still a profession. It will calculate the value which such qualifications command, and endeavour to give this value in a combination of social position, and the advantages arising from it, with money. It will boast of putting a gentleman in each parish to diffuse the refinements of social life, and exhibit the results of temperance, kindness, and all the civic virtues in his own person. It will connect such teachers by means of marriage with the great mass of the middle and upper classes throughout the country, and so give these classes a sort of personal and domestic interest in the stability of religion; thus calling forth a homage to all that is respectable and dignified, all the more cordial on the part of the givers, because no slight temporal advantage and convenience will be connected with it. This in countries where the Christian religion has been established and prevails. But should it attempt to propagate that religion into heathen countries, what measures will it take? Viewing religion as the chief means of civilising men, by introducing order, peace, industry, commerce, and prosperity, it will endeavour to attract agents by the offer of competent salaries and adequate social position, who may exert in these new countries a similar influence to that possessed by the ministers of religion at home. Thus the missionary will have a profession by which himself, his wife, and children may live abroad,[1] as the clergyman at home; and his business will be to teach religion, as that of the lawyer is to regulate men's civil contracts, and that of the physician to cure their bodily diseases.

Again, if there be any great work of which the pre-eminent importance will be acknowledged by the human society, it is the work of education. It will feel instinctively that the whole structure of civilised life is built thereon. Accordingly it will especially encourage those who communicate knowledge in all its branches. And how will it do this? By the great power which it sways, the power of remuneration. The work of education will be costly. Men will live in comfort and flourish by it as a profession.

[1] There is a missionary society which has gone so far as to bestow an increased salary on the missionary for every child born to him.

And thus, in the race for success, the competition for honour and wealth, great energies will be evoked, and distinguished results attained. Learning in the various arts and sciences, and the application of them to the purposes of life, will carry with it both rank and profit; and therefore learned men in all these will abound.

Nor will the human society neglect the works of mercy, which not only approve themselves to the natural feelings, but enter into the true doctrine of political economy. It will have hospitals admirably conducted as to the medical treatment of the patients and their material conveniences. Whatever means to such an effect wealth liberally poured forth can command, it will have; salubrious buildings, able physicians, well-instructed nurses, duly-provisioned chaplains. In such houses acts of kindness, zealous labours by day and night, abound. Only the basis of them all, that without which they would not exist, is, in some shape or other, adequate remuneration.

Such is the triple work of religion, education, and charity in the hands of the human society. It proceeds on the principle of regulating the natural desires of man for pleasure, wealth, and honour, giving, as it were, a fitting standard to the three concupiscences, guiding them into a good channel, and so disarming them of that fatal power wherewith they can hurry men to violent contests and mutual destruction.

How, in the meantime, does the divine society set about the same triple work?

First, as to the maintenance and propagation of religion. Now, the divine Founder of our Faith uttered some words to its first ministers which do not seem exactly to convey the sort of position assigned above to the ministers of religion by the human society. He said, "I send you forth as lambs among wolves." "Take nothing for the way." "Carry neither purse, nor scrip, nor sandals."[1] There is a notion of sacrifice and suffering conveyed here which was quite absent from the former position. And how did those whom He sent forth interpret His words? Far from seeking a home for themselves, and the possession of a house and family, and so endeavouring to act upon society as examples of decorum and respectability while they propagated the faith in a crucified God with which they were charged, one of their first acts was willingly to cut themselves off from the possibility of this. Clearly they sought not to influence others by an exhibition of the family life, for it was specifically this life which they renounced. As clearly they sought not the influence of wealth, for they considered it as the most dangerous snare, and chose to be poor. And as for human honour, their portion for ten generations was, more than all other Christians, to be outcasts, the refuse of men, as one of their chief leaders calls them. And by carrying out these three things they planted the Christian Faith through the Roman Empire. At length, when the Cross, from having been the gibbet of the slave, was woven into the standard of kings, and became the fairest ornament of their diadem, honour followed likewise to the special champions of the Cross, and gifts of piety surrounded them. But they still kept a guard against both by that signal mark of their Lord upon their bodies, the profession of the unmarried life. Still in this form they refused to take provision for the way, to furnish themselves with purse, scrip, or sandal;

[1] Luke x. 3; Mark vi. 8.

the way was still the way to them, not a home; a
journey, not a rest. And because it was so, and just
so far as it was so, they found an entrance into all
lands, and lived in the hearts of their people, and continued on, not by a carnal but by a spiritual generation, drawing to them from age to age the flower of
their flocks, the noble in mind, and the strong of
heart, who could choose that way of violence, and take
the kingdom by force. They do not therefore cultivate a profession, but perpetuate a sacrifice; they do
not recommend civil decency and social virtues, but
the crown of thorns on the head of Him whom they
follow has flourished on their head into the coronet of
the Virginal Life.

In virtue of this one institution in the Clergy and
the Religious Orders, the whole work of maintaining
the Catholic Faith and of propagating it has been
through eighteen centuries and is a work of divine
love, and not of human remuneration. It proceeds
and lives not by tempering the three concupiscences,
but by overcoming them. As St. Paul went forth
with Silvanus, Luke, Titus, and Timotheus, and each
city produced a Thecla as the answer of his teaching,
so now on the emigrant ship may be seen the missionary bishop and his attendant priests, and with
them likewise St. Thecla's representatives and successors, the Sisters of Mercy and Charity, and of so
many other religious rules, bearing to distant lands
their unbought love, unsalaried labours, and fruitful
sufferings. India, China, and Australia know them,
and recognise them now, as France, Spain, Germany,
and England knew them and recognised them of old;
and what the work of the past has been, the work of
the future shall be. But if they have done this of

old, and if they do it still, it is solely in virtue of the Virginal Life, and its attendant grace and strength, which they have chosen.

And inasmuch as there is in the religious life a special inspiration, which blows where it lists, and with unequal aspirations, this supernatural element is guided and administered by the unity and equability of the Church's spiritual rule. What is needed is a moderating hand, which shall distribute and apply the force which works through these various rules on the common basis of the three vows, and their root, the profession of celibacy. And the more so because these Orders have their own distinct impulse, as each plant that distinct life which draws it into the shape and produce proper to it; and again, because the life being something above and beyond nature, while it works in those subject to nature, has inequalities, excesses, and failures by turns. Therefore the guiding power arranges and orders the work and the field of work for each. The supremacy of spiritual jurisdiction, being necessarily one over the whole Church, because the Church is one, like an experienced general, directs the plan of the whole battle with the world, holds its reserves in hand, and so produces, from a source uncertain in the individual, but regular in the universal, that equable movement of discipline, that continual supply of forces, which is necessary to maintain action on any great scale, and which secular government rightly looks for in the work of teaching its people. Within the last two generations a great neighbouring nation has seen the Church, after losing, together with the proscription of her Clergy and her Religious Orders, the whole of her property, both that which belonged to her secular and that which belonged to her regular

Clergy, reproduce, as it were, anew the whole machinery requisite for the teaching of a people, springing up with the vigour of fresh youth, amid poverty and trial of every kind, from the inexhaustible root of religious celibacy.

Secondly, the work of education has ever been in the divine society one not of profit but of devotion, a dedication of the best gifts of mind and heart to the service of others. The function of teaching is one specially belonging to the Clergy and the Religious Orders. The time which they have gained by withdrawing from the pursuits and pleasures of the world they have freely bestowed on imparting knowledge. Who shall describe the patient sacrifice of long years in the flower of life given up to the instruction of youth by so many priests, by so many religious of both sexes? When their own inward life had been formed, this was their work in all the period from opening manhood to middle age, at the time that energy of mind and body is freshest; a work not pursued for praise or emolument, but simply to communicate to others what they had themselves received. Thus, during the Benedictine centuries, a period of at least five hundred years, the monasteries of that Order sowed Europe with spiritual seed. Each of these were centres of intellectual power and moral training, where the Christian life was first cultivated in its highest perfection, and then disseminated among the surrounding population. In the thirteenth century the Franciscan and Dominican Orders infused fresh vigour into this great work. In the sixteenth the Jesuits instituted a new and more perfect system of intellectual training, and became the founders

CREATION OF THE VIRGINAL LIFE 315

of modern education. Their schools were for a long time the most celebrated in Europe; their course of studies the most complete. And what these Orders did for one sex a multitude of religious congregations did for the other. None of these teachers had in view the making private fortunes for themselves: their own rule of life rendered such a purpose impossible. Accordingly the education which they gave was not costly, but so far as the expenditure of their own labour and the gift of their own talents were concerned, was even gratuitous. The pupils might pay for their own maintenance, but not for the value of their teachers' accomplishments. Thus teaching never became a livelihood, but remained a spiritual work of mercy. In this way the great institution of the Virginal Life fulfilled throughout the divine society the office of spiritual parentage. As from father and mother came the life of nature, so from it came the life of human science and divine knowledge; and the words of a great writer in the fourth century have been fulfilled over more than a thousand years in innumerable instances: " Christ is born of a Virgin: ye women, cultivate the Virginal Life, that you may become mothers of Christ."

But thirdly, works of corporal mercy have ever in the divine society fallen to the special lot of those who professed the Virginal Life. Acts of Parliament may establish poor-laws, by the operation of which, for the first time in the history of the world, those who are relieved will conceive for their supporters not love but hatred, and abodes for the poor be created, over the door of which the poor see written, " Who enter here must leave all hope behind." Voluntary subscriptions may even support hospitals of great efficiency as to the material aid of food and medical treatment. But to clothe the naked, feed the hungry, minister to the infirm, seeing in each one an image of Christ, to be treated with tenderness and honour; this, as a rule, and gratuitously, has been done by no class of men or women save those who have first made to God the sacrifice of the virginal, or at least the continent life; nor is there a single work of mercy, to repeat again the words of St. Thomas, for the execution of which a religious institution may not be formed, even if it be not yet formed. A single community, among the multitude created by the divine society, may serve to represent all this class of works, that of the Sisters of St. Vincent of Paul. From their central house in Paris they have gone into all lands, winning hearts, while they minister to bodily needs. Not from them do the poor turn with dread of their charity. Even the Mahometan revilers of their Faith have learnt to reverence the fold of their garments, from experience of the spirit which it covers. But for all this dedication of self for the good of others, force is given by the profession of the unmarried life. Thus alone is it rendered possible. Thus alone as a fact does it exist. And this is the secret of that unrepining cheerfulness which attends on their ministration, and communicates itself to others by the secret sympathy of charity.

Now the noblest works for the good of others in which man can be engaged fall under these three classes: that of maintaining and propagating religion; that of forming the human character by education; that of administering to human infirmities by acts of mercy. And the evidence of history, by induction from many times and countries, is this, that wherever the Virginal Life does not exist as an institution, these works, if pursued, are only pursued as a profession. They may be followed with much zeal and ability, and even with considerable success ; but still it will be as a means of livelihood; not for the sake of others, but for the sake of self. Remuneration in some shape will be their motive power. And no less does it follow from the evidence of history, that where the Virginal Life is cultivated, and exhibits itself in various institutions, it will throw itself especially upon these three classes of works. The dedication and sacrifice which lie at the root of it will communicate themselves to these works, as conducted by it, will give to them a high and superhuman character, a power of attraction over the hearts of men, which come from that divine Original of sacrifice, whose signet is the Virginal Life. And in this case no human remuneration will be the spring of these works ; neither praise, nor power, nor wealth, nor pleasure will call them forth or reward them. Rather they will flourish amid poverty, self-denial, and humility, in those who exercise them, and be the fruit not of political economy but of charity.

III. A great Christian writer, who stood between the old pagan world and the new society which was taking its place, and who was equally familiar with both, made, near the end of the fourth century, the following observation :[1] "The Greeks have had some men, though it was but few, among them, who, by the force of philosophy, came to despise riches ; and some, too, who could control the irascible part of man ; but the flower of Virginity was nowhere to be found among them. Here they always gave precedence to us, confessing that to succeed in such a thing was to

[1] St. Chrysostom, tom. i. 249 A.

be superior to nature, and more than man. Hence their profound admiration for the whole Christian people. The Christian host derived its chief lustre from this portion of its ranks." And again he notes the existence in his time of three different sentiments respecting this institution: "The Jews," he says,[1] "turn with abhorrence from the beauty of Virginity, which indeed is no wonder, since they treated with dishonour the very Son of the Virgin Himself; the Greeks, however, admire it, and look up to it with astonishment; but the Church of God alone cultivates it." After fifteen hundred years we find the same sentiments in three great classes of the world. The pagan nations among whom Catholic missionaries go forth reproduce the admiration of Greek and Latin pagans; they reverence that which they have not the strength to follow, and are often drawn by its exhibition into the fold. But there are nations who likewise reproduce the Jewish abhorrence of the Virginal Life. And as the Jews worshipped the unity of the Godhead, like the Christians, and so seemed to be far nearer to them than pagan idolaters, and yet turned with loathing from this product of Christian life, so these nations might seem from the large portions of Christian doctrine which they still hold to be nearer to Christianity than the Hindoo or the Chinese; and yet their contempt and dislike of the Virginal Life and its wonderful institutions seems to tell another tale. But now, as fifteen hundred years ago, whether men outside admire or abhor, the Church alone cultivates the Virginal Life. Now, as then, it is her glory and her strength, the mark of her Lord, and the standard of His power, the most *special* sign of His

[1] St. Chrys., περὶ παρθενίας, i. tom. i. 268.

CREATION OF THE VIRGINAL LIFE 319

presence and operation. If, says the same writer,[1] "you take away its seemliness and its continuity of devotion, you cut the very sinews of the Virginal Estate: so, when it is possessed together with the best conduct of life, you have in it the root and support of all good things. Just as a rich, fruitful soil nurtures a root, so a good conduct bears the fruits of Virginity. Or, to speak with greater truth, the crucified life is at once both its root and its fruit." Which words we may interpret to mean that the special imitation of our Lord, which gives birth to it, likewise leads it on to unworldliness, piety, and disregard of everything which fetters the soul's free flight to its Maker.

Nor is it possible that such an example, produced again and again in the midst of society, should not have a wide effect beyond those in whom it works, and beyond all the works which it produces, though these be the fairest fruits of denying self in behalf of others. How great is the number of those who have been hurried away by the passions of youth and the seductions of sense into all sorts of disorder, who yet have had, by the example of this superhuman life, impressed upon them, all through this riot of passion, the sense and the craving for better things! And when the time of awakening comes, how often has the victim of the world become the victim of divine love! and one who, without this standard of purity, self-denial, and unworldliness set up continually before her eyes, would have ended at best with a skin-deep repentance, becomes through long years a model of penance, from a Duchess de la Vallière, Sister Louisa of Mercy. How often has the Carmelite, Benedictine, Dominican, or

[1] περί παρθενίας, lxxx. 332.

Franciscan robe covered hearts the sublimity of whose penitence has rivalled the fairest fruits of innocence? as in the long line of the Church's doctors none shines with so bright a light as he who wasted many years of his youth among the false pleasures of Carthage, but who, when the moment of conversion came, was wrought upon not by the Christian life in the exhibition of common virtues, but by the tale of those two youths who, being in the Emperor's court, with fair prospects and affianced brides, were moved to give up all this by meeting with a little book containing the life of St. Anthony in the desert. Of such conversions history during eighteen hundred years has been full. They are due to the glorious and enchanting light which the Virginal Life casts out beyond itself into the darkness of the world around. It is the sight of those who pass over the ocean of the world without being tossed by its billows (to quote again the words of St. Ambrose) which kindles the ray of hope and then of desire in so many souls all but merged in the waves, and moves them to seek that haven of peace.

Thus the honour and excellence of Virginity, springing forth from the very cradle of Christianity and the Person of its Author, are found in the course of centuries to be a new element communicated to human life, of power sufficient to make society other than it was before its introduction. Its work on each individual heart we have touched upon; but on its collective work a few words remain to be said. When we glanced over Europe as it was under the brilliant civilisation of the reign of Augustus, we found it in possession of great material prosperity, of a general peace and an advancing commerce. Examined more accurately from the moral point of view, society is seen to be dominated by the three main desires of the human heart—the love of pleasure, the love of wealth, the love of honour. There is no resistance anywhere to these desires; they are in full possession of man.

Look again upon Europe at the end of fifteen centuries, and what do we see? A circle of kindred nations has sprung up, possessing similar political and social institutions, and one religion. In all the countries from the Mediterranean to the farthest inhabited northern land, great houses are found in which men and women severally dwell, who have, under different rules, each by a distinct solemn act accepted and bound themselves to the Virginal Life. These houses, springing up at various intervals in the preceding centuries, were each of them the fruit not of compulsion but of free choice; not imposed by force on the conquered, or established by means of taxes, but produced by the gifts of men in the first instance, continued on from generation to generation by such gifts, when men and women gave not only their wealth but themselves. These houses were one and all the fruit of a free choice in man of the supernatural over the natural; not a transient choice, but a choice for life; not a choice of one generation, but a choice of many. At that time there were houses which numbered thirty continuous generations of men among their inhabitants, who from age to age chose poverty instead of riches, humility and subordination to others, and resignation of their own will, instead of pride; purity and self-denial instead of bodily pleasures and the heart's affections. They were houses of penitence; houses of prayer; houses, too, of intellectual thought and training. They formed even collectively but a small portion of

the population, a portion replenishing itself by a
spiritual attraction, but sufficiently numerous that
there should not be a single range of country from
the north of Norway to the Straits of Gibraltar and
the sunny Cyclades, not a city or town within these
vast limits, which did not see at least one example of
a house wherein men or women lived together under
the triple vow of Continence, Poverty, and Obedience.
In these countries there was to be seen at times and
in various proportions violence, cruelty, and wrong,
shedding of blood, and sensual living; but there was
always, thanks to the institution on which we have been
dwelling, a higher and nobler example, bearing witness
against violence and worldliness, breathing peace, suggesting penitence, calling back the wandering, maintaining and supporting the innocent, or, what sums up
all this and much more in one word, exhibiting the
life of Christ on earth. For on what did these religious
houses live? What was their very reason for being?
Let everything else in the world be as before, but take
away one fact, that the Son of God had become Man,
had lived on earth and died for man, and these houses
would have had nothing to live upon, nothing which
should originally call them into being, nothing which
should support and prolong their life, nothing which
could enable them for a single year to exist. Their
poverty would have no meaning; their obedience no
bond; their continence no prototype; their vows no
constraining power, no influence of ever-present aid;
their austere life no justification and no attraction.
But given this one fact, and their life has found its
proper original, its standard, and its strength. From
the Incarnation they were born; upon it they lived;
in it they hoped; through it they flourished. They

are the progeny of the Virgin and the Virgin's Son. In them the creative Word of their Lord has found its perpetual execution: they have seen, loved, and followed Him, making themselves as He was for the kingdom of heaven by the force of a powerful will, which was their own, and yet His working in them, and stronger than earth's strongest things. Therefore in them the old prophecy of the sweetest prophet concerning Messiah's times is fulfilled, and they have given them in His house and within His walls a place and a name better than of sons and daughters. Theirs is something beyond even the inheritance of children, an everlasting name which shall never perish. For they are the carrying out through the long ages of Christendom in time and space of the very life which their Lord led on earth: they are those in whom even the pagan of old and now discerns and reverences the image of their Lord. St. Augustine has given us both the order of their birth and the power of their life. "No corporeal fecundity produces this race of virgins; they are no offspring of flesh and blood. Ask you the mother of these? It is the Church. None other bears these sacred virgins but that one espoused to a single husband, Christ. Each of these so loved that beautiful One among the sons of men, that, unable to conceive Him in the flesh as Mary did, they conceived Him in their heart, and kept for Him even the body in integrity."[1]

[1] St. Aug. *de s. Virginitate*, 11, 12.

INDEX

Afra, St., her martyrdom, 192-4.
Agnes, St., her martyrdom, 191.
Alexandria compared with Rome, 43.
Antioch compared with Rome, 42.
Athens compared with Rome, 41.
Augustine, St., his judgment on the moral state of Rome, 63.
    sketch of his life to his conversion, 157.
    his conversion, 159.
    death of his mother, 159.
    his genius and character, 166.
    how instinct with thought of Providence, 169.
    his doctrine of the City of God, 172.
    which is the first philosophy of history, 173.
    key to his life and writings in his treatise *De vera Religione*, 176-7.
Augustus, his effort to improve Roman morality by law, 241.

Cato of Utica, why not chosen as representative of Rome, 139.
Charity, the supreme Christian virtue, 110.
    infused by the Holy Spirit, 112.
    the soul and root of other virtues, 112.
    new to all the heathen nations, 113.
Christianity, its description by Diognetus, 180-4.
    restores the value of human life, 186.
    corrects heathen impurity, 189.
    elevates man's natural to a supernatural end, 195.
    gives inwardness to life and virtue, 199.
    transforms the natural virtues by the theological, 201.
    action on society by its Sacerdotium, 204.
    gives seven attributes to it, 207-220.
    what it had done in the first 400 years, 222.
    what it does for marriage, 225-269.

INDEX

Christianity, what it does for the Virginal Life, 273-323.
    creates obedience to civil government, 121.
    contrasts the human with the Christian commonwealth, 129-130.
Cicero, his choice as representing Rome, 144.
    sketch of his life and doctrines, 145.
    his treatise on social duties, 146.
    on the nature of the gods, 150.
    his exile, 153.
    his daughter's death, 154.
    his conduct at the break-up of the republic, 155.
    his inferiority in natural genius to St. Augustine, 166.
    his statement of the one supreme law, 223.

EPICTETUS, why not chosen to represent heathenism, 141.

FAITH, Hope and Charity, their relation to Prudence, Justice, Temperance, and Fortitude, 109.
    which they complete and form, 201.

GOD, how the idea of Him was lost in heathenism, 67.
    His sevenfold idea restored, 91.
    His grace touches the individual, 184.

HEATHENISM, six points common to it in Greeks and Romans, 136-8.
History, its growth as a picture of human society and civilisation, 2-10.
    advanced by Christianity, 10-16.
    philosophic history, 16.
    its course from the Flood to the Advent of Christ, 78.

INDIVIDUAL, all Christian progress springs from the, 185.

JOHN, St., his picture of Roman civilisation, 76.

MAN, three things at once—a personality, a race, and a society, 225.
    his primary relation with woman, 226.
    his marriage instituted by God, the founder of human society, 227-230.
    of infinitely greater value than human society, 185.
    his imitation of one model, Christ, the source of all restoration to him, 185, 273.
Marcus Aurelius, his philosophy, 100, 140.

INDEX

PANTHEISM, 70.
Paul, St., his picture of Roman civilisation, 77.
    applies the Incarnation to all virtues of man, 107-126.
Pax Romana, its majesty, 36.
    its commerce, 37.
    its life at Rome in the baths, 38.
Personality of man lost in heathenism, 72.
    the one great subject with which the Christian faith dealt, 132, 225.
    that of Christ, the object on which all minds were centred, 273.
Peter, St., and his coming to Rome, 84.
    the execution and the banquet which he witnessed there, 83-4.
    what he rested on in his encounter with Rome, 85, 90.
✓ Philosophy of History, what it is, 1, 20.
    created by the Christian faith, 24.
    first instance in St. Augustine's *De Civitate Dei*, 26.
    second instance by Bossuet, 26.
    attempts at it by Guizot, 27; by Balmez, 28; by Frederic Schlegel, 28.
    Newman's history of the Turks, 29.
    Dante's statement of it, 32.
    sketch of it at present, 30-3.
Potamiæna, St., her martyrdom, 191.
Priesthood of the Church, its unity, uniformity, and universality, as derived from Christ, seen in seven attributes, 204-220.
    centred in the act of sacrifice, which constituted the Sacerdotium, 219.
    everywhere practised from the beginning, 220.

ROME, its legislation, 40.
    its citizenship, 44.
    its coloniæ, 45.
    its sovereignty, 47.
    its magistrates, 49.
    its language, 50.
    its slavery, 51-8.

SLAVERY at Rome, 51-64.

VIRGINAL Life springs from our Lord's personal character, 273.
    its influence illustrated by that of civilisation, 274.
    created by the Virginal Son of a Virgin Mother, 275.
    preluded by our Lady's choice of it, 276.
    its source a special imitation of Christ and His Mother, 278.

Virginal Life described by St. Methodius, 280.
    summed up by the great Fathers, 281.
    carried into practice through the world, 283-7.
    virgins called by St. Cyprian the brides of Christ, 284.
    by St. Athanasius, the image of angelic sanctity, 285.
    by St. Augustine the Church's race drawn from the example of Christ, 285.
    its office, the propagation of Christianity, 291.
    development in the secular clergy, 294.
    in the religious orders, 299.
    the three vows and their reason, 300.
    the Church's marriage, 306.
    distinguishes the divine from the human society, 308-315.
    raises the propagation of religion, works of mercy, and education, from a profession to an act of devotion, 316.
    a new element given to society, 320.
    what it made out of Europe, 321.

WOMAN, her first position, 227.
    her position at Rome under Augustus, 231.
    her original condition in Greece, 231.
    and in Rome, 230.
    and in Persia, 235.
    and in Israel, 235.
    and in the East and South, 237.
    and among the Germans, 237.
    ruined by divorce, adultery, and polygamy, 238.
    moral state of the world in consequence, 240.
    her restoration springs from the birth of our Lord, 246.
    and from the conduct of our Lady, 248.
    and is carried out by the Church through various times, 251-7.
    being the security of the family and of education, 261-6.
    as ranking with man as his companion, as the mother, as the nurturer and teacher, 269-271.

END OF VOL. I.

1898.

Selection

FROM

Burns & Oates'

Catalogue of Publications.

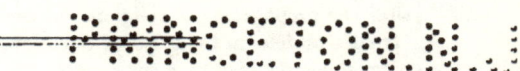

Messrs. BURNS & OATES have compiled the following Catalogues, which they will be happy to forward post free on application.

New Classified Catalogue of Standard Catholic Books (84 pages), comprising every class of book in demand among Catholic Readers.

Illustrated Catalogue of Catholic Prayer Books, Bibles, Manuals of Devotion, Hymn Books, etc., in English.

Catalogue of Liturgical Works in Latin, comprising Breviaries, Missals, and other books used in the Office of the Church, with an Appendix of Books relating to the Liturgy, Ceremonial, etc.

Catalogue of School Books and Stationery.

Illustrated Catalogue of School Furniture.

Illustrated Catalogue of Church Furniture, Vestments, Statuary, etc.

Illustrated Catalogue of Ecclesiastical Brass Work.

Lists of New English and Foreign Publications are issued periodically.

BURNS & OATES, LIMITED,
Granville Mansions, 28 Orchard Street, London, W.

Latest Publications
AND
Announcements.

New Testament. New large type Edition. Crown 8vo. Size, 7½ by 5 inches.
 Messrs. Burns & Oates have just issued an entirely New Edition with bold clear type. The volume contains some 500 pages, and is printed on specially selected paper. Of convenient size and in attractive binding, the Publishers confidently anticipate a large demand for this Edition, and are consequently issuing it at the extremely low price of TWO SHILLINGS. For further particulars see page 5.

Scripture Manuals for Catholic Schools. Edited by the Rev. SYDNEY F. SMITH, S.J.
 ACTS, Part I. By Very Rev. T. A. BURGE, O.S.B. Crown 8vo, boards. 2/- [*Ready.*
 ST. MATTHEW. By Rev. SYDNEY F. SMITH, S.J. [*In preparation.*
 A commentary on St. Mark will follow in due course. The other books of the new Testament are not required for examination purposes, but it will be a matter for later consideration whether they shall be included in the series to meet the needs of other readers.

Oxford Conferences. Given by Rev. JOSEPH RICKABY, S.J. Lent and Summer Terms, 1897. Stiff wrapper. 1/- net (postage 2d.). [*Ready.*

A Short History of the Catholic Church. By F. GOULBURN WALPOLE. Crown 8vo, cloth. 3/-. [*Ready.*

Carmel in Ireland. By the Very Rev. JAMES P. RUSHE, Prior of the Discalced Carmelites in Dublin. Crown 8vo, cloth. 3/6 net (postage 4d.). [*Ready.*

Imitation of Christ. By THOMAS A KEMPIS. A newly revised Translation, based upon Bishop Challoner's Text of 1737. Strongly bound in cloth, red edges. 6d. Roan, red edges. 1/-. [*Ready.*

Two Little Pilgrims. A Story for Children. By M. M. Cloth. 2/-. [*Ready.*

Bruno and Lucy. A Story from the German of W. HERCHENBACH. Cloth, gilt. 3/. [*Ready,*

India. A Sketch of the Madura Mission. By the Rev. H. WHITEHEAD, S.J. Cloth. Illustrated. 3/6. [*Ready.*

Life of St. Hugh of Lincoln. Translated from the French Carthusian Life and Edited with considerable additions by Rev. FR. THURSTON, S.J. Crown 8vo, cloth. Quarterly Series. [*In preparation.*

Life of Blessed John Avila. From the Italian of PADRE DEGLI ODDI. Edited by Rev. J. G. MACLEOD, S.J. Crown 8vo, cloth. Quarterly Series. [*In preparation.*

A Study of the Life of St. Augustine, Apostle of England. By the Right Rev. ABBOT BERGH, O.S.B. [*In preparation.*

The Divinity of Jesus Christ. From Pascal. With Commentary by Rev. W. B. MORRIS, of the Oratory. [*In the press.*

Life of Don Bosco, Founder of the Salesian Society. Translated from the French of J. M. VILLEFRANCHE by Lady MARTIN. New Popular Edition. Wrapper. 1/- net. [*Ready in January.*

St. Francis de Sales as a Preacher. By the Very Rev. CANON MACKEY, O.S.B. [*Ready shortly.*

Jewels of Prayer and Meditation from Unfamiliar Sources. By PERCY FITZGERALD, M.A. [*In the press.*

1898.

Selection

FROM

Burns & Oates'

Catalogue of Publications.

ALETHEA: At the Parting of the Ways. An Historical Tale, dealing with Christian Life in Constantinople in the Ninth Century. By Cyril (Canon Dennehy). Two Vols. Crown 8vo, cloth, gilt. 8/-.
"From the hill-top and the gutter-bottom, novels with their bad philosophy, bad manners, and bad grammar, from the religious sophistry and the rickety history of too much writing of the day, *Alethea* is indeed a relief. The religion in it is sound, its history historical, and its philosophy of life clean and worth looking into."—*Tablet.*

ALEXIS-LOUIS, PÈRE (O.C.D.).
Five Thrones of Divine Love upon the Earth, The. The Womb of Mary, the Crib, the Cross, the Eucharist and the Faithful Soul. From the French. Crown 8vo, cloth. 3/6.
"A book of devotion, consisting of a series of short readings or meditations, chiefly on the Incarnation, the Blessed Eucharist, the Crucifixion and the principles which underlie and govern the spiritual life, whether among the Priesthood, the cloistered Religious or the laity. The sum of the experimental knowledge of a Carmelite priest, it breathes the very inner spirit of St. John of the Cross, and contains the essence of affective theology."—*Monitor.*

ALLIES, T. W. (K.C.S.G).
A Life's Decision. Second and Cheaper Edition. Crown 8vo, cloth. 5/-.
"Interesting, not only in the way in which all genuine personal narratives are interesting, but also for the many letters from well-known persons that it contains. It is a valuable contribution to the history of the Anglican Church in the eventful years which followed Newman's secession."—*Guardian.*

THE FORMATION OF CHRISTENDOM SERIES.
Vol. I. The Christian Faith and the Individual. Popular Edition. Crown 8vo, cloth. 5/-.
Vol. II. The Christian Faith and Society. Popular Edition. Crown 8vo, cloth. 5/-.
Vol. III. The Christian Faith and Philosophy. Popular Edition. Crown 8vo, cloth. 5/-.
H. E. CARDINAL VAUGHAN says:—"It it one of the noblest historical works I have ever read. Now that its price has placed it within the reach of all, I earnestly pray that it may become widely known and appreciatively studied. We have nothing like it in the English language."
Holy See and the Wandering of the Nations, The. Demy 8vo, cloth. 10/6.
Peter's Rock in Mohammed's Flood. Being the Seventh Volume of Mr. Allies' great work on the "Formation of Christendom". Demy 8vo, cloth. 10/6.

ALLIES, T. W. (K.C.S.G.)—*(continued)*.

The Throne of the Fisherman, built by the Carpenter's Son. The Root, the Bond, and the Crown of Christendom. Demy 8vo, cloth. 10/6.

"The most important contribution to ecclesiastical history which has been given to the world for many a long day."—*Tablet.*

ALLIES, MARY.

Pius the Seventh, 1800-1823. Crown 8vo, cloth gilt. 5/-.

"Miss Allies has narrated the history of the long and memorable Pontificate of the first Pope of this century with a thoroughness of research and a dignity of style worthy of her illustrious father."—*Irish Monthly.*

Leaves from St. John Chrysostom. With Introduction by T. W. Allies, K.C.S.G. Crown 8vo, cloth. 6/-.

"The selections are well chosen, and Miss Allies' rendering is smooth, idiomatic, and faithful to the original. There is no existing book which is better adapted to make the English reader acquainted with the most eloquent of the Fathers of the Church."—*Dublin Review.*

History of the Church in England, from the Beginning of the Christian Era to the Death of Queen Elizabeth. In Two Vols. Crown 8vo, cloth. Vol. I. From the Beginning of the Christian Era to the Accession of Henry VIII. 6/- Vol. II. From the Accession of Henry VIII. to the Death of Queen Elizabeth. 3/6.

"Miss Allies has admirably compressed the substance, or such as was necessary to her purpose, of a number of authorities, judiciously selected. . . . As a narrative the volume is capitally written, as a summary it is skilful, and not its least excellence is its value as an index of the best available sources which deal with the period it covers."—*Birmingham Daily Gazette.*

ANNE, MRS. CHARLTON.

A Woman of Moods. A Social Cinematograph. Crown 8vo, fancy cloth. 5/-.

"Mrs. Charlton Anne's second work, and it marks her out as a novelist of undoubted originality and power. . . . She has scored a distinct success."—*Gentlewoman.*

"*A Woman of Moods* may be commended for its spirited picture of country life, and for its fresh and often suggestive handling of some very serious themes. The opinions expressed are bold and original, and expressed in a bright and entertaining way."—*Tablet.*

ARNOLD, REV. FR. (S.J.).

Imitation of the Sacred Heart of Jesus. In Four Books. New Edition. With a Notice of the Author by the Rev. Matthew Russell, S.J. Cloth. 4/6. Cloth gilt, red edges. 5/-. Calf, red edges, or in morocco, gilt edges. 8/6 each.

ARNOLD, THOMAS (M.A., Fellow of the Royal University of Ireland).

Notes on the Sacrifice of the Altar. Crown 12mo, cloth gilt. 1/6.

"In this well-printed and neatly bound little volume, Mr. Arnold has given a very useful treatise on the Mass. The end of the Holy Sacrifice is first explained. Then the author takes occasion to point out the essential difference between the Anglican service and the Mass. Lastly, Mr. Arnold, following the course of the ritual, brings out clearly the meaning and object of each part of the sacred function. In his illustrative remarks he imparts a good deal of interesting information."—*Catholic Times.*

CATALOGUE OF PUBLICATIONS. 5

BAKER, VEN. FATHER AUGUSTIN (O.S.B.).
Holy Wisdom (*Sancta Sophia*). Directions for the Prayer of Contemplation, etc. Edited by Abbot Sweeney, D.D. New and Cheaper Edition. Crown 8vo. Handsomely bound in half leather, xx., 667 pp. 6/-.
"The thanks of the Catholic public are due to Dr. Sweeney for re-editing this famous work. It does not belong to the catalogue of ephemeral publications. It is of a totally different standard. . . . To lovers of prayer and meditation it will be a most acceptable guide and friend."—*The Tablet.*

BELLASIS, EDWARD. (*Lancaster Herald.*)
Memorials of Mr. Serjeant Bellasis. New and Cheaper Edition. 8vo, 250 pp., bound in cloth. With fifteen Portraits and Illustrations. 6/-.
"A noteworthy contribution to the history of the Tractarian Movement."—*Times.*

BIBLES, etc.
N.B.—*For full particulars of Bindings, etc., see Illustrated Prayer Book Catalogue, sent post free on application.*
Holy Bible. POCKET EDITION (size, 5¼ by 3¼ inches). Embossed cloth, red edges, 2/6 ; and in leather bindings, from 4/6 to 7/6. MEDIUM EDITION (size, 7¼ by 4¾ inches). Cloth, 3/6 ; and in leather bindings, from 6/- net to 10/6 net (postage 6d.). OCTAVO EDITION (size, 9 by 6 inches). Cloth, 6/- ; and in a great variety of leather bindings, from 8/- to 35/- net. Family Editions in quarto and folio Prices upon application.
New Testament, The. POCKET EDITION. Limp cloth. 6d. (postage 2d.). Cloth, red edges, 1/-. Roan, 1/6. Paste grain round corners, 3/-. Best calf or morocco, 4/6 each. ROYAL 8vo EDITION (size, 9 by 6 inches). Cloth, 1/- net (postage 3d.). NEW MEDIUM EDITION. Crown 8vo (size, 7½ by 5 inches). Large type. 500 pp. Cloth, boards, gilt lettered, 2/-. Paste grain, limp, round corners, red or gold edges, 4/6. German calf, limp, round corners, red under gold edges, 8/6. Morocco, limp, round corners, red under gold edges, 8/6. Also in better bindings for presentation.
Book of Psalms, The. Translated from the Latin Vulgate. Revised by Cardinal Wiseman and Edited by Very Rev. Dr. Richards. Ninth Edition. 32mo, cloth, red edges, 1/6. Best calf, red edges, 5/-.

BLESSED SACRAMENT, OUR GOD; or, Practical Thoughts on the Mystery of Love, The. By a Child of St. Teresa. Cloth gilt. 1/-.

BRIDGETT, REV. T. E. (C.SS.R.).
Discipline of Drink, The. An Historical Inquiry into the Principles and Practice of the Catholic Church regarding the Use, Abuse, and Disuse of Alcoholic Liquors, especially in England, Ireland, and Scotland from the 6th to the 16th century. With an Introductory Letter by H. E. Cardinal Manning. Fcap. 8vo, cloth. 3/6.
Life and Writings of Blessed Thomas More, Lord Chancellor of England and Martyr under Henry VIII. With Portrait of the Martyr taken from the Crayon Sketch made by Holbein in 1527. Second Edition. Crown 8vo, cloth. 7/6.

BRIDGETT, REV. T. E. (C.SS.R.)—*(continued).*

Life of the Blessed John Fisher. With a reproduction of the famous Portrait of Blessed John Fisher by Holbein, and other Illustrations. Second Edition. Crown 8vo, cloth. 7/6.

Lyra Hieratica: Poems on the Priesthood. Collected from many sources by the Rev. T. E. Bridgett, C.SS.R. Fcap. 8vo, cloth. 2/6 net (postage 3d.).
"The idea of gathering an anthology of Poems on the Priesthood was a happy one, and has been happily carried out. Priests and laity alike owe a debt of gratitude to Father Bridgett for the many beautiful things he has brought together."—*Tablet.*

Our Lady's Dowry. How England gained that Title. New and Revised Edition. Illustrated. Crown 8vo, cloth extra, gilt top, 506 pp. 5/-.
The Cardinal Archbishop of Westminster says: "The most excellent, the most interesting, and the most original work of its kind, and for its purpose, that has been published in the English language."

Ritual of the New Testament. An Essay on the Principles and Origin of Catholic Ritual in Reference to the New Testament. Third Edition. Crown 8vo, cloth. 5/-.
"It is solid and most useful, and deserving of high commendation as a mine of sacred learning."—*Catholic World.*

The True Story of the Catholic Hierarchy deposed by Queen Elizabeth, with fuller Memoirs of its Last Two Survivors. By the Rev. T. E. Bridgett, C.SS.R., and the late Rev. T. F. Knox, D.D., of the London Oratory. Crown 8vo, cloth. 7/6.
"We gladly acknowledge the value of this work on a subject which has been obscured by prejudice and carelessness."—*Saturday Review.*

Wisdom and Wit of Sir Thomas More, The. Edited, with Introduction, by Rev. T. E. Bridgett, C.SS.R. Crown 8vo, cloth. 5/-.
"Every page in this delightful volume bespeaks the master hand, the clear head, the deep and tender heart. It is lively, eloquent, impressive, genial; without stiffness or parade of learning, but as full of good things as it can hold."—*Catholic Times.*

BOWDEN, REV. H. S. (of the Oratory), edited by.

Dante's Divina Commedia: Its Scope and Value. From the German of Franz Hettinger, D.D., Professor of Theology at the University of Würzburg. Second Edition. Crown 8vo, cloth. With an Engraving of Dante. 10/6.
"We rise from the reading of Dr. Hettinger's book knowing Dante, and, we will add, loving him, as we have never known or loved him before. . . . The translation is exceedingly well done. There is not a dry, or ill-written, or uninteresting page in the book from beginning to end."—*Month.*

Miniature Lives of the Saints, for every Day in the Year. Twentieth Edition. Two Vols. 18mo. cloth gilt, 767 pp. 4/-. Also, in Packets of Single Leaves for distribution, each Packet containing the Lives of the Saints for One Month. 4d. per Packet. Or, the Complete Set of Packets for the year. 3/6.

Natural Religion. Being Vol. I. of Dr. Hettinger's "Evidences of Christianity". With an Introduction on "Certainty". Second Edition. Crown 8vo, cloth. 7/6.

BOWDEN, REV. H. S. (of the Oratory), edited by—(*continued*).
  Revealed Religion. The Second Volume of Dr. Hettinger's
    " Evidences of Christianity ". With an Introduction on the " Assent
    of Faith ". Crown 8vo, cloth. 5/-.
    " The two together (' Natural Religion ' and ' Revealed Religion ') supply a real
    want in our Catholic literature. Nothing is more common nowadays than for a
    priest to be asked to recommend a book, written from a Catholic point of view, on
    the evidence for the Christian religion. And in future he will be able to recommend
    Father Bowden's ' Hettinger '. . . . It may be confidently affirmed that all who have
    taken interest in the war against religion raised by its modern adversaries will find
    in Father Bowden's pages many of their chief difficulties helpfully dealt with."—
    Month.

BROWNE, REV. R. D.
  Plain Sermons. Sixty-eight Plain Sermons on the Fundamental Truths of the Catholic Church. Crown 8vo, cloth. 6/-.
    " These are good Sermons . . . the great merit of which is that they might be
    read verbatim to any congregation, and they would be understood and appreciated
    by the uneducated almost as fully as by the cultured. They have been carefully put
    together ; their language is simple, and their matter is solid."—*Catholic News.*

BROWNE, MRS. INNES.
  Three Daughters of the United Kingdom. Crown 8vo,
    cloth, extra gilt. 5/-.
    " A very charming book for girls. The whole tone of the book is pure and elevating, and, at the same time, both characters and incidents, are pleasantly natural
    and home-like."—*The Lady.*

BROWNLOW, BISHOP.
  Memoir of Mother Rose Columba Adams, O.P., first Prioress of St. Dominic's Convent, and Foundress of the Perpetual Adoration at North Adelaide. With Portrait and Plates. Crown 8vo,
    cloth, 384 pp. 6/6.
    " It is a work of the deepest interest and edification. In a handsomely printed
    and beautifully illustrated volume, Bishop Brownlow tells us the story of a remarkable woman's life and work, drawing on his own recollections of her career,
    and with the help of her own letters and the reminiscences of many friends, giving
    us a life-like picture of a singularly earnest, devoted, and saintly soul."—*Tablet.*
  Lectures on Slavery and Serfdom in Europe. Crown 8vo,
    cloth. 3/6.
  Sir James Marshall, C.M.G., K.C.S.G., A Memoir of.
    Taken chiefly from his own Letters. Crown 8vo, cloth. 3/6.

BUCKLER, REV. REGINALD (O.P.).
  The Perfection of Man by Charity. A Spiritual Treatise.
    Second Edition. Crown 8vo, cloth. 5/-.
    " The object of Father Buckler's useful and interesting book is to lay down the
    principles of the spiritual life for the benefit of Religious and Seculars. The book
    is written in an easy and effective style, and the apt citations with which he enriches
    his pages would of themselves make the treatise valuable."—*Dublin Review.*

BURNAND, F. C.
  My Time, and what I've done with it. An Autobiography.
    Compiled from the Diary, Notes, and Personal Recollections of Cecil
    Colvin. With Portrait of the Author. Crown 8vo, cloth. 5/-.
    " Interweaves with a partly fictitious plot Mr. Burnand's impressions of his boyhood and youth, especially of that period which he spent at College. The author
    of *Happy Thoughts* is an acute analyst of the sensations and unconscious reflections
    of boyhood as well as of manhood. For various reasons, then, this volume will be
    found entertaining."—*The Times.*

BUTLER, REV. ALBAN.
  People's Edition of the Lives of the Saints. Twelve Pocket Volumes, each Volume containing the Saints of the Month. Superfine paper, neat cloth binding, gilt lettered. 1/6 each; or the complete set (comprising over 6000 pages), in handsome cloth case to match, 18/-.
  "If any inducement to spiritual reading can be given apart from the intrinsic merits of such a work as Alban Butler's *Lives of the Saints*, by volumes that are characterised by handiness of size, clearness of type, and neatness of appearance, that inducement ought assuredly to be supplied by this People's Edition of that standard work. Alban Butler's *Lives of the Saints* is a monument of painstaking labour, performed single-handed in difficult days; it is full of varied interest and information, and breathes a healthy spirit of Catholic piety; it has stood the test of time, and still holds its own as the best compendious hagiological work in our language."—*Tablet.*

CATHOLIC BELIEF: or, A Short and Simple Exposition of Catholic Doctrine. By Very Rev. Joseph Faà di Bruno, D.D. Sixteenth Edition. 18mo, 427 pp. Wrapper, 6d. net (postage 2½d.); cloth boards, lettered, 10d. (postage 2½d.). Also an edition printed on better paper and strongly bound in cloth. With Steel Frontispiece. 2/-.
  "One of the most complete and useful manuals of doctrine, devotion, and elementary information for the instruction of those who are seeking the truth; and not for them only, but for those who have inherited it."—*H. E. Cardinal Manning in Preface.*

CATHOLIC GIRL IN THE WORLD, THE. By Whyte Avis. With Preface by Rev. R. F. Clarke, S.J. Crown 8vo, buckram gilt. 3/6.
  "We cannot recommend too highly this treatise. It begins by laying down the first and only possible principle of social life—unselfishness. In each of the subsequent divisions—music, painting, dress, sick-nursing, and the rest—there is much good, sound advice, conveyed in a pleasant, readable fashion."—*Tablet.*

CAVANAGH, REV. PIUS (O.P.), edited by.
  Life of St. Thomas Aquinas, The Angelic Doctor. With eleven Illustrations. 8vo, cloth. 4/6.
  "An honest, faithful, and very readable account of the saint's life."—*Scotsman.*

CAVE, ROBERT HAYNES (M.A.).
  In the Days of Good Queen Bess: the Narrative of Sir Adrian Trafford, Knight, of Trafford Place in the County of Suffolk. Edited by the Rev. R. H. Cave, M.A. Crown 8vo, cloth gilt. 3/6.
  "A story, the unflagging interest of which is heightened by the sound knowledge and critical sagacity which has been called to its aid. We feel that living men and women are playing their part before us amid the surroundings of their own times. The style owes its power to a simple directness which is relieved with a humour, quiet indeed, but telling."—*Tablet.*

CHALLONER, BISHOP.
  Meditations for Every Day in the Year. Revised and Edited by the Right Rev. John Virtue, D.D., Bishop of Portsmouth. Seventh Edition. Crown 8vo, 554 pp., cloth. 3/-.

CHAMPAGNAT, FATHER, LIFE OF. Founder of the Society of the Little Brothers of Mary (1789-1840). By one of his first Disciples. Translated from the French. With five Illustrations. Demy 8vo, cloth, 525 pp. 8/-.
  "A work of great practical utility, and one eminently suited to these times."—*Tablet.*

CHRISTIAN VIRGIN IN HER FAMILY AND IN THE WORLD,
The. Her Virtues and her Mission at the Present Time. From the Third French Edition. Fcap. 8vo, half-bound in leather, gilt top. 6/-.
"Shows how all those who, whether from choice or necessity, are led to live with their families or alone in the world, may, by consecrating and sanctifying their state, lead a life, not only useful and meritorious, but amiable and pleasant to themselves and to society in general."—*Tablet.*

CLIFTON TALES. In Two Volumes. Fcap. 8vo, bright cloth. 6/-.
Containing: "James Chapman"—"Joe Baker"—"Lucy Ward"—"Rich and Poor"—"Robert May"—"The Poor Man's Child" and "Winefride Jones."
(The Tales may be had separately in paper wrapper, 6d. each. Cloth gilt, 1/- each.)

CLIFTON TRACTS. The English and Foreign Reformation, Historical Fallacies, Christian Doctrine and Miscellaneous Tracts. Complete in Two Vols. Globe 8vo, cloth. 9/-.
Extremely useful for lending libraries. Cardinal Manning frequently referred to this work as "the best series of tracts he knew".

Clifton Tracts, Selections from the. In limp cloth, gilt lettered, in handy form for lending.
Mary and Elizabeth, 1/-. Catholic Worship and Devotion, 1/-. Protestantism Weighed in its own Balance, 10d. The Church and the Bible, 9d. The Protestant Reformers: their Lives and Deeds, 10d. How the Popes obtained their Temporal Power, 8d. The Doctrine of the Sacrifice of the Mass explained, 8d. Rites and Ceremonies of the Church, 6d. Points of History: the Inquisition, the Gunpowder Plot, St. Bartholomew, &c., 1/-. Narratives and Dialogues. 1/. The Catholic Church in England before the Reformation, 8d.
(The Tracts may also be had separately. List on Application.)

COLERIDGE, REV. H. J. (S.J.) (*See Quarterly Series and Classified Catalogue*).

DALE, REV. J. D. HILARIUS.
Ceremonial According to the Roman Rite. Translated from the Italian of JOSEPH BALDESCHI. New and Revised Edition. Crown 8vo, cloth. 6/6.
"This work is our standard English directory on the subject. Few functions of any importance are carried on without a glance at it. It is a familiar guide and friend—in short, a classic."—*Catholic Times.*

The Sacristan's Manual; or, Handbook of Church Furniture, Ornament, etc. Fourth and Enlarged Edition. Crown 8vo, cloth. 2/6.

DE ANDRADE, ALONSO (S.J.).
Daily Meditations on the Mysteries of our Holy Faith, and on the Lives of our Lord Jesus Christ and of the Saints, for all Seasons of the Year. Four Vols. Fcap. 8vo, cloth. Each 3/6.
These Meditations are arranged in four points for each day of the year, commencing with the First Sunday in Advent.

DE CHÉRANCÉ, FATHER LEOPOLD (O.S.F.C.).
St. Anthony of Padua. Rendered into English by Rev. Fr. Marianus, O.S.F.C. With an Introduction by Rev. Fr. Anselm, O.S.F.C. Crown 8vo, brown boards, gilt. 2/6 net (postage 4d.).
"It is a book which will rank with the best works on hagiography."—*Catholic Times.*

D'EREMAO, REV. J. P. VAL (D.D.).
  The Hail Mary: or, Popular Instructions and Considerations on the Angelical Salutation. Crown 8vo, cloth. 3/6.

DE MONTFORD, BLESSED GRIGNON.
  Treatise on the True Devotion to the Blessed Virgin Mary. Father Faber's Translation. Seventh Edition. Fcap. 8vo, cloth. 2/-.
  Edited by the Cardinal Archbishop of Westminster, who says: I should be glad to see it in the hands of every priest, as experience has taught me the power of this most persuasive treatise in propagating a solid devotion to the Blessed Mother of God.

DE SÉGUR, MGR.
  Familiar Instructions and Evening Lectures on all the Truths of Religion. Second Edition. Two Vols. Fcap. 8vo, cloth. 3/- each.
  These familiar instructions, almost 200 in number, form a complete course of Christian doctrine, and a collection of very simple elementary lectures well adapted to the religious need of our times.

✓ **DEVAS, C. S. (M.A. Oxon.).**
  Studies of Family Life: A Contribution to Social Science. Crown 8vo, cloth. 5/-.
  "We recommend these pages and the remarkable evidence brought together in them to the careful attention of all who are interested in the well-being of our common humanity."—*Guardian.*

DE VERE, AUBREY,
  The Household Poetry Book. An Anthology of English-speaking Poets from Chaucer to Faber. With Notes and Portrait of the Editor. Neat cloth. 2/-.
  "We may most cordially recommend the 'Household Poetry Book'. It contains over three hundred pages of excellent verse. The editor's name may be accepted as a guarantee for the judgment and poetical insight with which the selection has been made."—*Month.*

DIGNAM, FATHER (S.J.).
  Conferences given by Father Dignam, S.J., with Retreats, Sermons and Notes of Spiritual Direction. With a Preface by His Eminence Cardinal Mazzella, S.J. Crown 8vo, cloth gilt. 6/- net (postage 4d.).
  "To our mind this third volume of Father Dignam's remains, if we may so style it, consisting of spiritual gems of special lustre and spiritual flowers of special attractiveness, contains very much that is not to be found in its predecessors, and that we are grateful to have saved for us from destruction."—*Tablet.*

DRANE, AUGUSTA THEODOSIA.
  History of England. For Family Use, and for the Upper Classes of Schools. New Edition, revised and corrected to date. Crown 8vo, cloth gilt, 830 pp. 6/-.
  The Very Rev. Canon Northcote, D.D., says in his preface to the volume: "Having used the book for several years in St. Mary's College, Oscott, I can testify to its success as an able and attractive introduction to English history for purposes of education, and I believe it has been found no less acceptable as a reading book for all classes."

  Knights of St. John. A Sketch of the Order of Knights Hospitallers, especially of their efforts to stem the Moslem Invasion of Europe, with an Account of Lepanto and the Siege of Vienna. Cloth gilt extra. 3/-.

DRANE, AUGUSTA THEODOSIA—*(continued)*.

Songs in the Night, and other Poems. Third Edition. Crown 8vo, cloth gilt. 5/-.

Three Chancellors, The. Contains Lives of William of Wykeham, William of Waynflete, and of Blessed Thomas More. Cloth gilt extra. 3/6. Also separately, Wykeham, 1/-; Waynflete, 1/-; More, 1/6.

ECCLESIASTICAL CHART OF THE CATHOLIC CHURCH, Giving full Information concerning the Popes, Councils, Fathers, Schisms, Heresies, etc., in proof of the Church's Teaching. Size, 3 ft. by 2 ft. Unmounted, 1/- net (postage 3d.). Mounted, for hanging upon a wall, 1/6 net (postage 4d.).
"It contains a marvellous mass of most useful information."—*Catholic Times.*

EMMERICH (SISTER).

Dolorous Passion of Our Lord Jesus Christ. From the Meditations of Anne Catherine Emmerich. With a Preface by the Abbé de Cazalès, and a Life of Anne Catherine Emmerich. Sixteenth Edition. Fcap. 8vo, cloth, 352 pp. 3/6.

The Flight into Egypt. From the Meditations of Sister Anne Catherine Emmerich. Translated from the French by George Richardson. Tastefully printed, and bound in cloth gilt. 3/-.
"Those who love the realistic in literature could hardly have a better instance of its felicitous use than that afforded in this volume."—*Catholic World.*

EYRE, MOST REV. CHARLES (Archbishop of Glasgow).

The History of St. Cuthbert: or, an Account of his Life, Decease, and Miracles. Third Edition. With Maps, Charts, etc. Royal 8vo, handsomely bound in cloth. 14/-.

FABER, FATHER.

All for Jesus: or, The Easy Ways of Divine Love. New Edition. Crown 8vo, cloth, 407 pp. 5/-.
Contents: The Interests of Jesus—Sympathy with Jesus—Love Wounded by Sin—Intercessory Prayer—The Riches of our Poverty—Minting Money—Thanksgiving—Praise and Desire—Purgatory, etc., etc.

Bethlehem. New Edition. Crown 8vo, cloth, 500 pp. 7/-.
Contents: The Bosom of the Eternal Father—The Bosom of Mary—The Midnight Cave—The First Worshippers—The Infant God—Soul and Body—Calvary before its Time—Heaven Already—The Feet of the Eternal Father.

Ethel's Book: or, Tales of the Angels. A New and Cheaper Edition. Beautifully bound in cloth, extra gilt, gilt edges. 2/6.

Growth in Holiness: or, The Progress of the Spiritual Life. New Edition. Crown 8vo, cloth, 464 pp. 6/-.
Contents: True Signs of Progress in the Spiritual Life—The Spirit in which we Serve God—What holds us back?—Patience—Human Respect—The Human Spirit—Spiritual Idleness—Prayer—Temptations—Scruples—The Right View of our Faults—True Idea of Devotion—Lukewarmness—Fervour—Discretion, etc. etc.

Hymns. Complete Edition. Crown 8vo, cloth, 427 pp. 6/-.

FABER, FATHER—*(continued).*

Notes on Doctrinal and Spiritual Subjects. Fourth Edition. Two Vols. Crown 8vo, cloth, 759 pp. 10/-.
Contents: Mysteries and Festivals—God and the Most Holy Trinity—The Holy Ghost—The Sacred Humanity of Jesus—Our Blessed Lord—The Passion—Our Blessed Lady and the Saints—The Faith and the Spiritual Life—The Church—Sacraments—Controversy—The Spiritual Life—Old Testament History—Special Occasions—Life—The Four Last Things—Purgatory.

Poems. Complete Edition. Crown 8vo, cloth, 582 pp. 5/-.
Contains over 200 poems on: The Styrian Lake—Memorials of a Happy Time—The Mourner's Death—Oxford—Hope—The Holy Angels—Birthday Thoughts—The Four Religious Heathens—Thoughts while reading History—The Four Gospels—Prince Armadis—The Feast of the Invention of the Holy Cross, etc., etc.

Sir Lancelot. A Legend of the Middle Ages. Crown 8vo, cloth, 347 pp. 5/-.
Contents: The Ash-Tree Hermitage—The Books—The Beautiful Year—The Journey—Black Combe—Spirit of the Sea—The Leprosy—The Confession—The Absolution—The Communion.

Spiritual Conferences. Eighth Edition. Crown 8vo, cloth, 403 pp. 6/-.
Contents: On Kindness in General—Kind Words, Thoughts, and Actions—On Death: its Aspects and Characteristics—Preparation for Death—A Death Precious in the Sight of God—On Self-deceit—Simplicity—Weariness in Well-doing—Why so little comes of Frequent Confession—Wounded Feelings, etc., etc.

The Blessed Sacrament: or, the Works and Ways of God. New Edition. Crown 8vo, cloth, 548 pp. 7/6.
Contents: Prologue—On Triumph—The Blessed Sacrament, the Greatest Work of God—The Blessed Sacrament, the Devotion of Catholics—The Blessed Sacrament, a Picture of God—The Blessed Sacrament, a Picture of Jesus—Epilogue—On Reparation.

The Creator and the Creature: or, The Wonders of Divine Love. New Edition. Crown 8vo, cloth, 416 pp. 6/-.
Contents: A new Fashion of an old Sin—What it is to be a Creature—What it is to have a Creator—Why God wishes us to love Him—Why God loves us—Our Means of loving God—Our Actual Love of God—In what way God repays our Love—The Easiness of Salvation—The Great Mass of Believers—The World—Our own God.

The Easiness of Salvation. Cloth gilt. 1/-.

The Foot of the Cross: or, The Sorrows of Mary. Crown 8vo, cloth, 432 pp. 6/-.
Contents: The Martyrdom of Mary—The Prophecy of St. Simeon—The Flight into Egypt—The Three Days' Loss—Meeting Jesus with the Cross—The Crucifixion—The Taking Down from the Cross—The Burial of Jesus—The Compassion of Mary.

The Precious Blood: or, The Price of our Salvation. Fifth Edition. Crown 8vo, cloth, 308 pp. 5/-.
Contents: The Mystery of the Precious Blood—The Necessity of the Precious Blood—The Empire of the Precious Blood—The History of the Precious Blood—The Prodigality of the Precious Blood—The Devotion to the Precious Blood.

The Life and Letters of Frederick William Faber, D.D. By Rev. John E. Bowden, of the Oratory. Third Edition. Crown 8vo., cloth, 447 pp. 6/-.
"We know no man who has done more to make the men of his day love God and aspire to a higher path of the interior life; and we know of no man who so nearly represents to us the mind and preaching of St. Bernard and St. Bernardine of Siena in the tenderness and beauty with which he has surrounded the names of Jesus and Mary."—*Dublin Review.*

FABER, FATHER—(continued).
    Father Faber's May Book. Compiled by an Oblate of Mary Immaculate. A New Month of May, arranged for Daily Reading, from the Writings of Father Faber. 18mo, cloth, gilt edges, with Steel Frontispiece. 2/-.
    A Brief Sketch of the Early Life of Frederick William Faber, D.D. By his Brother. Limp cloth. 1/-.

FANDER'S CATECHISM OF THE CATHOLIC RELIGION.
    Preceded by a Short History of Religion. By Rev. Joseph Deharbe, S.J. New Edition. Collated with the latest German Edition by the Most Rev. Archbishop Porter, S.J. Fcap. 8vo, cloth. 2/-.

FAWKES, REV. ALFRED.
    Sacred Heart, and other Sermons, The. Red buckram, gilt. 2/6.
    "Bright, scholarly, thoughtful, and redolent of the modern spirit."—*Academy.*

FIDELIS, SISTER MARY.
    Growth in the Knowledge of our Lord. Meditations for every Day of the Year. Adapted from the Original of the Abbé de Brandt. Second Edition. In Three Volumes. Crown 8vo, cloth. 22/6. (Sold only in sets.)
    Lesser Imitation of Christ, The. By Thomas à Kempis. A Sequel to the "Imitation". Now done into English for the first time. 18mo, cloth gilt, 230 pp. 2/6.

FITZGERALD, PERCY.
    Jewels of the Imitation. A Selection of Passages with a Little Commentary. Cloth, extra gilt. 2/-.
    "It is an excellent book for spiritual reading in itself, and it will help its readers to read that holiest of books with more relish and fruit. Mr. Fitzgerald's pithy up-to-date comments throw a new light on many a wise saying of Thomas à Kempis."—*Irish Monthly.*
    Eucharistic Jewels. Second Edition. Fancy cloth. 2/6.
    "Every page is bright with some exquisite passage, and Mr. Fitzgerald's little commentaries, as he carries us along, are not unworthy of the glorious companionship in which he has placed them."—*Freeman's Journal.*
    Jewels of the Mass. A Short Account of the Rites and Prayers used in the Holy Sacrifice. Sixth Edition. Fancy cloth. 2/-.
    "A treatise on the Mass, in which the author proves himself a sound theologian, an accomplished master of ecclesiastical history bearing on the question, a cultured scholar, and the possessor of a very charming style."—*Nation.*
    The Layman's Day: or, Jewels of Practical Piety. Second Edition. Cloth, extra gilt. 2/-.
    "An effort to induce people to consider their every-day life from the point of view of practical common-sense. . . . Admirably done."—*Catholic News.*

FLORA, the Roman Martyr. New One Volume Edition. Crown 8vo, cloth gilt. 6/-.
    "A vivid picture of a far-off time in which the characters are so strongly and so naturally portrayed that they unconsciously inspire us with some of their own ardour and appreciation for the faith for which they died."—*Tablet.*

FORMBY, REV. H.
    Book of the Holy Rosary: a Popular Doctrinal Exposition of its Fifteen Mysteries. Embellished with thirty-six Full-page Illustrations. New Edition. Handsomely bound in cloth. 3/6.

FORMBY, REV. H.—*(continued).*

Martyrs of the City of Rome, Little Book of the. With numerous Illustrations of the Methods of Torture which the Christian Martyrs suffered. Crown 8vo, cloth limp. 1/- net (postage 2d.). Also a better Paper Edition. Cloth gilt. 2/- net (postage 3d.).

Monotheism, mainly derived from the Hebrew Nation and from the Law of Moses. The Primitive Religion of the City of Rome. An Historical Investigation. Demy 8vo, cloth, 360 pp. 5/-.

Pictorial Bible and Church History Stories. Copiously Illustrated. Parts I., II., III., Old Testament History. IV., Life of Christ (Vol. II.). V., VI., VII., Church History. The seven Parts may be had in canvas, 1/3 each. Or bound in Three Volumes, in canvas, 8/3. Also a better Edition, in green cloth, lettered. Volumes I. and III., 5/- each. Volume II. (The Life of Christ), 2/-.

Pictorial Bible and Church History Stories (Abridged). Complete in One Volume. Crown 8vo, 320 pp. With Panoramic Frontispiece, and Bird's-eye View of Jerusalem. Numerous Cuts throughout. School Edition. Cloth 1/4 (postage 4d.). Better Paper Edition, cloth extra, richly gilt, gilt edges, 3/6.

Pictorial Life of Jesus Christ. Complete Edition. Green cloth, illustrated. 2/-. Also an Abridged Edition, 64 pp. With 30 Vignettes in the Text. Cloth. 6d.

FRASSINETTI, VERY REV. JOSEPH.

Consolation of a Devout Soul, The. With an Appendix on the Holy Fear of God. Translated by Georgiana, Lady Chatterton. Popular Edition. Cloth, red edges. 1/6.

New Parish Priest's Practical Manual. A Work useful also for other Ecclesiastics, especially for Confessors and for Preachers. Translated by Very Rev. Canon Hutch, D.D. Third Edition. Crown 8vo, 556 pp., cloth. 6/-.

St. Teresa's Paternoster: A Treatise on Prayer. Translated by Very Rev. Canon Hutch, D.D. Third Edition. Cloth, 18mo, 368 pp. 4/-.

"Frassinetti has woven together the words of St. Teresa and of St. John of the Cross, with a commentary so practical, so clear, and yet so spiritual, that it would be difficult to imagine anything more perfect in its way."—*Tablet.*

FROM THE CRIB TO THE CROSS. Meditations for the Young. With a Preface by Very Rev. Fr. Purbrick, S.J. Fcap. 8vo, cloth. 4/-.

"It contains 107 simple, easy meditations on the Life of Our Lord from the Crib to the Cross, each ending with a Resolution and Prayer. The applications are such as are most suited to the needs and faults of childhood, and the scenes are pictured with a skill which fixes the attention and tends to fill the imagination with holy and pious images. We strongly recommend these meditations to Colleges and Convent Schools."—*Month.*

FULLERTON, LADY GEORGIANA.

Grantley Manor. An Interesting Story of Catholic Life and Society. New Edition. Cloth gilt, gilt edges, 349 pp. 3/6.

Life of St. Frances of Rome. New Edition. Cloth gilt. 2/-.

Life of Madame Duchesne, Religious of the Society of the Sacred Heart of Jesus, and Foundress of that Society in America. Crown 8vo, cloth. 7/6.

FULLERTON, LADY GEORGIANA—*(continued).*

Life of Mère Marie de la Providence, Foundress of the Helpers of the Holy Souls. Third Edition. With Preface and Appendix by Rev. Sydney F. Smith, S.J. Cloth. 1/6 net (postage 3d.).

Life of the Venerable Madeleine Barat, Foundress of the Society of the Sacred Heart of Jesus. Crown 8vo, cloth gilt, 368 pp. 7/6.

Seven Stories. New and Cheaper Edition. Cloth, gilt extra. 2/6.
Contents: "Rosemary"—"Reparation"—"The Blacksmith of Antwerp"—"The Beggar of the Steps of St. Roch"—"Trouvaille"—"Earth without Heaven"—"Ad Majorem Dei Gloriam".

Strawcutter's Daughter, and The Portrait in my Uncle's Dining-Room, The. New and Cheaper Edition. Cloth, gilt extra. 2/6.

GALLWEY, REV. PETER (S.J.).

Precious Pearl of Hope in the Mercy of God, The. Translated from the Italian. With Preface by the Rev. Fr. Gallwey. Cloth. 4/6.

GIBBONS, CARDINAL.

The Faith of our Fathers. A Plain Exposition and Vindication of the Church founded by our Lord Jesus Christ. Forty-eighth Revised and Enlarged Edition. With Portrait. Limp cloth, 2/- net (postage 4d.). Cloth boards, gilt lettered, 3/- net (postage 4d.).

GIBBS, HENRY.

A Long Probation. A Novel. Dedicated by permission to His Eminence Cardinal Vaughan. Crown 8vo, cloth gilt. 6/-.
"A beautiful story—the interest is well sustained from beginning to end, the sentiment is thoroughly Catholic, and the characters are deftly drawn."—*Month.*

GIBSON, REV. HENRY.

Catechism made Easy: being a Familiar Explanation of the Catechism of Christian Doctrine. Eleventh Edition. Two Vols. Fcap. 8vo, cloth, 800 pp. 7/6.
Contains a course of fifty-eight instructions on Catholic doctrines, each accompanied by from one to eleven stories, legends, anecdotes, etc., expressly designed to illustrate their meanings and to fix them in the minds of children.
"This work must be of priceless worth to any who are engaged in any form of catechetical instruction. The best book of the kind that we have seen in English."
—*Irish Monthly.*

GILBERT, RT. REV. MGR.

Love of Jesus: or, Visits to the Blessed Sacrament for every Day in the Month. Thirty-ninth Edition. 32mo, cloth. 1/6. Also in calf, red edges. 5/-. Morocco, gilt edges. 5/6. German calf limp. 5/6.

Reflections on the Stations of the Cross: or, The Love of Jesus in His Passion. With the Devotion of the *Via Crucis.* Ninth Edition. 32mo, cloth. 1/6.

GILLOW, JOSEPH.

Biographical History, and Bibliographical Dictionary of the English Catholics. From the Breach with Rome in 1534 to the Present Time. Vol. I., A-C, 612 pp. Vol. II., D-Grad, 557 pp. Vol. III., Grah-Kem, 688 pp. Vol. IV., Kem-Met, 572 pp. Demy 8vo, cloth. 15/- each.

"The patient research of Mr. Gillow, his conscientious record of minute particulars, and especially his exhaustive bibliographical information in connection with each name are beyond praise."—*British Quarterly Review.*

The Haydock Papers. Illustrated. Demy 8vo, half bound. 7/6.

St. Thomas's Priory: or, The Story of St. Austin's, Stafford. With three Illustrations. Crown 8vo, half leather, gilt top. 5/-.

GRADWELL, MONSIGNOR.

Succat: The Story of Sixty Years of the Life of St. Patrick. Crown 8vo, cloth. 5/-.

Monsignor Gradwell in this work has treated his subject from a novel point of view. In the first place, he has chosen a portion only of the life of St. Patrick. Again, he has attempted to exhibit him in the light in which he was seen by his contemporaries. The style is eminently readable, the descriptions are vivid, and the narrative of events is clear and accurate.

GRANDE CHARTREUSE, MONASTERY OF THE.

By a Carthusian Monk. English Edition. With four Full-page Phototints. Crown 8vo, wrapper. 2/6.

"All who are desirous of obtaining a precise idea of the sort of life led by the members of the Order (the Carthusians) should procure this little book."—*Catholic Times.*

GRANVILLE POPULAR LIBRARY

of Entertaining, Instructive, and Amusing Books. All handsomely bound in cloth, extra gilt (new designs), and suitable for Prizes.

Special Descriptive List post free on application.

One Hundred Books selected from this Library, varying in price from 1/- to 3/-, sent, carriage paid, to any part of the United Kingdom on receipt of £5 5/-.

HAMMERSTEIN, REV. L. VON (S.J.).

Foundations of Faith: The Existence of God Demonstrated. From the German of Fr. Ludwig von Hammerstein, S.J. With an Introduction by the Rev. W. L. Gildea, D.D. Crown 8vo, cloth. 6/-.

"Popular, interesting, forcible and sound. It is well to have a book like Father von Hammerstein's to put into the hands of serious inquirers; it forms a valuable addition to our apologetic literature."—*Tablet.*

HAYWARDEN, RICHARD T.

Pilate's Wife. A Tale of the Time of Christ. Fcap. 8vo, fancy cloth. 2/6.

"One of the most remarkable little books of the day. . . . Each character is drawn as by a master hand, a literary artist; and very impressive are his pictures of the suffering Saviour, of whose trial and crucifixion a vivid and realistic account is given, which recalls very graphically the stupendous scene enacted on Calvary."—*Devon County Standard.*

HEDLEY, BISHOP.

The Christian Inheritance. Second Edition. Crown 8vo, cloth gilt, 430 pp. 6/-.

"We do not know any book we could more confidently recommend to intelligent inquirers after truth, perplexed by the prevailing unbelief, than this new volume, in which the Bishop of Newport prints some twenty discourses preached by him on various occasions."—*Tablet*.

Our Divine Saviour, and other Discourses. Second Edition. Crown 8vo, cloth gilt. 6/-.

"This volume is made up of eighteen Discourses, which treat chiefly of the Incarnation, the Mass, the Blessed Sacrament, the Sacramental System, and kindred subjects. They are not controversial in form, yet they have constant reference to current errors of our day. They are brief, concise, lucid, profoundly philosophical, yet so direct and simple in the arrangement of their thoughts and in their language, that any person of ordinary intelligence can understand and profit by them."—*American Catholic Quarterly*.

A Retreat: consisting of Thirty-three Discourses, with Meditations: for the Use of the Clergy, Religious, and Others. Third Edition. In handsome half-leather binding. Crown 8vo, 428 pp. 6/-.

"The book is one which, beyond the purpose for which it is directly intended, may be strongly recommended for spiritual reading."—*Month*.

"Everywhere will be found a freshness of thought and polished beauty of expression that readily impress the memory, and render meditation on the subject proposed comparatively easy."—*Irish Ecclesiastical Record*.

HERBERT OF LEA, LADY.

Life of Mgr. Berneux, Bishop of Capse and Vicar-Apostolic of Corea. Translated from the French. Fcap. 8vo, cloth gilt, red edges. 3/-.

Month of March in Honour of St. Joseph, Protector of the Church and Model of Christians. By Madame de Gentilles. Translated by Lady Herbert. 32mo, cloth. 2/-.

Thekla. An Autobiography. Fancy cloth, gilt. 3/.

"The autobiography of Thekla is described with a picturesqueness and reality which prove it to be sketched from life, and gives a remarkable fascination to this charming little book."—*Month*.

HEYWOOD, J. C.

Lady Merton. A Tale of the Eternal City. In two Volumes. Crown 8vo, fancy cloth, gilt. 8/-.

Poetical Works. Two Volumes. Cloth. 5/-.

HOPE, MRS.

Conversion of the Teutonic Race, The. Edited by Rev. J. B. Dalgairns. A New and Popular Edition. Two Volumes, each complete in itself. Vol. I., Conversion of the Franks and English. Vol. II., St. Boniface and the Conversion of Germany. Fcap. 8vo. 2/6 each.

"Mrs. Hope was capable of the best original work, as her studies on the 'Conversion of the Teutonic Race' abundantly attest."—*Month*.

Early Martyrs, The. A Martyrology from the Apostles to A.D. 320. Eighth Edition. Fcap. 8vo, cloth, 360 pp. 2/6.

This interesting volume gives accounts of the martyrdoms of nearly all the early Saints of the Church.

HOPE, MRS.—(*continued*).
    Franciscan Martyrs in England. Third Edition. Fcap. 8vo, cloth, lettered, 250 pp. 1/6.
    Life of St. Philip Neri, Apostle of Rome and Founder of the Congregation of the Oratory. Sixth Edition. Fcap. 8vo, cloth, 202 pp. 1/-.
    Life of St. Thomas of Canterbury. With Preface by Rev. Fr. Dalgairns. Third and Cheaper Edition. Revised and Corrected, with Memoir of the Author. Fcap. 8vo, neat cloth, 298 pp. 2/-.
    "Mrs. Hope's works have become standard books of our Catholic literature."—*Tablet.*

HUMPHREY, REV. W. (S.J.).
    Divine Teacher, The. A Letter to a Friend. With a Preface in Reply to the English Church Defence Tract "Papal Infallibility". Seventh Edition. Demy 8vo, cloth. 2/6.
    "We cannot speak in terms too high of the matter contained in this excellent and able volume."—*Westminster Gazette.*

INNER LIFE OF FATHER THOMAS BURKE, O.P. By a Dominican Friar of the English Province. Dark green buckram, gilt. 2/-.
    In this little work the writer has endeavoured to depict that side of Father Burke's character which, if it is least known, gives the truer as well as the higher idea of the well-known preacher.

KEENAN, REV. STEPHEN.
    Controversial Catechism: or, Protestantism Refuted and Catholicism Established by an Appeal to the Holy Scriptures, the Testimony of the Holy Fathers, and the Dictates of Reason; in which such portions of Scheffmacher's Catechism as suit modern Controversy are embodied. New Edition, with latest Revisions by Rev. George Cormack and a Preface by the Right Rev. Bishop Hedley O.S.B. Fcap. 8vo, cloth. 2/-.

KOLBE, REV. F. C.
    Minnie Caldwell, and other Stories, for Girls and for their Elders. Cloth gilt, bevelled boards. 3/-.
    "Excellent reading for young girls about to enter into the world of society."—*Morning Post.*

LAMBERT, REV. L. A.
    Answers to Atheists: or, Notes on Ingersoll. Crown 8vo, wrapper, 203 pp. 6d. (postage 2d.). Also in cloth, lettered. 1/-.
    Over 200,000 copies of this remarkable book have been sold in America.

LASSERRE, HENRI.
    Our Lady of Lourdes. The History of the Miraculous Sanctuary of Our Lady of Lourdes. Translated by Rev. F. Ignatius Sisk, O.C. New Edition. Crown 8vo, cloth gilt. 3/6.
    Miraculous Episodes of Lourdes. Continuation and Second Volume of "Our Lady of Lourdes". Translated from the Seventeenth Edition, with the express permission of the Author, by M. E. Martin. Crown 8vo, cloth, extra gilt. 5/-.
    Month of Mary of Our Lady of Lourdes. Translated by Mrs. Crosier. Fourth Edition. Fcap. 8vo, cloth gilt. 2/6.
    "There is no devotional work with which we are acquainted that can for an instant be brought into comparison with it. The exquisite charm and attraction of this beautiful prayer book it would be difficult to exaggerate."—*Weekly Register.*

LE MASSON, REV. DOM INNOCENT.
    Spiritual Reading for every Day in the Year. Translated and slightly Abridged by Rev. K. D. Best, of the Oratory. Fifth Edition. Cloth. 2/-. Suitable for all Readers, young and old.

LESCHER, REV. WILFRID (O.P.).
    Rosary, The: its History, Confraternity and Indulgences. New Edition. Wrapper. 3d. Also better Edition in neat cloth, gilt extra. 1/-.
    Evolution of the Human Body, The. Wrapper. 6d.
    Scholastic Idea of the Universal, The. Second Edition. Wrapper. 6d.

LIGUORI, ST. ALPHONSUS.
    A Translation of the Works of St. Alphonsus, edited by the late Bishop Coffin :—
    Vol. I. Christian Virtues, and the Means for obtaining them, The. Cloth gilt. 3/-. Or separately, cloth flush—1. The Love of Our Lord Jesus Christ. 1/-. 2. Treatise on Prayer (in many editions a great part of this work is omitted). 1/-. 3. A Christian's Rule of Life. 1/-.
    Vol. II. The Mysteries of the Faith—The Incarnation ; containing Meditations and Devotions on the Birth and Infancy of Jesus Christ, etc., suited for Advent and Christmas. 2/6.
    Vol. III. The Mysteries of the Faith—The Blessed Sacrament. 2/6.
    Vol. IV. Eternal Truths—Preparation for Death. 2/6.
    Vol. V. The Redemption—Meditations on the Passion. 2/6.
    Vol. VI. Glories of Mary. New Edition. 3/6.
    Reflections on Spiritual Subjects and on the Passion of Jesus Christ. 2/6.

LILLY, W. S.
    Ancient Religion and Modern Thought. Second Edition. Demy 8vo, cloth, xxvi.-367 pp. Reduced to 6/-.
    Contents : The Message of Modern Thought—The Claim of Ancient Religion—Religious and Religion—Naturalism and Christianity—Matter and Spirit.

LITURGICAL WORKS.
    Manuale Officiorum Quorundam, ex ordine Administrandi Sacramenta excerptorum. 48mo, roan, 1/6. Persian calf, 2/6. English calf, 3/6. Morocco, 4/.
    Ordo Administrandi Sacramenta, et alia quædam officia ecclesiastica rite peragendi in Missione Anglicana; ex Rituali Romano extractus; nonnullis adjectis ex Antiquo Rituali Anglicano. 18mo, French morocco, gilt edges, 4/-. Calf, red edges, 5/-. Morocco, gilt edges, 6/-.
    Ritus Servandus in Expositione et Benedictione Sanctissimi Sacramenti. Ex Decreto XVIII. N4 Concilii Provincialis Westmonasteriensis I. ubique in Anglia adhibendus. New and Enlarged Edition, recently approved by the Bishops of England. Beautifully printed in red and black from new type on superfine paper. Quarto, solidly bound in red cloth, with gilt cross. Price 5/- net (postage 6d.). Full red calf, 15/- net. Red morocco, 17/6 net.

LIVIUS, REV. T. (M.A., C.SS.R.).
   St. Peter, Bishop of Rome: or, The Roman Episcopate of the Prince of the Apostles. Demy 8vo, cloth. 12/-.
   Explanation of the Psalms and Canticles in the Divine Office. By St. Alphonsus Liguori. Translated from the Italian by Thomas Livius, C.SS.R. With a Preface by his Eminence Cardinal Manning. Crown 8vo, cloth, xxx.-512 pp. 7/6.
   Mary in the Epistles: or, The Implicit Teaching of the Apostles concerning the Blessed Virgin. Crown 8vo, cloth. 5/-.
   The Blessed Virgin in the Fathers of the First Six Centuries. Demy 8vo, cloth. 12/-.
   Cardinal Vaughan says in his preface to the volume: "I trust that this most valuable addition to our literature upon the Office of Mary in the work of our Redemption and Sanctification, will meet with the cordial reception which it deserves; from devout Catholics on the one hand, and from sincere and earnest inquirers outside the Church on the other.

MADDEN, REV. W. J.
   Disunion and Reunion. Crown 8vo, cloth. 3/-.
   "A useful, interesting and well-written book."—*Irish Monthly.*
   "The volume contains a good deal of practical information in a plain and popular style."—*Catholic Times.*

McLAUGHLIN, REV. J.
   Is One Religion as Good as Another? Fortieth Thousand. Wrapper. 6d. net (postage 2d.). Cloth. 1/6 net.

MALTUS, VERY REV. J. A. (O.P.).
   Many Incentives to Love Jesus and His Sacred Heart. Cloth gilt. 2/6.
   "The work consists, for the most part, of sentences from the writings of the Saints, arranged in sections for devout meditation, and deserves to be widely known among priests and Religious."—*Tablet.*
   The Pure Love of God. In which are Incorporated "Heaven, our Eternal Home," "The Everlasting Life and Love of Jesus," "The Triumph of Charity on Earth and in Purgatory," and "Charity is the Greatest Created Gift of God to Man". Cloth gilt. 2/-.
   "In this beautiful little volume practical Catholics will find a series of eloquent prayers and ejaculations appropriate to all the vast variety of devotions which the Church enjoins. They constitute a very valuable incentive to religious fervour."—*Scotsman.*

MANNING, CARDINAL.
   Confidence in God. Seventh Edition. 32mo, neat cloth gilt. 1/-.
   Lost Sheep Found. A Sermon. Wrapper. 6d. Being an Appeal for the Convents of the Good Shepherd.
   Miscellanies. First Series. Crown 8vo, cloth, 387 pp. 6/-.
   Contents: Roma Æterna—Work and Wants of the Church in England—On the Subjects Proper to the Academia—Father Faber—Cardinal Wiseman—Ireland—On Progress—The Dæmon of Socrates, etc., etc.
   Miscellanies. Second Series. Crown 8vo, cloth, 391 pp. 6/-.
   Contents: The Church of Rome—Cæsarism and Ultramontanism—Dignity and Rights of Labour—Christianity and Anti-Christianism—The Pope and Magna Charta—Philosophy without Assumptions—Frederick Ozanam, etc., etc.

MANNING, CARDINAL—*(continued).*

Religio Viatoris. Fifth Edition. Crown 8vo, cloth. 1/6.
"The four following truths are the four corners of my faith: The Existence of God—That God hath revealed himself to me—That this Revelation is Christianity—That Historical Christianity is the Catholic Faith."—*Preface.*

Sermons on Ecclesiastical Subjects. Crown 8vo, cloth, 456 pp. 6/-.
Contents: Introduction on the Relations of England to Christianity—Help Nearest when Need Greatest—Dogmatic Authority Supernatural and Infallible—Perpetual Office of the Council of Trent—Name and Patience of Jesus—The Certainty of Divine Faith—Strength in Weakness—The Good Shepherd—The Resurrection of Dry Bones, etc., etc.

Sin and its Consequences. Tenth and Cheaper Edition. Crown 8vo, cloth. 4/-.
Contents: The Nature of Sin—Mortal Sin—Venial Sin—Sins of Omission—The Grace and Works of Penance—Temptation—The Dereliction on the Cross—The Joys of the Resurrection.

The Blessed Sacrament the Centre of Immutable Truth. 32mo, neat cloth gilt. 1/-.

The Eternal Priesthood. Twelfth and Cheaper Edition. Crown 8vo, cloth. 2/6.
Contents: The Nature, Powers, Three Relations, Obligations of Sanctity, and the Instrumental Means of Perfection of the Priesthood—The End of the Priest—The Priest's Dangers, Sorrows, Friends, Liberty, Obedience, Rewards, House, Life and Death, etc., etc.

The Four Great Evils of the Day. Seventh and Cheaper Edition. Crown 8vo, cloth. 2/6.
Contents: The Revolt of the Intellect against God—The Revolt of the Will against God—The Revolt of Society from God—The Spirit of Anti-Christ.

The Fourfold Sovereignty of God. Fourth and Cheaper Edition. Crown 8vo, cloth. 2/6.
Contents: Six Lectures on the Sovereignty of God over the Intellect and the Will of Man and over Society—The Sovereignty of the Divine Head of the Church—The Sovereignty of the Church derived from its Divine Head—The Sovereignty of God over the Course of the World.

The Glories of the Sacred Heart. Seventh and Cheaper Edition. Crown 8vo, cloth. 4/-.
Contents: The Divine Glory of the Sacred Heart—The Sacred Heart God's Way of Love—Dogma, the Source of Devotion—The Science, the Last Will, the Temporal Glory, the Transforming Power, the Signs of, and the Eternal Glory of the Sacred Heart—The Sure Way of Likeness to the Sacred Heart.

The Grounds of Faith. Eleventh Edition. Crown 8vo, cloth. 1/6.
Four Lectures: Revealed Truth Definite and Certain—The Choice of a Historical Witness—The Church a Divine Witness—Rationalism the Legitimate Consequence of Private Judgment.

The Holy Ghost the Sanctifier. 32mo, neat cloth gilt. 2/-.

The Independence of the Holy See. Second and Cheaper Edition. Crown 8vo, cloth. 2/6.
Contents: The Temporal Sovereignty of the Pope a Divine Ordinance and a Provision for the Independence of the Spiritual Power—The Violation of the Providential Order of the Christian World—The Revolt and its Nemesis. With three Appendices.

MANNING, CARDINAL—(*continued*).

The Internal Mission of the Holy Ghost. Seventh and Cheaper Edition. Crown 8vo, cloth, 494 pp. 5/-.

Contents: Grace the Work of a Person—Salvation by Grace—The Virtues of Faith, Hope and Charity—The Glory of Sons—The Seven Gifts of the Holy Ghost—The Gifts of Holy Fear, Piety, Science, Fortitude, Counsel, Understanding, and of Wisdom—The Fruits of the Spirit—The Beatitudes—Devotion to the Holy Ghost.

The Love of Jesus to Penitents. Fourteenth Edition. 32mo, neat cloth gilt. 1/-.

The Office of the Church in Higher Catholic Education. 6d.

The Temporal Mission of the Holy Ghost: or, Reason and Revelation. Fourth and Cheaper Edition. Crown 8vo, cloth. 5/-.

Contents: The Relation of the Holy Ghost to the Church, to the Human Reason, to the Letter and to the Interpretation of Scripture, and to the Divine Tradition of the Faith.

The True Story of the Vatican Council. Second and Cheaper Edition. Crown 8vo, cloth. 2/6.

Contents: The Origin and Motive of the Vatican Council—The Centenary of St. Peter and Preparations for the Council—The Opening of the Council, and First Constitution on Faith—The First Constitution on the Church—The Definition of Infallibility.

The Workings of the Holy Spirit in the Church of England. New Edition. Crown 8vo, cloth. 1/6.

Being a letter to the Rev. E. B. Pusey, D.D., first published in 1864.

MANNING, CARDINAL, Edited by.

Life of the Curé d'Ars. From the French of the Abbé Monnin. Popular Edition. Fcap. 8vo, cloth. 2/6.

The authorised translation of the work by the Abbé Monnin, the friend and fellow-labourer of the Curé, written by command of the Bishop of Belley, and is the only authentic work published.

MANNOCK, REV. JOHN (O.S.B.).

Poor Man's Catechism: or, People's Catechism of Catholic Doctrine, The. Fcap. 8vo, cloth, 250 pp. 1/-.

MANRESA: or, The Spiritual Exercises of St. Ignatius. For general use. New Edition. Fcap. 8vo, cloth, 364 pp. 3/-.

The title of the original work, *viz.*: "Spiritual Exercises: chosen with a view to lead man to conquer himself, to disengage himself from the fatal influence of evil affections, and, with his heart thus set free, to trace out for himself the plan of a truly Christian life," clearly points out the object of this work.

MARTIN, LADY.

Life of Princess Borghese (*née* Gwendalin Talbot). Translated from the French. Crown 8vo, tastefully bound in cloth gilt. 4/-.

"The life of the charming and saint-like young Englishwoman will come as a welcome surprise to the readers of a later generation, who will find how completely the spirit of Catholic faith and charity was combined in the person of Lady Gwendalin Talbot with the rarest beauty and the most accomplished talents."—*Tablet*.

MEMORIES OF THE CRIMEA. By Sister Mary Aloysius. With Preface by the Very Rev. J. Fahey, D.D., V.G. Crown 8vo, cloth gilt. 2/6.
"The venerable Sister, upon whom Her Majesty the Queen bestowed the decoration of the Royal Red Cross a few months ago, tells her touching story of heroic self-abnegation with a modest simplicity that is far more impressive than the most elaborate and picturesque style of descriptive writing."—*Daily Telegraph.*

MÉRIC, ABBÉ.
The Blessed will know each other in Heaven. From the French of the Abbé Méric, by Mrs. Ringer. Second Edition. Tastefully bound in cloth, gilt edges. 3/-.
"Contains a limitless store of consolation and hope."—*Catholic Times.*

MEYNELL, ALICE.
Lourdes: Yesterday, To-day, and To-morrow. Translated from the French of Daniel Barbé, by Alice Meynell. With twelve Full-page Water Colour Drawings by Hoffbauer, reproduced in Colours. Royal 8vo, blue buckram, gilt. 6/-.
"The story has never before been so vividly conceived and so pointedly expressed; while the illustrations, twelve in number, not only mark a new era in artistic colour-printing, but bring home to the reader the shrine, and the scenes that yearly take place there, with a beauty and percision unattempted before."—*Tablet.*

MONTGOMERY, HON. MRS.
Life of the Blessed Angelina of Marsciano, Foundress of the First Convents of the Third Order Regular of St. Francis of Assisi. Fcap. 8vo, cloth. 2/6.
"Mrs. Montgomery has given us in a very simple and pleasing style, a life of the saintly promotress of the Third Order of St. Francis, filled in with much interesting matter illustrative of the habits and manners of the age."—*Catholic News.*

The Divine Ideal. New Edition. Crown 8vo, neat cloth. 3/6.
"In 'The Divine Ideal' we have essayed to elucidate the position of Mary the Mother of God, in Creation and in Redemption, showing the validity of her claim equally in both."—*Extract from Preface.*

The Eternal Years. With an Introduction by the Most Rev. Archbishop Porter, S.J. Crown 8vo, cloth. 3/6.
An endeavour to trace the hopes and expectations of the soul, and of the Church.

MORRIS, REV. JOHN (S.J.).
Devotions of the Lady Lucy Herbert of Powis. 3/6.
Letter Books of Sir Amias Poulet, Keeper of Mary, Queen of Scots. Demy 8vo. 3/6 net (postage 4½d.).
Two Missionaries under Elizabeth. Demy 8vo. 14/-.
The Catholics under Elizabeth. Demy 8vo. 14/-.
The Life of Father John Gerard, S.J. Third Edition, Rewritten and Enlarged. Demy 8vo. 14/-.
Life and Martyrdom of St. Thomas Becket. Second and Enlarged Edition. In One Vol. Large post 8vo, cloth, pp. xxxvi.-632. 12/6. Or bound in Two Vols. Cloth. 13/-.
Catholic England in Modern Times. 1/6 net (postage 3d.).

MORRIS, REV. W. B. (of the Oratory).

The Life of St. Patrick, Apostle of Ireland. Fifth and Revised Edition in the press. Crown 8vo, cloth. 5/-.

"The standard biography of Ireland's Apostle. For clear statement of facts, and calm judicious discussion of controverted points, it surpasses any work we know of in the literature of the subject."—*American Catholic Quarterly.*

Ireland and St. Patrick. A Study of the Saint's Character and of the Results of his Apostolate. Second Edition. Crown 8vo, cloth. 5/-.

"We read with pleasure this volume of essays, which, though the Saint's name is taken by no means in vain, really contains a sort of discussion of current events and current English views of Irish character."—*Saturday Review.*

MULHOLLAND, CLARA.

Little Merry Face and his Crown of Content, and other Tales. Crown 8vo, fancy cloth gilt. 2/6.

"Many of them are full of quiet pathos, and all breathe a spirit of true Catholic piety, which conveys the highest moral without obtruding it."—*Dublin Review.*

MULHOLLAND, ROSA (LADY GILBERT).

The Wicked Woods. Crown 8vo, cloth, gilt top, with Portrait. 5/-.

"An exceptionally bright, powerful and striking tale."—*Morning Post.*
"The tale is gracefully written, and its characteristic touches of true Irish romance will recommend it to many readers."—*Scotsman.*

The Wild Birds of Killeevy. Fourth Edition. Crown 8vo, fancy cloth, gilt extra. 3/6.

"One of the best Catholic stories of the century."—*Catholic News.*

NEWMAN, CARDINAL.

The Church of the Fathers. Fcap. 8vo, cloth, 361 pp. 4/-.

An attempt to illustrate the tone and modes of thought, the habits and manners, of the early times of the Church.

Detailed List of Cardinal Newman's Works on application.

NORTHCOTE, VERY REV. PROVOST (D.D.).

Mary in the Gospels: or, Lectures on the History of our Blessed Lady as Recorded by the Evangelists. Second Edition. Cloth gilt, 344 pp. 3/6.

OAKELEY, CANON.

Catholic Worship: A Manual of Popular Instruction on the Ceremonies and Devotions of the Church. New Edition. Cloth, lettered. 1/-.

Order and Ceremonial of the Sacrifice of the Mass Explained. Popular Edition. Cloth, lettered, 144 pp. 1/-.

Written as a dialogue between a Priest and a Catechumen, with an appendix on Vespers, Compline, and Benediction.

Voice of Creation as a Witness to the Mind of its Divine Author. Five Lectures. Cloth. 1/- net (postage 2d.).

Youthful Martyrs of Rome, The. A Christian Drama, adapted from "Fabiola". Eighth Edition. Cloth. 1/8.

O'MEARA, KATHLEEN.

The Blind Apostle, and A Heroine of Charity. Crown 8vo, fancy cloth, gilt. 4/6.

"The last bequest of the cultivated and pious intelligence to which we owe so many beautiful and instructive writings."—*Cardinal Manning.*

PAROCHIAL REGISTERS, A NEW AND UNIFORM SET OF.

Large quarto, 13 by 11 inches. Very strongly bound in half-leather, cloth sides and joints, coloured edges, gilt lettering. "Liber Baptizatorum." "Liber Confirmatorum." "Liber Matrimoniorum." "Liber Defunctorum." To suit the convenience of large or small Missions each book may be had in the following sizes and prices. 100 pp., 10/- each; 200 pp., 15/- each; 400 pp., £1 each; 600 pp., £1 10/- each.

The registers are bound in different colours, so that the volume needed may a once be recognised.

PARSONS, MRS.

Afternoons with Mrs. Maitland. Cloth gilt. 1/6.
A book of household instruction and entertainment. Each afternoon deals with the discussion of some virtue or useful quality, pleasantly and simply treated.

Life of St. Ignatius of Loyola. An Interesting Account of the Saint and of his Work. Cloth gilt. 2/-.

Thomas Rileton. His Family and Friends. Crown 8vo, fancy cloth. 3/6.
"A bright and simple controversial story, with a motive and a moral. . . . The reading of the book does one good."—*Weekly Register.*

Twelve Stories for Children. Cloth gilt. 2/-.
Entertaining and instructive stories for boys and girls.

Twelve Tales for the Young. First Series. Cloth, gilt extra. 2/6.

Twelve Tales for the Young. Second Series. Cloth, gilt extra. 2/6.

Wrecked and Saved. A Tale. New Edition. Crown 8vo, fancy cloth, gilt extra. 3/6.

PATTERSON, BISHOP.

Jesus Christ, Model of the Priest. Translated from the Italian. Fifth Edition. 32mo, cloth gilt. 1/4.

PERIODICALS.

Messrs. Burns & Oates *receive Subscriptions to any of the Reviews, Magazines, or Daily Papers published in the United Kingdom or America. Subscriptions may commence at any time, but cannot be received for less than six months; or in the case of Magazines, etc., published abroad, twelve months. They will be happy to forward Price List of the principal Periodicals on application.*

PERRY, REV. JOHN.

Practical Sermons, for all the Sundays of the Year. First and Second Series. Sixth Edition. Fcap. 8vo, cloth. 3/6 each.

"The price at which these are issued puts them within reach of the most moderate purse. We trust their circulation may be so extensive as to verify in Fr. Perry's regard, that which was written of another great Servant of God—'being dead he yet speaketh'".—*Tablet.*

POLICE, REV. A.
   Parochial Hymn Book. Fcap. 8vo, cloth boards, 1/- net (postage 3d.). Roan, red edges, 2/- net. French morocco, gilt edges, 2/6 net. Calf, red edges, 5/6 net.
   Parochial Hymn Tunes, containing Words and Melodies. Demy 8vo, cloth. 4/-.
   Contains some 575 hymns, vespers, compline, and prayers and devotions for all the faithful.

POPE, REV. T. A. (of the Oratory).
   Life of St. Philip Neri. Translated from the Italian of Cardinal Capecelatro. Second and Revised Edition. Two Volumes. Crown 8vo, cloth. 12/6.
   "Altogether this is a most facinating work, full of spiritual lore and historic erudition, and with all the intense interest of a remarkable biography. Take it up where you will, it is hard to lay it down. We think it one of the most completely satisfactory lives of a Saint that has been written in modern times."—*Tablet.*

PORTER, ARCHBISHOP (S.J.).
   The Banquet of the Angels: Preparation and Thanksgiving for Holy Communion. New Edition. 18mo, blue cloth, gilt. 2/-. Also bound in a variety of handsome leather bindings suitable for First Communion memorial gifts. From 6/6 to 12/6 net.
   "This little volume is intended chiefly for people in the world, and contains an excellent series of considerations and meditations suitable for the solemn occasion of Holy Communion."—*Irish Ecclesiastical Record.*

PRACTICAL MEDITATIONS FOR EVERY DAY IN THE
   Year, on the Life of our Lord Jesus Christ. Chiefly for the Use of Religious. By a Father of the Society of Jesus. With Imprimatur of Cardinal Manning. New Edition, Revised. In Two Volumes. Cloth, red edges. 9/-.
   These volumes give three different daily points for consideration and application. "A work of great practical utility, and we give it our earnest recommendation."—*Weekly Register.*

PRACTICAL NOTES ON MORAL TRAINING. Especially addressed to Parents and Teachers. With a Preface by Fr. Gallwey, S.J. Third Edition. Crown 8vo, cloth. 2/6.

PRAYER BOOKS, etc.
   N.B.—For full particulars of Prayer Books, see *Illustrated Prayer Book Catalogue,* sent post free on application.
   Catholic Child's Guide to Devotion. A First Prayer Book for the Young. In large Type. With Engravings. Cloth, 6d. and 1/-. Leather, 2/6.
   Catholic Piety. A Popular Manual of Catholic Devotion, containing all the ordinary Prayers and Services of the Church, with Epistles and Gospels. Three Editions, all approved by the Cardinal Archbishop of Westminster. 48mo EDITION (size, 3⅝ by 2¼ inches). In handsome leather bindings, from 1/- to 5/-. DEMY 32mo EDITION (size, 4 by 2¼ inches). In six different styles of leather bindings, from 1/6 to 3/6. ROYAL 32mo EDITION (size, 5 by 3¼ inches) without Epistles and Gospels. Cloth, 6d. Roan, 1/-. Or complete, in six different styles, from 1/6 to 4/6.

PRAYER BOOKS, etc.—*(continued).*

Catholic Prayer Book. Gives, in a small compass, an approved Selection of Private Devotions, with an excellent Summary of Christian Doctrine. Paste grain, 2/-. Calf limp, 4/-.

Catholic's Daily Companion. With Epistles and Gospels. From 1/- to 5/- each.

Catholic's Vade Mecum: or, Select Prayers for Daily Use, The. New and Beautiful Edition. Printed in red and black on superfine paper. (Size, 5½ by 3½ inches.) Calf, red edges, 5/6. German calf or morocco, four styles, 6/- each. German calf, padded, five styles, 7/- each. Russia, two styles, morocco circuit or with clasp, 8/6 each, and in handsome leather bindings, beautifully finished, at 10/6 to 21/-.

Child's Mass Book. From 1/- to 4/-.

Children's Pictorial Mass Book. Abridged. 2d. and 6d. Complete Editions. 1/-, 1/6, 3/-, 5/6.

Choir Manual for Sisters of Mercy. Cloth. 1/- net. With Office of B.V.M. 2/6 net (postage 3d.).

Christian's Manual. Royal 32mo, calf stiff or limp, red edges. Containing New Testament, Book of Psalms, and Following of Christ. 6/6 net (postage 4d.).

Church Manual. With Epistles and Gospels. New and Revised Edition. In leather bindings, 2/-, 3/6, 5/-, and 7/6 each.

Daily Exercise. New Edition. With Engravings. Cloth. 6d.

Daily Prayer Book. Compiled from various Sources. By the Rev. H. S. Bowden, of the Oratory. Cloth. 1/-.

Dawn of Day: A Prayer Book for the Young. Cloth. 1/-.

Devotional Library for Catholic Households. Containing New Testament, Book of Psalms, Imitation of Christ, Devout Life, Spiritual Combat. All neatly bound in cloth, red edges, with cloth case to match. 5/- net (postage 4d.).

Devotions for Ecclesiastical Year. Cl. 3/- net (postage 3d.).

Exercises of St. Gertrude. From 1/6 upwards.

Faithful Guide. Prayers and Devotions recommended to Catholic Youth. By Fr. V. Raymond, O.P. Cloth, 2/6. Leather, 4/- and 6/-.

Few Flowers from the Garden. Cloth. 1/-.

Flowers of Devotion: being a Collection of Favourite Devotions for Public and Private Use. Compiled from Approved Sources, and with the Imprimatur of H. E. Cardinal Vaughan. French morocco, limp, round corners, gilt edges, 1/6. Polished paste grain, limp, round corners, red under gold edges, gold rolled, 2/6. German calf, limp, 4/-. Polished morocco, limp, 4/-. Russia, limp, gold rolled, calf lined, 5/-. Polished morocco, silk lined, with pockets for Visiting Cards, etc. 6/-.

PRAYER BOOKS, etc.—*(continued).*

Garden of the Soul, The. By Bishop Challoner. Containing all the popular Devotions, with the Mass, Vespers, Benediction, and Epistles and Gospels for Sundays and Festivals. Five Editions are issued by Messrs. Burns & Oates, all bearing the Imprimatur of the Cardinal Archbishop of Westminster. 48mo EDITION (size, 3⅔ by 2¼ inches). In strong cloth binding, 6d., and in handsome leather bindings, with red line borders, from 1/- to 5/-; or in Two Volumes, in leather cases, in various styles, from 3/- to 12/6. DEMY 32mo EDITION (size, 4 by 2½ inches). In six different styles of leather binding, from 1/6 to 3/6. IMPERIAL 32mo EDITION (size, 5¾ by 3½ inches). Without Epistles and Gospels, cloth, 6d.; roan, 1/-. Or complete in 18 different styles, from 1/- to 10/6. 18mo EDITION, with larger type (size, 5½ by 3¾ inches). Cloth, 1/-, without Epistles and Gospels; or complete, from 1/4 to 5/6. SAILORS' EDITION. Strong leather binding. 2/-,

Golden Manual, The. A Complete Guide to Catholic Devotion, Public and Private. (Size, 5¾ by 3¾ inches.) Paste grain limp, or French morocco, stiff, 6/- each. Rutland roan, limp, round corners, 7/-. Best calf, red edges, 8/6. German calf, or morocco, limp, round corners, 8/6 each. Morocco boards, gilt edges, 8/6. Morocco boards, extra gilt, 11/-. Any of the above with Epistles and Gospels, 1/- extra. Also in handsome leather bindings, in a variety of styles, from 13/- net to 30/- net.

Imitation of Christ, Of the. By Thomas à Kempis. NEW POPULAR EDITION FOR DISTRIBUTION. Cloth, red edges, 6d. (postage 2d.). Leather, red edges, 1/-. SUPERFINE POCKET EDITION. Fancy cloth extra, with red borders, 1/6. And in leather bindings, from 2/6 to 10/-. PRESENTATION EDITION (size, 6¼ by 4¼ inches). With red border on each page. Cloth extra, 3/6. And in leather bindings, from 7/- to 15/-.

Imitation of Christ and New Testament. 3/6 and 6/-.

Imitation of Christ and Spiritual Combat. 3/6 and 6/-.

Instructions and Devotions for Confession, for the Use of Convents, Schools, etc. 32mo, cloth, 6d. Calf, red edges, 3/-.

Key of Heaven, The. Containing all the Popular Devotions, Prayers, and Services of the Church, together with the Epistles and Gospels. Three Editions, all issued by authority of the Cardinal Archbishop of Westminster. 48mo EDITION (size, 3⅝ by 2¼ inches). In handsome leather bindings, with red borders, from 1/- to 5/-. DEMY 32mo EDITION (size, 4 by 2¼ inches). In six different styles of leather bindings, from 1/6 to 3/6. ROYAL 32mo EDITION (size, 5 by 3¼ inches), without Epistles and Gospels. Cloth, 6d. Roan, 1/-. Or complete, in various styles, from 1/6 to 4/6.

Little Book of the Most Holy Child Jesus: A Prayer Book for His Children. Cloth. 1/-.

Manna of the New Covenant. A Sacramental Companion. Cloth. 2/.

Manual of the Holy Family, with the Hymns. Cloth. 6d.

Manual of Indulgences, or Collection of Prayers and Good Works, to which the Sovereign Pontiffs have attached Holy Indulgences. Authorised Translation. Royal 16mo, 576 pp., cloth. 4/-.

PRAYER BOOKS, etc.—*(continued).*
  Manual of Prayers for Congregational Use. With Hymns, Appendix, and Supplement. Authorised by the Archbishops and Bishops of England and Wales. Pocket Edition. Cloth, 1/-. Leather, 2/6, 5/-, and upwards. Also two larger Editions.
  Manual of Prayers, for the Use of Training Ships, Reformatory Schools, etc. Strong leather binding. 2/- net (postage 3d.).
  Manual of Prayers, for the Use of Catholic Youth, chiefly in Schools. Approved by the Cardinal Archbishop of Westminster. 32mo, cloth. 1/6.
  Manual of the Sacred Heart. New and Beautiful Edition. Cloth, 2/- and 2/6. Leather, 4/6, 5/6, and 6/6.
  Missal for the Laity. Abridged Edition. 32mo, cloth, 6d. Leather, 1/6, 2/6, 4/6, and 5/-.
  Missal. New and Complete Pocket Missal, with the Imprimatur of H. E. Cardinal Vaughan, in Latin and English, with all the New Offices, and the propers for Ireland, Scotland, and the Jesuits. (Size, 5⅞ by 3⅞ inches.) Roan or French morocco, 5/-. Rutland roan, limp, 7/-. Best calf or morocco, four styles, 8/6 each. Also in better bindings, from 11/- to 30/- net.
  Our Lady of Perpetual Succour. A Manual of Devotion for every Day of the Month. Translated from the French by Rev. T. Livius, C.SS.R. Ninth and Revised Edition, with coloured Frontispiece. 32mo, cloth, 1/- net. Imitation seal, 2/- net. Paste grain roan, 2/6 net. German, calf, 4/6 net (postage on single copies, 2d.).
  Our Lady of Perpetual Succour, Manual of. From the Writings of St. Alphonsus Liguori. By a Redemptorist Father. Twenty-fifth Thousand. 18mo, cloth, 1/- net. Leather, 2/- net. With Hymns. Cloth, red edges, 1/6 net. Leather, gilt edges, 3/- net (postage on single copies, 3d.).
  Our Lady's Manual, or Devotions to the Sacred Heart of Mary. Cloth, 2/- and 2/6. Leather, 4/6 and 5/6.
  Paradise of the Christian Soul. By Horstius. New Edition. Cloth, 4/-. Leather, 8/- and 10/-.
  Path to Heaven, The. The Cheapest and most Complete Book of Devotions for Public or Private Use ever issued. (Size, 5⅞ by 3½ inches.) Cloth, 2/-. Ditto, red edges, 2/6. Roan, 3/-. Paste grain, gilt edges, 4/-. French morocco, gilt, with clasp, 4/6. Persian calf, red edges, 4/6. Calf, red edges, 7/6. Morocco, gilt edges, 7/6. German calf, or morocco, limp, round corners, 7/6 each. Ditto, soft cushioned, round corners, 8/6 each.
  Pax Vobiscum. Specially adapted for Sick Persons and Invalids. Large type, cloth, 2/6. Leather, 4/-.
  Pray for Us. Little Chaplets for the Saints. Imperial 32mo, cloth extra, gilt edges. With Steel Frontispiece. 2/-.
  Prayers and Exercises of St. Gertrude. Two Volumes. In a case, in best calf or morocco. 12/- net. Or in calf, in one book. 6/6.
  Prayers for the People. By the Rev. F. D. Byrne. Imperial 32mo, cloth, extra gilt. 2/-.

PRAYER BOOKS, etc.—*(continued)*.

Prayers of St. Gertrude and St. Mechtilde. Cloth, 1/- and 1/6. Leather, 2/- and 4/6 each.

Psalter, The, or Psalms of David in English. Cloth, 1/6. Calf, 5/-.

Reflections and Prayers for Holy Communion. From the French. Two Series. Each, 4/6 and upwards.

Servite Manual. Compiled by the Servite Fathers. Cloth, 2/6. With Hymns, 3/-.

Spirit of the Sacred Heart. A new large type Manual of Prayers. Cloth, 3/6. Paste grain roan, gilt, 5/6. Also in better bindings.

Spiritual Combat: together with the Supplement to the same, and the Treatise of Inward Peace. A new Translation. Pocket Edition. Cloth, 1/-. Leather, 1/6, 2/6, and 4/6.

Treasury of Prayer, The: A Manual of Popular Devotion. Dedicated to the Frequenters of the Oratory of St. Philip Neri. New Edition. With Epistles and Gospels. Cloth, 16mo, 2/6. Leather, 4/- and 7/6.

Vesper Book. 32mo. Cloth, 1/-. Leather, 1/6 and 4/6.

Vesper Book. Complete. 16mo. Leather, 3/6 upwards.

PRIESTMAN, JOHN.

God's Birds. Small 4to, tastefully bound. 3/6.

"A charming volume. The raven, the dove, and many other birds of Scripture, occupy these fascinating pages, wherein we receive almost a new light on the meaning of the sacred text, and we see more clearly the love of God for his creatures."—*Tablet.*

QUARTERLY SERIES. Edited by the Jesuit Fathers. 96 volumes published to date.

SELECTION.

The Life and Letters of St. Francis Xavier. By the Rev. H. J. Coleridge, S.J. Second Edition. Two Volumes. 10/6.

The History of the Sacred Passion. By Father Luis de la Palma, of the Society of Jesus. Translated from the Spanish. 5/-.

The Life and Letters of St. Teresa. By Rev. H. J. Coleridge, S.J. Three Volumes. 7/6 each.

The Life of Mary Ward. By Mary Catherine Elizabeth Chalmers, of the Institute of the Blessed Virgin. Edited by the Rev. H. J. Coleridge, S.J. Two Volumes. 15/-.

The Return of the King. Discourses on the Latter Days. By the Rev. H. J. Coleridge, S.J. 7/6.

Pious Affections towards God and the Saints. Meditations for every Day in the Year, and for the principal Festivals. From the Latin of the Ven. Nicolas Lancicius, S.J. 7/6.

The Life and Teaching of Jesus Christ in Meditations for every Day in the Year. By Fr. Nicolas Avancino, S.J. Two Volumes. 10/6.

QUARTERLY SERIES—*(continued)*.

The Hours of the Passion. Taken from the *Life of Christ*. By Ludolph the Saxon. 7/6.

The Baptism of the King: Considerations on the Sacred Passion. By the Rev. H. J. Coleridge, S.J. 7/6.

The Mother of the King. Mary during the Life of our Lord. 7/6.

The Mother of the Church. Mary during the First Apostolic Age. 6/-.

The Life of St. Alonso Rodriguez. By Francis Goldie, of the Society of Jesus. 7/6.

Letters of St. Augustine. Selected and arranged by Mary H. Allies. 6/6.

Acts of the English Martyrs, hitherto unpublished. By the Rev. John H. Pollen, S.J. 7/6.

Life of St. Francis di Geronimo, S.J. By A. M. Clarke. 7/6.

Aquinas Ethicus: or, The Moral Teaching of St. Thomas. By the Rev. Joseph Rickaby, S.J. Second Edition. Two Volumes. 12/-.

The Spirit of St. Ignatius. From the French of the Rev. Fr. Xavier de Franciosi, S.J. 6/-.

Jesus, the All-Beautiful. A Devotional Treatise on the Character and Actions of our Lord. Edited by Rev. J. G. Macleod, S.J. Second Edition. 6/6.

The Manna of the Soul. By Fr. Paul Segneri. New Edition. In Two Volumes. 12/-.

Saturday Dedicated to Mary. From the Italian of Fr. Cabrini, S.J. 6/-.

Life of Fr. Augustus Law, S.J. By Ellis Schreiber. 6/-.

Life of Ven. Joseph Benedict Cottolengo. From the Italian of Don P. Gastaldi. 4/6.

Story of St. Stanislaus Kostka. Edited by Rev. F. Goldie, S.J. Third Edition. 4/6.

The Lights in Prayer of the Ven. Frs. Louis de la Puente and Claude de la Colombière, and the Rev. Fr. Paul Segneri. Edited by the Rev. J. Morris, S.J. 5/-.

Life of St. Francis Borgia. By A. M. Clarke. 6/6.

Life of Blessed Antony Baldinucci. By Rev. F. Goldie, S.J. 6/-.

Distinguished Irishmen of the Sixteenth Century. By Rev. E. Hogan, S.J. 6/-.

Journals kept during Times of Retreat. By the late Fr. John Morris, S.J. Edited by Rev. J. Pollen, S.J. 6/-.

Life of the Rev. Mother Mary of St. Euphrasia Pelletier. By A. M. Clarke. 6/-.

QUARTERLY SERIES—(*continued*).

Jesus: His Life, in the very Words of the Four Gospels. A Diatessaron by Henry Beauclerk, S.J. Cloth. 5/-.

First Communion. A Book of Preparation for First Communion. Edited by Fr. Thurston, S.J. Second Edition. With nineteen Illustrations. 6/6.

The Life and Letters of Fr. John Morris, S.J. By Fr. J. H. Pollen, S.J. Cloth. 6/-.

The Story of Mary Aikenhead, Foundress of the Irish Sisters of Charity. By Maria Nethercott. Crown 8vo, cloth. 3/-.

VOLUMES ON THE LIFE OF OUR LORD. By Fr. Coleridge.

The Preparation of the Incarnation. 7/6.

The Nine Months. The Life of our Lord in the Womb. 7/6.

The Thirty Years. Our Lord's Infancy and Early Life. 7/6.

The Ministry of St. John Baptist. 6/6.

The Preaching of the Beatitudes. 6/6.

The Sermon on the Mount. Continued. Two Parts. 6/6 each.

The Training of the Apostles. Parts I., II., III., IV. 6/6 each.

The Preaching of the Cross. Part I. 6/6.

The Preaching of the Cross. Parts II., III. 6/- each.

Passiontide. Parts I., II., III. 6/6 each.

Chapters on the Parables of our Lord. 7/6.

The Life of our Life. Harmony of the Life of our Lord, with Introductory Chapters and Indices. Second Edition. Two Volumes. 15/-.

The Passage of our Lord to the Father. Conclusion of *The Life of our Life.* 7/6.

The Works and Words of our Saviour, gathered from the Four Gospels. 7/6.

The Story of the Gospels. Harmonised for Meditation. 7/6.

RAM, MRS. ABEL.
"**Emmanuel.**" Being the Life of our Lord reproduced in the Mysteries of the Tabernacle. Crown 8vo, cloth gilt. 5/-.
"The arrangement of the matter, and the deep spirit of thoughtful devotion that pervades almost every sentence, render it specially suitable for the exercises of mental prayer."—*Irish Ecclesiastical Record.*

RAWES, VERY REV. FR. (D.D.).
Bread of Life: or, St. Thomas Aquinas on the Adorable Sacrament of the Altar, The. Arranged as Meditations, with Prayers and Thanksgivings, for Holy Communion. Second and Cheaper Edition. Cloth gilt. 3/6.

CATALOGUE OF PUBLICATIONS. 33

RAWES, VERY REV. FR. (D.D.)—*(continued).*
Devotions for the Souls in Purgatory. Fourth Edition.
32mo, neat cloth, red edges. 2/-.
A way of hearing Mass for the Dead, and the Doctrines of Suarez on Purgatory are also included in this Edition.

Foregleams of the Desired. Third Edition, with Frontispiece. Neat cloth, gilt. 2/6.
Contains Sacred Verses, Hymns and Translations on the Sacred Humanity of Jesus—The Mother of Jesus—Days of Jesus—Saints of Jesus, etc.

St. John the Evangelist: or, The Beloved Disciple. Third and Cheaper Edition. Fcap. 8vo, cloth. 2/6.
"Full of research and of tender and loving devotion."—*Tablet.*

Septem: or, Seven Ways of Hearing Mass. New Edition. 32mo, cloth flush, 1/-. Neat cloth, with red edges, 2/-. Best calf, 4/-. Turkey morocco, 4/6.
"A great assistance to hearing Mass with devotion."—*Tablet.*

Visits and Devotions. 32mo, neat cloth, red edges. 3/6.
This volume contains: The Eucharistic Month—Twelve Visits to Our Lady—Nine Visits to the Blessed Sacrament and Devotions for the Souls in Purgatory.

READINGS WITH THE SAINTS. Compiled from their Writings for the Use of Priests, Religious, and Christians in the World. By a Priest of the Diocese of Clifton. With a Letter of Approbation from Cardinal Manning. Crown 8vo, cloth gilt. 3/-.
"For spiritual reading it is most suitable, and to the preacher it will furnish admirable thoughts and topics on which to dwell."—*Month.*

REEKS, REV. J. W.
St. George's Hymn-Tune Book. New and Enlarged Edition. 1/6. Words for Above. Wrapper. 1d.

REEVE AND CHALLONER.
Bible History. New and Improved Edition. Containing both Old and New Testament History. Cloth. 2/-.

RENDU, A. (LL.D.).
The Jewish Race in Ancient and Roman History. Translated from the Eleventh Corrected Edition by S. T. Crook. Crown 8vo, 440 pp. 6/-.
"This should prove a very useful book."—*Dublin Review.*
"The story is well and lucidly told."—*Schoolmaster.*

RICHARDS, VERY REV. DR.
Manual of Scripture History. Eighth Edition. Complete in One Volume. Crown 8vo, cloth, 415 pp., with Maps, etc. 4/-.
Being a complete analysis of the historical books of the Old Testament. Adopted as a text-book in our colleges and training schools.

St. Francis of Sales, Introduction to the Devout Life. New Translation. Eleventh Edition. Cloth, red edges, 1/6. Best calf, red edges, 5/-. Morocco, gilt edges, 5/6.

RICKABY, REV. JOSEPH (S.J.).
Oxford Conferences. Lent and Summer Terms, 1897. Crown 8vo, wrapper, 1/- net (postage 2d.).

2

RIVINGTON, REV. LUKE (D.D.).
  Rome and England: or, Ecclesiastical Continuity. Crown 8vo, cloth, 3/6.
  "Fr. Rivington's method of exposition is admirable—brief and lucid without meagreness, pointed and telling without harshness. . . . A book to be grateful for; useful alike to the controversialist, the historical student, and the general reader."—*Tablet.*

ROBERTSON, MARY T.
  Dorothy Close. Crown 12mo, cloth gilt. 1/6.
  "A dainty little book, and a charmingly told story for girls."—*Teacher's Aid.*

RODRIGUEZ ON CHRISTIAN PERFECTION. For Persons living in the World. Fcap. 8vo, neat cloth, 800 pp. 6/-. Also an Edition for the Use of Religious, "Religious and Christian Perfection". In Three Volumes. Crown 8vo, cloth. 12/-.

ROSE, STEWART.
  St. Ignatius Loyola and the Early Jesuits. With more than 100 Illustrations, by H. W. and H. C. Brewer and L. Wain. Edited by the Rev. W. H. Eyre, S.J. Super royal 8vo, handsomely bound in cloth, extra gilt, 650 pp. 15/- net (postage 8d.).
  "The materials for the book have been gathered together with exemplary care and labour from authorities old and recent, and more particularly from authentic sources of information which have only become accessible within the last few years. Emphatic praise and recognition are due to the manner in which the volume is illustrated; the engravings and sketches so freely scattered through the book elucidate the life of St. Ignatius almost as much as the text."—*Scotsman.*

RUSHE, VERY REV. JAMES P. (O.D.C.) (Father Patrick of St. Joseph).
  Carmel in Ireland. A Narrative of the Irish Province of Teresian or Discalced Carmelites. A.D. 1625-1896. Crown 8vo, cloth, 3/6 net (postage 4d.).

RUSSELL, REV. MATTHEW (S.J.).
  Moments before the Tabernacle. Fourth Edition. Demy 32mo, cloth. 1/- net (postage 1d.).
  At Home near the Altar. Third Edition. With Steel Frontispiece. Cloth, gilt edges. 2/-.
  "Another of those exquisite gems which Father Russell is contributing to the literature of the Real Presence. Its charm of style and beautiful variety of thought, above all, its deep and tender devotion, will make it a welcome companion to the meditative moments of the devout, and perhaps awaken a throb of devotion in the hearts of the lukewarm."—*The Ave Maria.*

RYDER, REV. H. I. D. (of the Oratory).
  Catholic Controversy: A Reply to Dr. Littledale's "Plain Reasons". Eighth Edition. Fcap. 8vo, cloth. 2/6.

SACRED HEART, ANCIENT DEVOTIONS TO THE. By Carthusian Monks of the Fourteenth, Fifteenth, Sixteenth, and Seventeenth Centuries. Cloth gilt, 3/-. Best calf, red edges, 6/6.
  "The book deserves to be widely known and used, being a perfect treasure-house of devotions to the Sacred Heart by choice disciples of St. Bruno."—*Tablet.*

SALVATORI'S PRACTICAL INSTRUCTIONS FOR NEW Confessors. Edited by Fr. Anthony Ballerini, S.J., and Translated by Very Rev. William Hutch, D.D. Third Edition. 18mo, cloth gilt, 314 pp. 4/-.
  This work has been approved by His Lordship the Bishop of Cork as a text-book.

SCHOOL BOOKS, Stationery, and General School Requisites.
Complete Catalogue sent post free on application.

SCHOUPPE, REV. F. X. (S.J.).
  Purgatory: Illustrated by the Lives and Legends of the Saints. Second Edition. Crown 8vo, cloth. 6/-.
  "Solid, instructive, practical, and interesting as a romance, this book will go far to dispel the vague and erroneous ideas entertained among the faithful on the subject of Purgatory. Its careful perusal will repay the thoughtless Christian, the devout Catholic, and the zealous priest."—*Irish Ecclesiastical Record.*
  Short Sermons for the Low Masses of Sunday. Comprising a Methodical Exposition of Christian Doctrine. Second Edition. Crown 8vo, cloth. 5/- net (postage, 4d.).
  Abridged Course of Religious Instruction, Apologetic, Dogmatic, and Moral, for the Use of Catholic Colleges and Schools. New Edition. Thoroughly Revised. Crown 8vo, 405 pp. 3/-.
  Adopted as a text-book in our training schools, and approved by Cardinal Manning.

SCRIPTURE MANUALS FOR CATHOLIC SCHOOLS. Edited by the Rev. Sydney F. Smith, S.J. Arranged with a view to the Oxford and Cambridge Local Examinations.
  St. Luke. By the Rev. T. W. Darby, O.S.B., and the Rev. Sydney F. Smith, S.J. Crown 8vo, 308 pp., boards, with Map. 2/6.
  Acts, Part I. (Chapters i.-xii.). By the Very Rev. T. A. Burge, O.S.B. Crown 8vo, 130 pp., boards, with Map, and Supplement containing Chapters xiii.-xvi., pp. 40. 2/-.
  Acts, Part II. By the Very Rev. T. A. Burge, O.S.B. Crown 8vo, 132 pp., boards, with Map. 1/6.
  St. Matthew. By the Rev. Sydney F. Smith, S. J.
  [In preparation.

SHAPCOTE, EMILY MARY, Compiled by.
  Legends of the Blessed Sacrament, gathered from the History of the Church and the Lives of the Saints. With Illustrations. Handsomely bound for presentation. 4to, cloth, extra gilt. 6/-.
  "This very beautiful work will find a ready welcome from the Catholic reader. . . . The earnest feeling by which the whole is characterised, and the simple eloquence with which it is written, add greatly to its attractions."—*Weekly Register.*

SHIPLEY, ORBY (M.A.).
  Annus Sanctus. Hymns of the Church for the Ecclesiastical Year. Translated from the Sacred Offices by various Authors. With Modern, Original, and other Hymns, and an Appendix of Earlier Versions. Selected and arranged by Orby Shipley, M.A. Crown 8vo, cloth gilt. 5/- net (postage 4d.).
  Carmina Mariana. An English Anthology in Verse in honour of, or in relation to, the Blessed Virgin Mary. Collected and arranged by Orby Shipley, M.A. Second Edition. Cloth gilt. 7/6.
  Carmina Mariana. A Second Series is in preparation.

STANTON, REV. R. (of the Oratory).
  Menology of England and Wales: or, Brief Memorials of the British and English Saints, arranged according to the Calendar. Together with the Martyrs of the Sixteenth and Seventeenth Centuries. With a Supplement containing Notes, Enlarged Appendices, and an Index. Demy 8vo, cloth. 16/-.
    The Supplement can be had separately. Wrapper. 2/-.
  "As a work of reference it is invaluable."—*Month.*

ST. BERNARD ON THE LOVE OF GOD, and Three Rosaries of our Lady. Translated by Marianne Caroline and Coventry Patmore. Second Edition. Fcap. 8vo, cloth. 4/6.

ST. FRANCIS DE SALES, The Works of. Translated into the English Language by the Very Rev. Canon Mackey, O.S.B., under the Direction of the Right Rev. Bishop Hedley, O.S.B.

    Vol. I. Letters to Persons in the World. Third Edition. Crown 8vo, cloth. 6/-.

    Vol. II. The Treatise on the Love of God. Fr. Carr's Translation of 1630 has been taken as a basis, but it has been Modernised and thoroughly Revised and Corrected. Second Edition. 6/-.

    Vol. III. The Catholic Controversy. Crown 8vo, cloth. 6/-.

    Vol. IV. Letters to Persons in Religion, with Introduction by Bishop Hedley on "St. Francis de Sales and the Religious State". Second Edition. Crown 8vo, cloth. 6/-.

    "We earnestly commend these volumes to all readers, and we desire their widest diffusion, as we desire also that the doctrine and spirit of St. Francis may reign in all our hearts, both of pastors and of people."—Cardinal Manning in the *Dublin Review*.

STEWART, AGNES M., Cheap Uniform Edition of the Works of.

    Life and Letters of Blessed Thomas More. 3/-.

    Sir Thomas Gascoigne: or, The Yorkshire Plot. 3/-.

    The People's Martyr, a Legend of Canterbury. An Historical Tale, founded upon the Life and Death of St. Thomas à Becket. 3/-.

    Life of Cardinal Pole. 3/-.

    Last Abbot of Thornton: or, Lord Wake of Baynard Castle 3/-.

SWEENEY, RIGHT REV. ABBOT (O.S.B.).

    Sermons for all Sundays and Festivals of the Year. Fourth Edition. Crown 8vo, handsomely bound in half-leather. 10/6.

    "For such priests as are in search of matter to aid them in their round of Sunday discourses, and have not read this volume, we can assure them that they will find in these 600 pages a mine of solid and simple Catholic teaching."—*Tablet*.

TAYLOR, MISS.

    A Marvellous History: or, The Life of Jeanne de la Noue, Foundress of the Sisters of St. Anne of the Providence. Crown 8vo, cloth, with Portrait. 4/-.

    Lost, and other Tales for Children, adapted from the French. Second Edition. Cloth. 2/-.

    Tyborne, and who went thither, in the Days of Queen Elizabeth. New and Revised Edition. Cloth gilt. 3/6.

THOMPSON, EDWARD HEALY (M.A.).

Letters and Writings of Marie Lataste, with Critical and Expository Notes. By two Fathers of the Society of Jesus. Translated from the French. Three Volumes. 8vo, cloth. 5/- each.

Life of Jean-Jacques Olier, Founder of the Seminary of St. Sulpice. New and Enlarged Edition. Post 8vo, xxxvi.-628 pp. 15/-.
" M. Olier's life is a perfect mine of ecclesiastical thought and suggestion. I wish all our Ecclesiastical Colleges possessed many copies of it, so that it might form a kind of text-book, both for Superiors and for Ecclesiastical Students."— *H. E. Cardinal Vaughan.*

The Hidden Life of Jesus. A Lesson and Model to Christians. By Henri-Marie Boudon. Translated from the French by E. Healy Thompson, M.A. Third Edition. Cloth gilt. 3/-.
" It is very satisfactory to find that books of this nature are sufficiently in demand to call for a re-issue; and the volume in question is so full of holy teaching that we rejoice at the evidence of its being a special favourite."—*Month.*

The Life and Glories of St. Joseph, Husband of Mary, Foster-Father of Jesus, and Patron of the Universal Church. Grounded on the Dissertations of Canon Vitali, Fr. Josè Moreno, and other Writers. Second Edition. Crown 8vo, cloth. 6/-.
" A work which is without its equal."—*H. E. Cardinal Vaughan.*

The Unity of the Episcopate. Crown 8vo, cloth. 4/6.
" The book which made altogether the most decided impression on my mind was 'The Unity of the Episcopate'. The *principle* of unity was there unfolded in a way that was new to me, and which, I think, does away with a whole class of passages (and they the strongest) which are usually alleged against the Papacy."—The late Fr. Baker, Paulist, quoted in his Life by Fr. Hewit.

THOMPSON, EDWARD HEALY (M.A.), Edited by.

LIBRARY OF RELIGIOUS BIOGRAPHY.

Life of St. Aloysius Gonzaga, S.J. Eleventh Edition. Globe 8vo, cloth, xxiv.-373 pp. 5/-.
" The life before us brings out strongly a characteristic of the Saint, which is, perhaps, little appreciated by many who have been attracted to him chiefly by the purity and early holiness which have made him the chosen patron of the young. This characteristic is his intense energy of will. . . . We have seldom been more struck than in reading this record of his life, with the omnipotence of the human will when united with the will of God."—*Dublin Review.*

Life of Marie Eustelle Harpain: or, the Angel of the Eucharist. Fifth Edition. Cloth, xxi.-388 pp. 5/-.
" The life of Marie Eustelle Harpain possesses a special value and interest, apart from its extraordinary natural and supernatural beauty, from the fact that to her example and to the effect of her writings is attributed, in great measure, the wonderful revival of devotion to the Blessed Sacrament in France."—*Dublin Review.*

Life of St. Stanislaus Kostka. Fifth Edition. Cloth. 5/-.
" We strongly recommend this biography to our readers, earnestly hoping that the writer's object may thereby be attained, in an increase of affectionate veneration for one, of whom Urban VIII. exclaimed that, although 'a little youth,' he was indeed 'a great saint'."—*Tablet.*

Life of Marie Lataste, Lay Sister of the Congregation of the Sacred Heart. With a Brief Notice of her Sister Quitterie. Second Edition. Cloth. 5/-.

THOMPSON, EDWARD HEALY (M.A.), Edited by—*(continued)*.

Life of Leon Papin-Dupont, The Holy Man of Tours. Fourth Edition. Cloth. 5/-.

"It is an original compilation, written in that well-known style of devout suggestiveness and literary excellence which characterises the writer's former volumes of religious biography. The life is full of devout thought and touching stories."—*Dublin Review*.

Life of Jean Baptiste Muard, Founder of the Congregation of St. Edme and of the Monastery of La Pierre-qui-Vire. 8vo, cloth, xix.-540 pp. 6/-.

Life of St. Charles Borromeo, Cardinal Archbishop of Milan. Second Edition. Cloth gilt. 3/-.

"Well written and interesting, the work of a scholar and a man of judgment, as well as a devout Catholic."—*Weekly Register*.

TWO LITTLE PILGRIMS. A Tale. By the Author of "Gloomy Winter's Noo Awa'," etc. Prettily bound in cloth. 2/-.

ULLATHORNE, ARCHBISHOP.

Christian Patience, the Strength and Discipline of the Soul. Fifth and Cheaper Edition. Demy 8vo, cloth, 256 pp. 7/-.

Contents: The Work of Patience in the Soul—The Nature and Object of Christian Patience—Patience as a Universal Virtue—Christian Fortitude—The Patience of the Son of God—Patience as the Discipline of the Soul—Encouragements to Patience—The Gifts of the Holy Ghost—Prayer—Patience in Prayer—The Cheerfulness of Patience, etc.

The Endowments of Man considered in their Relations with his Final End. Fourth and Cheaper Edition. Demy 8vo, cloth, 404 pp. 7/-.

Contents: The Nature of Man—Why Man is made in the Image of God—Creation and Providence—Self and Conscience—On Evil and the Origin of Evil—On Justice and Moral Evil—Why Man was not Created Perfect—The Fall, the Restoration and the Regeneration of Man—From the Beginning to the End of Man, etc.

The Groundwork of the Christian Virtues. Fifth and Cheaper Edition. Demy 8vo, cloth, 411 pp. 7/-.

Contents: The Divine Law of Probation—The Nature of Christian Virtue—The Difficulties of Virtue—Nature of Humility—The Grounds of Humility—On Humility towards our Neighbour—The Divine Master of Humility—On the Detestable Vice of Pride—The World without Humility—The Humility of Faith—On the Schools of Humility—On Humility as the Counterpart of Charity, etc.

Memoir of Bishop Willson, First Bishop of Hobart, Tasmania. With Portrait. Crown 8vo, cloth. 2/6.

"The compassion of the Bishop for the Convicts and the noble firmness with which he besieged the authorities, until he obtained an amelioration of their condition will draw forth the admiration of every Philanthropist."—*Weekly Register*.

The Autobiography of Archbishop Ullathorne. Edited by Augusta Theodosia Drane. Second Edition. Demy 8vo, cloth. 7/6.

"As a plucky Yorkshireman, as a sailor, as a missionary, as a great traveller, as a ravenous reader, and as a great prelate, Dr. Ullathorne was able to write down most fascinating accounts of his experiences. The book is full of shrewd glimpses from a Roman point of view of the man himself, of the position of Roman Catholics in this country, of the condition of the country, of the Colonies, and of the Anglican Church in various parts of the world, in the earlier half of this century."—*Guardian*.

ULLATHORNE, ARCHBISHOP—*(continued)*.

The Letters of Archbishop Ullathorne. Arranged by A. T. Drane. (Sequel to the "Autobiography".) Demy 8vo, cloth, 550 pp. 9/-.

"Compiled with admirable judgment for the purpose of displaying in a thousand various ways the real man who was Archbishop Ullathorne. . . . This book is very cordially recommended, not only for the intrinsic interest, but also for the sage and prudent counsel which characterises the intimate correspondence of Archbishop Ullathorne."—*Tablet*.

Characteristics from the Writings of Archbishop Ullathorne, together with a Bibliographical Account of the Archbishop's Works. Crown 8vo, cloth. 6/-.

"The Archbishop's thoughts are expressed in choice, rich language. We have perused this book with interest, and have no hesitation in recommending our readers to possess themselves of it."—*Birmingham Weekly Mercury*.

VAUGHAN, CARDINAL.

On the Holy Sacrifice of the Mass. Large Paper Edition. Cloth, red edges. 1/-. Also a Cheap Edition for Distribution. Wrapper. 2d. net (postage ½d.).

The People's Manuals. In Two Volumes. Cloth 2/- net (postage 3d.). Or the Manuals may be had separately at 1d. and 2d. each.

VAUGHAN, REV. DOM JEROME (O.S.B.), Edited by.

The Life and Labours of St. Thomas of Aquin. By Archbishop Vaughan, O.S.B. Second Edition. Crown 8vo, cloth gilt, 544 pp. 6/6.

"Popularly written, in the best sense of the word; skilfully avoids all wearisome detail, whilst omitting nothing that is of importance in the incidents of the Saint's existence, or for a clear understanding of the nature and the purpose of his sublime theological works."—*Freeman's Journal*.

Pax Animæ. By St. Peter of Alcantara. Third Edition. Neat cloth. 1/-.

A short treatise on the tranquillity and peace of the soul, and how it may be obtained.

VAUGHAN, REV. DOM JEROME, Translated by.

The Practice of Humility. A Treatise edited by H. H. Leo XIII. Sixth Edition. Cloth gilt. 1/6. Cheaper Edition, in wrapper. 6d. net (postage 1d.).

WALPOLE, F. GOULBURN.

A Short History of the Catholic Church. Crown 8vo, cloth, 3/-.

This work may be described as a Skeleton History of the Church. It has been compiled from notes made by the author for his own instruction, and he hopes that it may prove useful to those who may not have leisure or inclination to study the voluminous standard works upon which it is based.

WISEMAN, CARDINAL.

Fabiola. A Tale of the Catacombs. New Cheap Edition. Crown 8vo, cloth, xii.-324 pp. 2/-. Also an Edition on better paper, bound in cloth, richly gilt, gilt edges. 3/6. And an *Edition de luxe* printed on large 4to Paper, embellished with thirty-one Full-page Illustrations and a Coloured Portrait of St. Agnes. Handsomely bound. £1 1/-.

This story of the persecutions of the early Christians contains as graphic and minute a description of the Catacombs as has ever been written.

"'Fabiola' has well maintained the high place in fiction which it obtained at the very outset, and to-day it may be said to be one of our English classics. . . . The present editions are brought out in most excellent style."—*Catholic Times.*

A Few Flowers from the Roman Campagna. Small 4to, cloth gilt, printed in red and black. 1/- net (postage 2d.).

New Visits to the Blessed Sacrament. Edited by Cardinal Wiseman. Containing Devotions for the Quarant' Ore and other Occasions of Exposition and Benediction. Cloth, red edges. 2/-.

Works by the Jesuit Fathers.

Arrangements have been made by which Messrs. Burns and Oates, Limited, shall have the entire control of the sale of the Quarterly Series (of which 96 volumes have been published already), and of other publications issued by Fathers of the Society of Jesus. The well-known works by the late Father Coleridge, S.J., and those of Father John Morris, S.J., and other Jesuit Fathers, and the "Ascetical Library" include Lives of the Saints and Holy Persons, Catholic Biographies, Theological Treatises, Books of Meditation, Scriptural Discourses and Explanations of various portions of the Scriptures. There are to be found also valuable Historical Books. These volumes should find a place in every Catholic library, and Messrs. Burns and Oates will be glad to receive a general order from their clients to subscribe for each volume issued from the Manresa Press, as it appears, and thus save delay of any kind.

BURNS & OATES, LIMITED,
28 Orchard Street, London, W.

www.ingramcontent.com/pod-product-compliance
Lightning Source LLC
Chambersburg PA
CBHW030408230426
43664CB00007BB/800